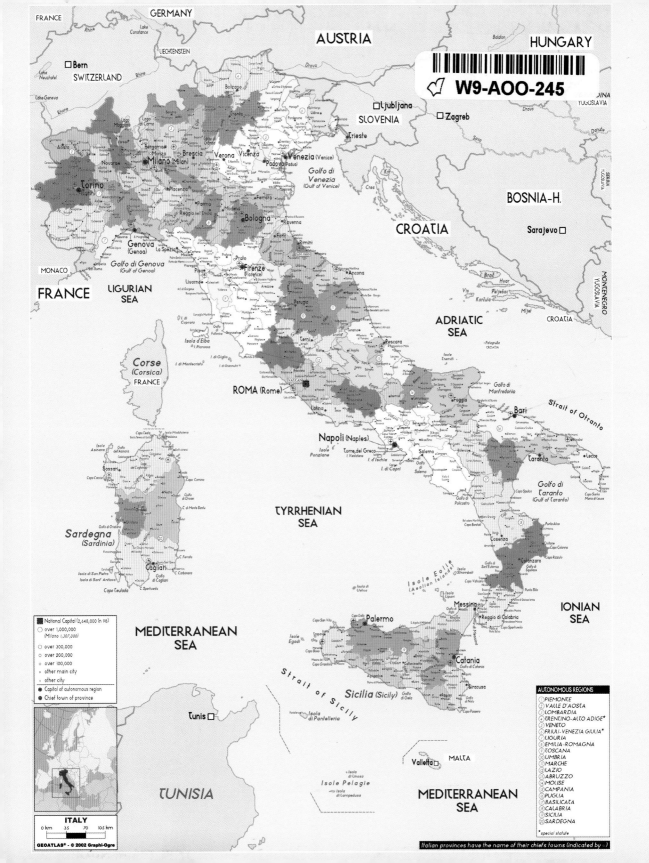

Fireside
A Division of Simon & Schuster, Inc.
1230 Avenue of the Americas
New York, NY 10020

Published originally under the title *L'Italia del Gusto*
Copyright © 2007 Food Editore srl
Via Bordoni, 8 - 20124 MILAN
Via Mazzini, 6 - 43100 PARMA
www.foodeditore.it

English translation by
Traduzioni Culinarie

English layout by
TGM

Photographs by
Davide Di Prato, Matteo Cervati, Massimo Fanti, Monia Petrolini, Cristina Bottari, Lidia Piras,
Gianluca Bergonzi, Claudio Mersoni, Leonello Savoretti, Giuseppe Pipita, Gettyimages

Recipes by
Simone Rugiati, Massimiliano Ciccarello, Diego Bongiovanni, Christian Bertol (p. 95)

First Fireside edition April 2009

FIRESIDE and colophon are registered trademarks of Simon & Schuster, Inc.

For information about special discounts for bulk purchases, please contact Simon & Schuster Special Sales
at 1-800-456-6798 or business@simonandschuster.com.

Printed in China in 2009

10 9 8 7 6 5 4 3 2 1

ISBN-13: 978-1-4391-1002-7
ISBN-10:   1-4391-1002-6

The Taste of Italy

300 Authentic Recipes from Each Region

A Fireside Book
Published by Simon & Schuster
New York   London   Toronto   Sydney

the traditional flavors,

original recipes, local products and wonderful photos highlighting Italian regional cuisine

olio d'oliva
lasagne
taralli
baccalà
peperoncino
salame
culatello
tartufo d'Alba

tigelle
tortellini
lardo
strolghino
Castelmagno
*pastiera
napoletana*
paccheri
brigidini

Contents

The fascinating complexity and delicious tastes of Italian cuisine stem from its rich and ancient history and the quality of its raw ingredients.

Italian cooking is not a static collection of rules and regulations drawn up by scholars and gourmets. Rather, it is an ever-evolving tradition that goes through a continuous, fertile stream of innovations from both chefs and experts, as well as from home cooks and amateurs. We could say that Italian cuisine was created and is growing thanks to a constant synergy of the professionals and inspired dabblers who have helped make it truly great—both a noble art with humble origins and a refined gastronomy that cannot be easily classified. Italian cooking, if it must be categorized under a single definition, is the product of a delicate, centuries-old balance

between the gastronomy of the aristocrats and the peasants.

This link between fancy urban cuisine and simple regional foods becomes even more pronounced when we leave the field of celebrated restaurants and instead immerse ourselves in the ordinary trattorias and osterias that dot the countryside and local neighborhoods. This is where we truly discover the unique and admirable qualities of Italian cooking. From the steep alleyways of Genoa to the cobbled streets of Emilia, from the winding medieval lanes of Tuscan hill towns to the avenues of Naples, from the rough cart tracks of the south to sun-soaked Mediterranean islands, Italy is not just *Il Bel Paese* ("the beautiful country") but an ensemble of *many* countries, profoundly diverse but in harmony.

This development of originality that we find in Italian architecture and art can also be found at the Italian table. The differences between the many regions of Italy pale in comparison with the thing that draws them together: something the Italians call *gusto*— taste, enjoyment, pleasure. And here we come to "our" *Taste of Italy*, a book that aims to describe a collection of flavors, fragrances and colors that define this multifaceted land. In truth, this book could also have been called *tastes* of Italy— together, we'll be exploring the many flavors, inventions, and regions of Italy. While other great international cuisines offer a more uniform gastronomical map, Italy is characterized not by regularity but by imagination, by the many offerings that co-exist within the same tradition. It is really the creativity, the

flair, and the joy of the Italians that makes their cuisine great. Beyond this, the country's varied landscape and rich agricultural tradition provides the high-quality raw materials necessary for magnificent creations.

Italian foods and wines enjoy the popularity precisely because of a *genius loci*, a spirit of place. This spirit seems to possess many parts of the Italian peninsula since time immemorial, a perfect combination of location, climate, atmosphere, tradition and imagination that produces many of the most appreciated, envied and imitated foods and wines of the planet.

In a world of fast food, rushed lunch breaks and five-minute dinners, Italy becomes not just an enchanting country to visit and to (re)discover, but it also represents a chance to seek out that basic ingredient of our lives, inexplicably oft-ignored: quality. This means paying attention to ourselves and our well-being, starting with what we eat and drink. In a country that offers so many different landscapes, different climates and different cultures, its taste and quality are able to amaze, to involve and to move us profoundly.

If the Valle d'Aosta knows how to win you over with its ancient mountain specialties (fontina cheese, cured lardo and tender veal stand out), then Sardinia will draw you in with the frankness and force of its Mediterranean flavors. If Sicily seduces you with the historic Arab traditions that live on in its cooking, then Liguria will bewitch you with the myriad of nuanced differences present in its coastal food. And who knows, as you continue to travel through the pages of this Italy of tastes, the opulent generosity of Emilia-Romagna could get mixed up with the austere rigor of Trentino-Alto Adige, the hidden treasures of little-known regions like Molise and Basilicata could blend with the great culinary inventions of Campania or Tuscany, while the power of Abruzzian cooking, all strong spices and herbs, could melt into the delicacy of Piedmont.

It's a voyage of flavors that destroys borders and prejudices —in the best Italian cooking, the land and the sea come together to create a tasty, pleasurable trip. Join us on this journey through the best-known recipes of the Italian tradition: a journey with gusto.

Valle d'Aosta

A *region encircled by* snowy **mountains,**

where imposing and austere medieval castles preside over deep valleys. The local cooking makes the most of the products of the Alpine pastures: cheeses (like world-famous *Fontina, Tome, Séras*) and special *ricotta aged in hay* accompany steaming *polenta* and hearty *soups*. Among cured meats, rarities such as *mocetta, lardo d'Arnad* and the noble *jambon de Bosses* flavor this high-altitude cuisine.

VALLE D'AOSTA
local products

Jambon de *Bosses*

A HIGHLY PRIZED AND VERY ORIGINAL HAM, WHOSE
UNUSUAL PRODUCTION METHODS MEAN IT'S OFTEN HARD
TO FIND. Jambon de Bosses is made using traditional
techniques in the community of Saint-Rhémy-en-Bosses,
5,250 feet (1,600 m) above sea level. Thanks to its high
quality and unique characteristics, the ham has earned
the coveted DOP (Denomination of Protected Origin)
classification. The secret to the unmistakable flavor of the
ham is the use of spices combined with time-tested aging
techniques. Pork legs are seasoned with natural flavorings
such as sage, rosemary, garlic, juniper, thyme and bay, as
well as salt and whole and ground black peppercorns. After
being salted and seasoned, the meat is wrapped in hay and
left to age for 18 to 24 months in wooden structures called
rascards. Located at 5,900 feet (1,800 meters) above sea
level, the *rascards* replicate the conditions of the old haylofts
that were originally used. The result is an extraordinary
cured meat, with a vivid red color run through with veins
of pale pink fat and a delicate but decisive and slightly
gamey flavor. Produced in small quantities, Jambon de Bosses
DOP is hard to find outside the region. Once purchased,
it should be kept in a cool, dry place. The cut surface should
be rubbed with oil and then covered with aluminum foil
or plastic wrap. It is excellent eaten sliced with crusty,
country-style bread.

Fontina *valdostana*

TRUE FONTINA IS MADE ONLY IN VALLE D'AOSTA IN EUROPE'S HIGHEST ALPINE PASTURES, one of the rare cheeses made from raw milk from a specific local breed of cow. The herds are brought to the mountain meadows in July. They are milked in the middle of the night and the milk must be processed no less than two hours later, using the purest calf rennet for curdling. The cheese is pressed into forms and aged in caves carved out of the rock. The low temperature (8-10°C/46-50°F) and the high humidity (90%) in the caves make them the ideal environment for the aging process. Fontina has a soft, elastic consistency, with a pale straw color; the sweet, full-bodied taste is flavorful but never sharp.

Lardo di Arnad

THIS CURED LARD (LARDO) IS AMONG THE REGION'S BEST-KNOWN PRODUCTS, and has been awarded DOP recognition. The lard is cured with water, salt, garlic, rosemary and bay, then cut into large pieces and packed into containers called *doils*, layered with more salt and herbs. The *doils* are then filled with boiling salted water and left to age for at least three months. The lardo can be used in various dishes, or enjoyed simply sliced over slices of toasted brown bread, perhaps with a drizzle of honey.

Grappa *valdostana*

GRAPPA IS DISTILLED FROM VINACCE, THE RESIDUE OF GRAPE SKINS, STEMS AND SEEDS LEFT OVER AFTER WINEMAKING. Valle d'Aosta's grappa is usually single-varietal, produced artisanally in alembics and cauldrons. The resulting spirits are of the best quality, available only in limited quantities, and truly express the grape variety used—whether soft and semi-aromatic from Müller Thurgau, spiced from Petit Rouge, or intense and strong from Pinot Noir.

Risotto alla valdostana
Valle d'Aosta-Style Risotto

Serves 4

1 large pat of butter
1/2 onion, minced
1 ½ cups (10 ½ oz or 300 g) Carnaroli rice
3/4 cup (180 ml) white wine
4 cups (1 l) beef broth
5 ½ oz (150 g) Valle d'Aosta Fontina cheese, diced

Preparation time **10 minutes**
Cooking time **20 minutes**
Level **easy**
Wine **Valle d'Aosta Torrette**

Melt the butter in a heavy-bottomed saucepan. Add the onion and sauté until golden.

Add the rice and toast, stirring constantly, for a few minutes, then add the white wine.

Once the wine has evaporated start adding the broth, little by little. After about 15 minutes add the Fontina cheese.

Lower the heat and stir the rice until the cheese has completely melted and been absorbed by the rice, and the rice is tender. Serve immediumtely.

Note *This is the classic recipe, but there are several variations, such as adding chopped, seedless tomatoes to the sautéed onions before adding the rice.*

Crespelle alla valdostana
Valle d'Aosta-Style Crêpes

Serves 4

2 eggs
1 egg yolk
1 ⅔ cups (7 oz or 200 g) all-purpose flour
salt
2 cups (500 ml) warm milk
7 Tbsps (3 ½ oz or 100 g) butter
7 oz (200 g) ham, sliced
9 oz (250 g) Valle d'Aosta Fontina cheese, sliced

Preparation time **15 minutes**
Cooking time **20 minutes**
Level **easy**
Wine **Blanc del Morgex et De La Salle**

Preheat the oven to 450°F (230°C or Gas Mark 8). Beat the eggs and egg yolk together in a bowl. Sift in the flour, add salt and whisk together. Add a little water to the warm milk and then whisk gently into the egg mixture. The batter should be fairly thick.

Melt a pat of butter in a frying pan. Wipe the pan with a paper towel, then pour in a ladleful of batter. Cook briefly then flip over to cook the other side. Remove from the pan and continue making more crêpes in the same way until the batter is finished. Place a slice of ham and a slice of Fontina cheese on each crêpe, roll them up and place in a baking dish.

Lay the remaining Fontina over the top, then bake in the oven for a few minutes until the cheese melts and turns golden.

Crespelle alla valdostana

Minestra di porri
Leek Soup

Serves 4

1 large pat of butter
1 onion, minced
1 Tbsp minced parsley
5-6 leeks, trimmed and sliced
2 large potatoes, peeled and sliced
6 cups (1 ½ l) beef broth
grated nutmeg
freshly ground black pepper
1/2 cup (3 ½ oz or 100 g) rice
5 Tbsps grated Parmesan cheese

Preparation time **15 minutes**
Cooking time **1 hour 40 minutes**
Level **easy**
Wine **Valle d'Aosta Bianco**

Melt the butter in a large saucepan and sauté the onion and parsley over medium-low heat for 3-4 minutes. Raise the heat slightly and add the leeks and potatoes.

After 3 minutes add the broth, a grating of nutmeg and a pinch of pepper. Let cook for about 1 hour 10 minutes, then add the rice and cook for another 20 minutes.

Sprinkle with Parmesan and serve hot.

Note *The rice can be replaced by 3 ½ oz (100 g) short pasta.*

Zuppa alla valpellinentze
Valpelline-Style Soup

Serves 4-6

1 Savoy cabbage, shredded
12 slices dry bread
3 ½ oz (100 g) salted lardo (cured lard), thinly sliced
9 oz (250 g) Fontina cheese, thinly sliced
4 cups (1 l) beef broth
ground cinnamon
2 Tbsps (1 oz or 30 g) butter, cut into pieces
salt and pepper

Preparation time **20 minutes**
Cooking time **1 hour 20 minutes**
Level **easy**
Wine **Valle d'Aosta Nus Rosso**

Preheat the oven to 350°F (180°C or Gas Mark 4). Bring a large pot of salted water to the boil. Cook the shredded cabbage in the salted water until tender, then drain.

Toast the bread in the oven until golden-brown on both sides. Sauté the lardo in a frying pan yo render some of the fat and make it crispy. In an oven-proof terracotta baking dish, make alternating layers of bread slices, shredded boiled cabbage, sautéed lardo and Fontina cheese slices, finishing with a layer of bread slices.

Mix a little ground cinnamon into the broth to taste, add pepper, and pour the seasoned broth over the bread layers. Bake for 30 minutes, top with pieces of butter, then bake for another 30 minutes. Serve very hot.

Zuppa alla valpellinentze

fonduta
Valle d'Aosta-style fondue

Serves 4

14 oz (400 g) Fontina cheese
1 garlic clove, smashed
3/4 cup (180 ml) milk
1 pat of butter
4 egg yolks
salt
8 slices of crusty bread, toasted
1 truffle, shaved (optional)

Preparation time **10 minutes**
Cooking time **40 minutes**
Level **medium**
Wine **Valle d'Aosta Chambave Rosso**

Remove any rind from the Fontina cheese and cut the cheese into cubes. Place the cheese in a saucepan with the garlic and milk. Let sit for 2 hours in a cool, dry place (not the refrigerator).

Drain the cheese from the milk and discard the garlic and milk. Place the cheese a saucepan with the butter and cook over a low flame, stirring constantly. As soon as the cheese starts to melt, add the egg yolks one at a time, stirring quickly. Season with salt. When the mixture is smooth and creamy, pour into serving plates and serve with the toasted bread.

The fonduta can also be sprinkled with truffle shavings if desired.

Costolette alla valdostana
Valle d'Aostan Veal Cutlets

Serves 4

4 veal cutlets (about 7 oz or 200 g each)
3 ½ oz (100 g) Fontina cheese, sliced
salt and pepper
1 egg
3 Tbsps all-purpose flour
3 Tbsps breadcrumbs
7 Tbsps (3 ½ oz or 100 g) butter
1 truffle, shaved (optional)

Preparation time **15 minutes**
Cooking time **20 minutes**
Level **easy**
Wine **Valle d'Aosta Donnas**

Slice into the cutlets horizontally with a sharp knife, creating a pocket. Fill with Fontina and close, pounding the edges with a meat tenderizer to seal. Season with salt and pepper.

Beat the egg in a bowl and place the flour and breadcrumbs in separate bowls. Dip the cutlets in the flour, then the egg, and then the breadcrumbs, and press down with the palm of the hand so the breadcrumbs adhere.

Melt the butter in a wide saucepan over high heat and sauté the cutlets, browning well on both sides. Lower the heat and continue cooking until the cheese melts and the meat is done. Serve hot, with shavings of truffle if desired.

Carbonade
Beef Stew

Serves 4

1 ¾ lb (800 g) lean beef, cubed
1 garlic clove, minced
2 rosemary sprigs, minced
2 sage leaves, minced
2 fresh bay leaves, minced
salt and pepper
3 Tbsps all-purpose flour
1 pat of butter
1 onion, minced
3/4 cup (180 ml) wine (red or white)
cooked polenta, sliced (optional)

Preparation time **15 minutes**
Cooking time **1 hour 20 minutes**
Level **medium**
Wine **Valle d'Aosta Torrette**

Mix together the beef, garlic, rosemary, sage and bay. Season with salt and pepper and refrigerate for at least a day or overnight. Remove the beef from the refrigerator and dip the pieces in the flour.

Melt the butter in a saucepan and brown the beef for a few minutes. Remove from the pan, then add the onion. As soon as the onion has softened, return the beef to the pan, add the wine and continue to cook over low heat for 1 hour 20 minutes, seasoning with salt and pepper to taste. Serve hot, accompanied by slices of polenta if desired.

Carbonade

Polenta grassa
Creamy Polenta

Serves 4-6

8 cups (2 l) water
salt
2 ⅓ cups (14 oz or 400 g) polenta cornmeal
(not instant polenta)
14 oz (400 g) Valle d'Aosta Fontina cheese,
very thinly sliced
14 Tbsps (7 oz or 200 g) butter, chopped
freshly ground black pepper

Preparation time **10 minutes**
Cooking time **1 hour 30 minutes**
Level **easy**
Wine **Valle d'Aosta Pinot Nero**

Bring the water to boil in a copper cauldron
or a large saucepan. Add salt, then sprinkle
in the polenta. Whisk to break up any
lumps, then stir with a wooden spoon.
Continue cooking for 1 hour, then add
the Fontina and butter. Stir well to melt
the cheese and butter.

Cook for another 15 minutes, until
the mixture is firm, smooth and comes
away from the sides of the pan.

Serve the polenta hot with a sprinkling
of freshly ground black pepper.

Soça
Beef, Cabbage and Fontina Bake

Serves 6-8

6 cups (1 ½ l) water
salt
1 garlic clove
2 sage leaves
2 ¼ lb (1 kg) beef, cubed
1 medium cabbage, shredded
3 ½ lb (1 ½ kg) potatoes, diced
9 oz (250 g) Fontina cheese, sliced
7 Tbsps (3 ½ oz or 100 g) butter, melted

Preparation time **20 minutes**
Cooking time **1 hour 30 minutes**
Level **medium**
Wine **Valle d'Aosta Rosso**

Salt the water and bring to a boil with the
garlic and sage. Add the beef, cabbage and
potatoes to the boiling water. Cook, covered,
for 45 minutes, skimming off the foam when
necessary.

Preheat the oven to 350°F (180°C or Gas
Mark 4). Make layers in a baking dish of the
beef mixture and the Fontina cheese slices.
Finish with a layer of cheese. Pour over the
melted butter. Bake for a few minutes, until
the cheese melts. Serve very hot.

Trota alla valdostana
Valle d'Aosta-Style Trout

Serves 4

4 Tbsps extra-virgin olive oil
1 garlic clove, smashed
1 carrot, diced
1 celery stalk, diced
1 rosemary sprig
2 sage leaves
4 whole trout, cleaned
1/2 cup (120 ml) white wine vinegar
grated zest of 1 organic lemon
3 Tbsps raisins
salt and pepper
3 ⅓ cups (800 ml) vegetable broth
1 pat of butter
1 Tbsp all-purpose flour

Preparation time **35 minutes**
Cooking time **20 minutes**
Level **easy**
Wine **Blanc de Morgex et De La Salle**

Heat the olive oil in a large frying pan with the garlic. Sauté the carrot and celery with the rosemary and sage until soft. Add the trout and brown on both sides. Add the vinegar and let evaporate. Add the lemon zest and raisins, season with salt and pepper and continue cooking, adding hot broth as necessary. Once the trout is cooked through, remove from the pan and keep warm. Return the pan to the heat.

Mix together the butter and flour, then whisk into the cooking liquid to thicken. Pour the sauce over the trout and serve.

Trota alla valdostana

Blanc-Manger
Blancmange

Serves 6

3 gelatin sheets
1 ½ cups (7 oz or 200 g) blanched almonds,
roughly chopped
1 ¾ cups (400 ml) water
1/2 cup (3 ½ oz or 100 g) sugar
3 Tbsps Chantilly cream
1 Tbsp orange-flower water
strawberry sauce or diced strawberries (optional)

Refrigeration time **2 hours**
Preparation time **20 minutes**
Level **easy**
Wine **Valle d'Aosta Nus Pinot Grigio Passito**

Soak the gelatin in a little warm water.
Meanwhile pound the almonds with a mortar
and pestle (ideally made of stone), adding
the water little by little. Strain the mixture,
pressing lightly to obtain the milky liquid.

Dissolve the sugar in the almond milk and
transfer to a saucepan. Heat briefly and add
the drained gelatin, stir until dissolved and let
sit until the mixture reaches room temperature.

Stir in the Chantilly cream and orange-flower
water. Pour the mixture into small molds
and refrigerate for at least 2 hours.

Just before serving, remove from the
refrigerator and unmold. Serve with strawberry
sauce or diced fresh strawberries if desired.

Pere Martine al forno
Baked Martine Pears

Serves 4

2 ¼ lb (1 kg) Martine mountain pears,
peeled, halved and cored
1 tsp ground cinnamon
grated nutmeg
5 cloves
1 cup (7 oz or 200 g) sugar
3/4 cup (180 ml) red wine
1 cup (250 ml) heavy cream

Preparation time **20 minutes**
Cooking time **30 minutes**
Level **easy**

Preheat the oven to 350°F (180°C or Gas
Mark 4). Arrange the pear halves in a large
baking dish and add the cinnamon, nutmeg
and cloves.

Dissolve the sugar in the wine and pour
over the pears. Bake in the oven for
30 minutes. Whip the cream. Remove
the pears from the oven and let cool.

Serve drizzled with the cooking liquid
and garnished with whipped cream.

Note *Small and pot-bellied, Martine pears have
a rough, rust-colored skin and a grainy, dry flesh.
They are very hard and need long cooking times.*

Mont Blanc
Chestnut Pudding

Serves 6

3 ½ lb (1 ½ kg) chestnuts
3/4 cup (180 ml) milk
2 cups (14 oz or 400 g) sugar
1/2 cup (2 oz or 50 g) cocoa powder
1/4 cup (60 ml) rum
2 cups (1/2 l) heavy cream
4 Tbsps confectioners' sugar

Preparation time **25 minutes**
Cooking time **45 minutes**
Level **easy**
Wine **Valle d'Aosta Moscato**
Chambave Passito

Boil the chestnuts for about 45 minutes, then drain and peel, removing the outer shell and inner skin. Pass the chestnuts through a food mill or potato ricer.

Bring the milk to a boil and dissolve the sugar and cocoa powder in it. Add the rum, then stir the mixture into the chestnut puree. Pass the mixture through the food mill or a potato ricer, letting the resulting strings fall gently onto a serving plate to create a small mountain.

Whip the cream with the confectioners' sugar and use to garnish the mountain.

Pere Martine al forno

Mont Blanc

Piedmont

The region "at the foot of the mountains"

has a long farming tradition, but is also one of Italy's industrial powerhouses. Piedmontese cuisine is based on the excellence of its local products, with *rice* from the Po plains, great *wines* from its hills, *truffles* from the forests and flavorful *cheeses* from Alpine pastures.

PIEDMONT
local products

Toma *piemontese*

A HIGH-QUALITY AND VERY TYPICAL CHEESE, granted a DOP (Denomination of Protected Origin). Piedmontese Toma actually refers to a group of cheeses with different appearances, production techniques and origins.

Toma is produced with cow's milk cheese. *Semigrassa* (semi-fat) Toma is made with skim milk, formed into a cylinder and has a semi-hard, straw-white-colored paste and a thick, rough rind. Whole-milk Toma is the same shape, but has an elastic texture, a smooth, soft crust and a sweet, delicate flavor.

Castelmagno

AN EXTRAORDINARY CHEESE WHOSE HISTORY DATES BACK TO THE 12TH CENTURY, with an unmistakable aroma and flavor. Today it has gained DOP recognition and can be produced only in the areas around Castelmagno, Pradleves and Monterosso Grana. Castelmagno is made from cow's milk with small additions of goat's and sheep's milks; it has a cylindrical shape and a semi-hard paste. When aged for less than five months, the color is ivory with green speckles. More mature versions have a darker color with bluish veins and a sharper flavor. Castelmagno is aged in special caves with a microclimate that favors the production of molds.

Tartufi *pregiati*

TRUFFLES (*TARTUFI*) ARE A PRIZED DELICACY, and Piedmontese truffles are among the best in the world. Alba's white truffles are the most expensive and coveted, but white and black truffles are also collected from the Monferrato, Langhe and Roero hills. Truffles cannot be cultivated—they must be harvested in the wild—and they are closely interconnected with the local environment: The earth and the trees, particularly oaks, are of prime importance. In fact, Alba white truffles take on a different scent and flavor depending on the type of tree they've grown under.

Grissini *torinesi*

GRISSINI, LONG, THIN BREADSTICKS, ARE A TYPICALLY TURINESE PRODUCT, invented in the city near the end of the seventeenth century by baker Antonio Brunero, who was trying to satisfy a finicky royal request. Since then, breadsticks have spread around Italy and can be made with olives or herbs, artisanally or industrially. However the classic *grissini torinesi* are always long and crunchy, hand-pulled and made from a simple dough of flour and water with little or no salt, with malt or oil sometimes added to give them a flaky texture.

Tonda *gentile* delle Langhe

THE LANGHE HAZELNUT VARIETY, known as "Tonda gentile delle Langhe," has been recognized at a European level with an IGP designation (Indication of Protected Origin).

Small and round (*tondo*), with a shiny brown shell with paler streaks, they have a delicate but persistent flavor. Hazelnuts are much used in Piedmontese desserts and are featured in torrone, gianduiotti, hazelnut chocolate, croccanti, hazelnut cake and baci di dama cookies.

Barolo

THE KING OF WINES, THIS NOBLE RED IS KNOWN AROUND THE WORLD. Protected by strict DOCG (Denomination of Controlled Geographic Origin) rules, Barolo can only be made in the province of Cuneo within the municipalities of Barolo, Castiglione Falletto, Cherasco, Grinzane Cavour, La Morra, Monforte d'Alba, Novello, Roddi d'Alba, Serralunga d'Alba and Verduno. Made exclusively from Nebbiolo grapes, Barolo must be aged at least three years (at least two of them in oak or chestnut barrels), or five years for the Reserve. It needs at least four years to come into its own, and improves over the following decades.

Best served in large, balloon glasses to complement its full-bodied warmth, it pairs perfectly with roasted red meats, braises, game and aged cheeses. Nebbiolo grapes are also made into other noted Piedmontese wines such as Barbaresco, Nebbiolo d'Alba, Gattinara, Ghemme and Roero.

Krumiri

THIS TYPICAL PIEDMONTESE COOKIE IS RICH IN HISTORY AND TRADITION, with a grainy texture and a gently curved shape said to imitate King Vittorio Emanuele II's moustache. Originally from Casale Monferrato, the classic version is made from flour, sugar, fresh eggs and natural vanilla.

Cioccolato e *Bicerin*

PIEDMONT WOULDN'T BE THE SAME WITHOUT ITS BAKERIES, CAFÉS AND BARS serving delicious local specialties, many based on cioccolato (chocolate). Turin is famous for its confectionery, particularly gianduiotti, chocolates flavored with toasted hazelnuts, vanilla and sugar and shaped into little wedges. The chocolate's name comes from Gianduia, a Piedmontese carnival character. Chocolate in Piedmont means more than gianduiotti, however, with baci di dama

and baci di Cherasco cookies also making good use of it, plus Turin's famous bicerin, a mix of coffee, cream and hot chocolate.

Torta verde del Monferrato
Monferrato-Style Spinach Pie

Serves 6

1 Tbsp extra-virgin olive oil
2 leeks, julienned
2 ¼ lb (1 kg) spinach
1 ½ cups (10 ½ oz or 300 g) rice
5 cups (1 ¼ l) vegetable broth - 5 eggs
1 ½ cups (5 ½ oz or 150 g)
grated Parmesan cheese
1 pat of butter
2 Tbsps breadcrumbs
1 rosemary sprig, minced

Preparation time **25 minutes**
Cooking time **1 hour 20 minutes**
Level **easy**
Wine **Roero Arneis**

Preheat the oven to 350°F (180°C or Gas Mark 4). Heat the olive oil in a frying pan and sauté the leeks until soft. Meanwhile, in another pan, wilt the spinach, then squeeze out excess liquid and chop finely.

Add the rice to the leeks and toast, stirring constantly. Continue to cook, adding vegetable broth as necessary, until the rice is cooked but still al dente. Add the spinach and stir. Let the mixture cool. Reserve one egg yolk and beat the remaining eggs. Stir the eggs and Parmesan into the rice mixture.

Butter a baking dish and sprinkle with 1 tablespoon of breadcrumbs. Pour in the rice mixture and level off the surface. Brush with the remaining egg yolk, then sprinkle over some more breadcrumbs and the rosemary. Bake for 1 hour, then serve warm.

Tartrà
Savory Herbed Flan

Serves 4

3 ½ Tbsps (2 oz or 50 g) butter
1 white onion, minced
4 eggs - 2 egg yolks
2 cups (500 ml) milk
1 cup (250 ml) heavy cream
2 Tbsps grated Parmesan cheese
2 sage leaves, minced
1 fresh bay leaf, minced
1 rosemary sprig, minced
grated nutmeg
salt and pepper
1 Tbsp extra-virgin olive oil

Preparation time **25 minutes**
Cooking time **35 minutes**
Level **easy**
Wine **Grignolino d'Asti**

Preheat the oven to 400°F (200°C or Gas Mark 6). Melt half the butter in a small frying pan and sauté the onion until golden, then let cool. Beat the eggs and yolks in a bowl together with the milk, cream, Parmesan, sage, bay leaf, rosemary and nutmeg and season with salt and pepper. Stir in the onion and mix well. Pour the mixture into a mold or individual molds, oiled with olive oil and buttered with the remaining butter. Bake in a water bath for about 30 minutes. Serve warm.

Note *This is a traditional Piedmontese peasant recipe, whose name suggests it comes from outside Italy, perhaps Spain. There is also a sweet version.*

Tortino di funghi e tartufi
Truffled Porcini Gratin

Serves 6

1 Tbsp extra-virgin olive oil

1 garlic clove

2 bay leaves

2-3 fresh porcini mushrooms,
cleaned and chopped

4 eggs

2 oz (50 g) black truffle, shaved

3 ½ oz (100 g) Fontina cheese, thinly sliced

3 ½ Tbsps (2 oz or 50 g) butter, diced

Preparation time **20 minutes**
Cooking time **15 minutes**
Level **easy**
Wine **Dolcetto d'Alba**

Preheat the broiler. Heat the olive oil in
a frying pan with the garlic and bay leaves.

Sauté the porcini, then transfer them to
a baking dish. Lightly beat the eggs then
pour over the mushrooms.

Sprinkle over some shaved truffle, then
cover with slices of Fontina and some pieces
of butter. Broil for a few minutes until the
cheese melts and forms a golden crust.

Top with more truffle shavings and serve
immediumtely. The heat will help bring out
the truffle fragrance.

Tortino di funghi e tartufi

Rabatòn
Swiss Chard Dumplings

Serves 4-6

10 ½ oz (300 g) Swiss chard
1 lb (500 g) ricotta
1 ½ cups (5 ½ oz or 150 g) grated Parmesan cheese, plus extra for topping
2/3 cup (2 ½ oz or 75 g) breadcrumbs
3 eggs
salt and pepper
grated nutmeg
all-purpose flour for flouring
3 Tbsps (1 ½ oz or 40 g) butter, diced

Preparation time **25 minutes**
Cooking time **20 minutes**
Level **easy**
Wine **Roero Arneis**

Preheat the oven to 350°F (180°C or Gas Mark 4). Blanch the Swiss chard for a few minutes in water, drain, dry and chop finely.

Place in a bowl and mix in the ricotta, then add the Parmesan, breadcrumbs, eggs, pinches of salt and pepper and some nutmeg. Mix well; the consistency should be fairly dense. If it is too soft, add some flour.

Form walnut-sized balls in the palm of the hand, then roll on a floured work surface to obtain a more elongated shape.

Bring a large pot of salted water to a boil and boil the dumplings for 5 minutes.

Drain with a slotted spoon and arrange in a baking dish. Top with grated Parmesan and pieces of butter. Bake for a few minutes to brown, then serve hot.

Paniscia di Novara
Novara-Style Risotto

Serves 4

1/2 Savoy cabbage, chopped
1 carrot, diced
1 celery stalk, diced
1 cup (7 oz or 200 g) dried cranberry (borlotti) beans
3 ½ Tbsps (2 oz or 50 g) butter
1 onion, thinly sliced
2 oz (50 g) lardo (cured lard), minced
2 ½ oz (70 g) pork rind
1 small, soft salami, chopped
1 tsp ready-made tomato sauce
1 ¾ cups (13 oz or 360 g) Carnaroli rice
3/4 cup (180 ml) red wine
pepper

Preparation time **20 minutes**
Cooking time **3 hours 20 minutes**
Level **medium**
Wine **Gattinara**

Boil the cabbage, carrot and celery with the beans in salted water for about 3 hours.

Melt half the butter in a saucepan and add the onion, lardo, pork rind, salami and tomato sauce. Cook for a few minutes, then add the rice and toast for 1 minute, stirring.

Add the red wine and when evaporated, start gradually adding the cooking liquid from the beans, together with the cooked vegetables.

When the rice is cooked through stir in the rest of the butter and any remaining beans and vegetables. Finish with a sprinkling of pepper.

Paniscia di Novara

Tajarin delle Langhe
Langhe-Style Egg Noodles

Serves 4-6

4 cups (1 lb 2 oz or 500 g) all-purpose flour
4 eggs
2 egg yolks
1 Tbsp extra-virgin olive oil
salt
finely ground cornmeal for dusting
3 ½ Tbsps (2 oz or 50 g) butter
1 Alba white truffle

Preparation time **20 minutes**
Cooking time **8 minutes**
Level **easy**
Wine **Nebbiolo d'Alba**

Mound the flour on a wooden pastry board and make a well in the center. Break in the eggs and add the egg yolks, olive oil and a pinch of salt. Mix well to obtain a smooth and uniform dough.

Form into a ball, cover with a clean kitchen towel and leave to rest for 2 hours. Roll the dough out into a very thin sheet.

Sprinkle with a little cornmeal and let sit for a few minutes, then roll up the sheet and use a sharp knife to cut it into very thin strips. Unroll the tajarin and lay them out on a kitchen towel to dry.

Bring a pot of salted water to a boil and cook the tajarin. Drain and toss with the butter. Shave or grate the truffle on top and serve immediately.

Gnocchi al Castelmagno
Gnocchi with Castelmagno

Serves 4

2 ¼ lb (1 kg) yellow-fleshed potatoes
salt and pepper
1 Tbsp extra-virgin olive oil
2 egg yolks
2 cups (9 oz or 250 g) all-purpose flour
3 Tbsps milk or heavy cream
5 ½ oz (150 g) Castelmagno cheese, chopped
3 ½ Tbsps (2 oz or 50 g) butter
4 walnuts, minced

Preparation time **30 minutes**
Cooking time **35 minutes**
Level **easy**
Wine **Carema**

Boil the potatoes until tender, about 20 minutes. Drain and peel. Mash until smooth or pass through a potato ricer. Season with salt and pepper and stir in the olive oil, egg yolks and 1 ½ cups plus 1 ½ Tbsps (7 oz or 200 g) flour. Mix to obtain a smooth dough. Form the dough into ropes, then cut them into small pieces and lightly squash each piece with the tines of a fork, using the remaining flour to prevent sticking.

Heat the milk or cream in a saucepan and add the Castelmagno and butter. Melt over low heat, stirring constantly. Bring a large pot of salted water to a boil and cook the gnocchi.

As they rise to the surface, drain them with a slotted spoon. Add the cooked gnocchi to the saucepan with the cheese sauce and stir for a few minutes. Serve hot with a sprinkling of pepper and walnuts.

Zuppa alla Canavesana
Canavese-Style Soup

Serves 4

2 oz (50 g) lardo (cured lard), minced
7 Tbsps (3 ½ oz or 100 g) butter
2 garlic cloves, smashed
peppercorns, ground with a mortar and pestle
1 cabbage, shredded
8 cups (2 l) vegetable broth
salt
6 slices of crusty bread
1 cup (3 ½ oz or 100 g) grated Parmesan cheese
grated nutmeg

Preparation time **15 minutes**
Cooking time **50 minutes**
Level **easy**
Wine **Ghemme**

Heat the lardo, butter and garlic together in a large saucepan. Add the pepper and then the cabbage. Pour over the vegetable broth.

Salt to taste, then bring to a boil and cook until the cabbage is soft.

Preheat the oven to 350°F (180°C or Gas Mark 4). Toast the bread in a non-stick frying pan or under the broiler. Arrange the toasted bread in the bottom of a soup tureen, then pour over the soup. Sprinkle with half the Parmesan and a pinch of nutmeg. Bake for a few minutes.

Serve the soup hot, sprinkled with more Parmesan cheese.

Cabiette alle ortiche
Nettle Dumplings

Serves 4

5 ½ oz (150 g) nettles
1 ¾ lb (800 g) potatoes
2 oz (50 g) Toma cheese, diced
2 cups (7 oz or 200 g) rye flour, sifted
salt - 2 eggs
7 Tbsps (3 ½ oz or 100 g) butter
1 ¾ lb (800 g) onions, sliced
3 Tbsps rye breadcrumbs

Preparation time **15 minutes**
Cooking time **40 minutes**
Level **easy**
Wine **Gavi**

Preheat the oven to 350°F (180°C or Gas Mark 4). Wearing plastic gloves, wash the nettles, squeeze out excess water and finely chop. Boil the potatoes until tender, drain, peel and mash or pass through a potato ricer.

In a bowl, mix together the mashed potatoes, nettles, Toma cheese and rye flour. Season with salt and mix in the eggs. Form the dough into ropes and cut them into small pieces. Using your fingers, form them into slightly flattened ovals. Melt half the butter in a large frying pan and sauté the onions until soft. Melt the remaining butter in another saucepan.

Bring a large pot of water to a boil and cook the dumplings, draining them with a slotted spoon when they rise to the surface. In a baking dish, make layers of gnocchi, sautéed onions and melted butter. Sprinkle the top with the rye breadcrumbs. Bake for 30 minutes, then serve.

"Civet" alla lepre
Braised Hare

Serves 6

6 onions, minced
7 oz (200 g) lardo (cured lard), minced
1 bunch of parsley, minced
14 Tbsps (7 oz or 200 g) butter
5 Tbsps all-purpose flour
1 hare or rabbit, cut into pieces
(including heart and liver)
2 cups (500 ml) Barbera or other red wine
1/2 cup (120 ml) beef broth
1 Tbsp white wine vinegar
2 ½ Tbsps sugar
salt and pepper

Preparation time **25 minutes**
Cooking time **40 minutes**
Level **easy**
Wine **Barolo**

Heat the onions, lardo, parsley, butter and flour together in a saucepan.

Let sauté for a few minutes stirring constantly, then add the hare or rabbit.

Brown for a few minutes, then add the wine, broth, vinegar, sugar, salt and pepper. Let cook for about 30 minutes, until the hare or rabbit is tender and cooked through.

Stufato di vitello al Barolo
Beef Stew with Barolo

Serves 4

3 ½ lb (1 ½ kg) beef for stewing in 1 piece
1 bottle (750 ml) of Barolo wine
7 oz (200 g) lardo (cured lard) in 1 piece
1/2 celery stalk - 4 onions, minced
10 juniper berries - 3 carrots - 3 bay leaves
3 garlic cloves - 3 cloves - 3 Tbsps sugar
sprigs of thyme, sage, marjoram, tarragon and savory
1/2 cup (120 ml) Marsala wine
3 Tbsps extra-virgin olive oil - salt and pepper
7 Tbsps (3 ½ oz or 100 g) butter
1 Tbsp all-purpose flour
1 pinch of ground cinnamon
boiled potatoes or polenta (optional)

Preparation time **35 minutes**
Cooking time **2 hours 30 minutes**
Level **medium**
Wine **Barolo**

Cut the beef into pieces and place in a bowl with the Barolo, the lardo cut into 4 pieces, celery, onions, carrots, bay, garlic, cloves, juniper, thyme, sage, marjoram, tarragon, savory, 2 tablespoons of sugar, Marsala, salt and pepper. Let sit for at least 2 hours or overnight. Drain. Mince the celery and carrot and sauté the onion, celery and carrot with the olive oil and butter. Pat dry the pieces of beef and lardo, dust with flour and brown with the vegetables. Strain the marinade and add to the meat with salt, cinnamon and the remaining sugar.

Cook, covered, for 2-3 hours. Remove the meat and lardo. Puree the cooking liquid and vegetables with an immersion blender. Mince the lardo and return to the cooking liquid with the beef. Serve hot, with boiled potatoes or polenta, if desired.

Galletto all'agro
Flavorful Chicken

Serves 4

1 young, tender chicken, cut into 4 pieces
salt and pepper
4 Tbsps extra-virgin olive oil
1 bay leaf
2 sage leaves
1 onion, minced
2 celery stalks, minced
3 oz (80 g) pancetta, diced
3/4 cup (180 ml) dry white wine
2 garlic cloves
2 anchovy fillets
3 Tbsps red wine vinegar
1/2 tsp yellow mustard
salad leaves (optional)

Preparation time **20 minutes**
Cooking time **40 minutes**
Level **easy**
Wine **Barbera del Monferrato**

Season the chicken pieces with salt and pepper. Heat the olive oil in a saucepan over medium heat and brown the chicken together with the bay leaf, sage, onion and celery. When the pieces are well browned, add the pancetta and wine.

Cover the saucepan and continue cooking for 20 minutes. Pound the garlic and anchovies together with a mortar and pestle to make a paste. Stir in the vinegar and mustard.

Add this mixture to the chicken and continue cooking for another 5-10 minutes. Serve the chicken hot, with the cooking sauce, garnished with salad leaves if desired.

Stufato di vitello al Barolo

Galletto all'agro

bagna càôda
garlic and anchovy dip

Serves 4

Bagna Càôda

5 garlic cloves
1 ¼ cups (300 ml) milk
7 oz (200 g) salted anchovies
1/2 cup (120 ml) white wine
3/4 cup (200 ml) extra-virgin olive oil
5 Tbsps (2 ½ oz or 70 g) butter
3 Tbsps heavy cream

Vegetables

a selection of the following: squash, beets, onions, potatoes, leeks, cauliflower, Jerusalem artichokes, turnips, bell peppers, Savoy cabbage, red cabbage, celery, fennel, carrots, escarole, endive, lemon juice

Preparation time **20 minutes**
Cooking time **25 minutes**
Level **easy**
Wine **Carema**

Preheat the oven to 375°F (190°C or Gas Mark 5). Cut the squash, beets and onions into bite-sized pieces and roast for 45 minutes. Blanch the potatoes, leeks, cauliflower, Jerusalem artichokes and turnips until just barely tender, then cut into bite-size pieces. Roast the bell peppers, peel, deseed and slice.

Chop the cabbage, celery, fennel, carrots, escarole and endive into bite-sized pieces. Soak the garlic in the milk for 1 hour.

Rinse the anchovies and soak in the wine. Drain the garlic and the anchovies, place in a heavy-bottomed saucepan and cover with olive oil. Cook over low heat for 10 minutes, stirring to dissolve the ingredients. Add the butter and cook, stirring, for another 10 minutes. Stir in the cream. Bring the saucepan to the table and divide the sauce between individual terracotta serving bowls set over candles. The sauce should simmer continually throughout the meal. Serve the vegetables to be dipped into sauce.

Traditional recipe

Torta di cardi
Artichoke Gratin

Serves 6

2 ¼ lb (1 kg) artichokes
juice of 1 lemon
salt
1 cup plus 3 Tbsps (5 ½ oz or 150 g)
all-purpose flour
2 eggs, beaten
extra-virgin olive oil for frying
1 ¼ cups (4 oz or 120 g) grated Parmesan cheese
grated nutmeg
5 Tbsps (2 ½ oz or 70 g) butter, diced

Preparation time **20 minutes**
Cooking time **40 minutes**
Level **easy**
Wine **Freisa di Chieri**

Clean the artichokes and cut the stalks into pieces about 2-inch (5 cm) long. Soak them in water and lemon juice for about 30 minutes.

Preheat the oven to 375°F (190°C or Gas Mark 5). Drain the cardoons and boil in salted water, adding 1 tablespoon flour to the water.

Drain and pat dry. Dip the pieces first in egg, then in flour. Heat olive oil and fry the artichoke pieces. Drain and dry on paper towels.

Butter a baking dish and fill it with layers of artichoke pieces. Top each layer with Parmesan cheese, nutmeg and pieces of butter. Bake for about 15 minutes. Serve hot.

Polenta al Castelmagno
Polenta with Castelmagno Sauce

Serves 4

12 cups (3 l) water
salt
4 ¾ cups (1 ¾ lb or 800 g) polenta cornmeal
(not instant polenta)
8 oz (225 g) Castelmagno cheese, chopped
2 cups (500 ml) heavy cream
5 Tbsps grated Parmesan cheese
black pepper
1 pat of butter

Preparation time **25 minutes**
Cooking time **55 minutes**
Level **easy**
Wine **Dolcetto di Dogliani**

Bring the water to a boil in a large saucepan and add 1 ½ tablespoons salt. Sprinkle in the polenta and start stirring continuously, lowering the heat as soon as the water returns to a boil. Continue cooking for about 45 minutes, until the polenta starts to come away from the sides of the pan.

Stir in 3 ½ oz (100 g) Castelmagno until well mixed, then pour the polenta into a mold and let cool. Preheat the oven to 400°F (200°C or Gas Mark 6). Heat the cream, then transfer it to a bowl with the Parmesan and remaining Castelmagno. Add pinches of salt and pepper and whisk to obtain a smooth sauce.

Once firm, unmold the polenta and cut into slices. Arrange them in a buttered baking dish and pour over the cheese sauce. Bake for 10 minutes, until the sauce starts to color. Remove from the oven and serve hot.

Insalata tiepida di fagioli
Warm Bean Salad

Serves 4

1 ½ cups (10 ½ oz or 300 g)
dried cranberry beans
1 celery stalk
1 carrot
1 bay leaf
1 sage leaf
1 white onion, thinly sliced
1 smoked herring, chopped
1 pinch of chili pepper flakes
extra-virgin olive oil for dressing
vinegar for dressing

Preparation time **15 minutes**
Cooking time **20 minutes**
Level **easy**
Wine **Grignolino del Monferrato**

Soak the beans overnight. Drain the beans
and cook in fresh water together with
the celery, carrot, bay and sage until tender.

Drain and remove the celery, carrot, bay
and sage leaves and discard. Meanwhile
mix together onion, herring and chili pepper
in a bowl. Stir in the warm beans, then dress
with olive oil and vinegar to taste.

Cover the bowl and let sit for about
2 hours before serving.

Note *This is the "lean" version, for Fridays
or fast days, of a traditional Monferrato salad
which uses sliced leftover boiled beef instead
of herring.*

Polenta al castelmagno

Insalata tiepida di fagioli

Bunêt astigiano
Asti-Style Chocolate Pudding

Serves 10

4 cups (1 l) milk

3 ½ oz (100 g) ladyfingers, finely chopped

4 oz (120 g) small amaretti cookies, finely chopped

1/4 cup (60 ml) prepared espresso coffee

1 Tbsp instant coffee granules

2 Tbsps rum

2 Tbsps Marsala wine

5 eggs

1 cup (7 oz or 200 g) sugar, plus extra for sprinkling

1/2 cup (2 oz or 50 g) unsweetened cocoa powder

Preparation time **15 minutes**
Cooking time **50 minutes**
Level **medium**
Wine **Asti Moscato Spumante**

Preheat the oven to 400°F (200°C or Gas Mark 6). Bring the milk to a boil in a saucepan and let cool. Stir in the ladyfingers and amaretti. Mix well then stir in the espresso, instant coffee, rum and Marsala. Beat the eggs, sugar and cocoa powder together in a bowl until smooth and fluffy. Stir in the milk mixture.

Sprinkle a pudding mold with sugar, then heat it on the stove until the sugar caramelizes. Roll the mold around so the caramel is evenly distributed. Let cool and harden.

Pour the batter into the mold, then bake in a water bath for about 40 minutes. Remove from the oven and let cool before unmolding and serving.

Note *The word* bunêt *means cap, and this pudding is traditionally prepared in a circular mold, raised in the center, which resembles a kind of hat common in the 18th century.*

Baci di dama
Hazelnut Sandwich Cookies

Serves 6-8

1 cup (4 ½ oz or 125 g) hazelnuts
1 cup (4 ½ oz or 125 g) all-purpose flour
2/3 cup (4 ½ oz or 125 g) sugar
4 ½ oz (125 g) candied orange rind, minced
1 stick plus 1 Tbsp (4 ½ oz or 125 g)
butter, chopped
milk
4 ½ oz (125 g) dark chocolate, chopped

Preparation time **20 minutes**
Cooking time **30 minutes**
Level **medium**
Wine **Malvasia di Castelnuovo Don Bosco**

Preheat the oven to 320°F (160°C or Gas
Mark 3). Blanch the hazelnuts for a few minutes
in boiling water, then drain, cool and rub off
the skins. Finely chop the nuts.

Mix together the flour, hazelnuts, sugar,
candied orange rind and butter on a wooden
pastry board. Knead the dough well, adding
a little milk if it seems too stiff. Transfer the
mixture to a pastry bag.

Butter a baking sheet and pipe the dough into
small balls the size of a walnut. Bake for about
30 minutes. Meanwhile melt the chocolate
in a small bowl over a double boiler.

Remove the cookies from the oven, let cool
and then spread the flat bottoms with melted
chocolate. Stick the cookies together to form
small sandwiches. Let cool before serving.

Krumiri
Crumiri Cookies

Serves 6-8

2 cups (9 oz or 250 g) all-purpose flour
1 ½ cups (9 oz or 250 g) finely ground cornmeal
3/4 cup (5 ½ oz or 150 g) sugar
2 ½ sticks plus 1 Tbsp (10 ½ oz or 300 g) butter
at room temperature, plus extra for buttering
4 eggs
1 tsp vanilla extract

Preparation time **20 minutes**
Cooking time **30 minutes**
Level **easy**
Wine **Malvasia di Castelnuovo Don Bosco**

Mix together the flour and cornmeal in
a bowl. Add the sugar, butter, eggs and
vanilla. Mix well with the hands to obtain
a smooth, uniform dough. Form it into
a ball and cover with a kitchen towel. Let
rest for 30 minutes. Preheat the oven to
400°F (200°C or Gas Mark 6).

Transfer the dough to a pastry bag and pipe
cookies in the shape of an arc onto a buttered
baking sheet. Bake for 30 minutes. Remove from
the oven and let cool slightly before serving.

Torta di nocciole
Hazelnut Cake

Serves 6-8

1 ½ cups (7 oz or 200 g) hazelnuts
4 eggs
1 cup (7 oz or 200 g) sugar
1 ⅔ cups (7 oz or 200 g) all-purpose flour
10 ½ Tbsps (5 ½ oz or 150 g) butter at room temperature, plus extra for buttering
1 Tbsp extra-virgin olive oil
1 tsp vanilla extract
2 tsps baking powder
confectioners' sugar for dusting (optional)

Preparation time **15 minutes**
Cooking time **40 minutes**
Level **easy**
Wine **Asti Moscato Spumante**

Preheat the oven to 350°F (180°C or Gas Mark 4). Toast the hazelnuts in the oven for a few minutes, let cool and then rub with a kitchen towel to remove the skins. Chop finely in a food processor.

Beat the eggs in a bowl with the sugar, flour, butter, hazelnuts, olive oil, vanilla and baking powder. Mix well until smooth and uniform, without lumps.

Butter and flour a cake tin and pour in the batter. Bake for around 40 minutes. Serve the cake warm or at room temperature, dusted with confectioners' sugar if desired.

Krumiri

Torta di nocciole

Lombardy

Mountains in the north
and placid plains to the south,

a region whose cuisine has strong roots in peasant culture, yet which created noble dishes such as *saffron risotto* with gold leaf. *Cheeses* and *polenta*, simple and poor foods, but a region defined by business and power: apparent contrasts for this solid land with a solid work ethic.

LOMBARDY
local products

Vini di Franciacorta

THE MORAINE HILLS IN THE PROVINCE OF BRESCIA, south of Lake Iseo, are known as Franciacorta. Here wine (*vino*) has been made since the Middle Ages, and in significant quantities since the nineteenth century. The reputation of Franciacorta rose greatly in the twentieth century thanks to the experiments with sparkling wines carried out by Guido Berlucchi of Borgonato, a true pioneer. Today Franciacorta has around 1,500 hectares of vineyards, of which 840 are used for producing the prestigious sparkling DOCG (Denomination of Controlled Geographic Origin). It is made from Chardonnay, Pinot Blanc and Pinot Noir grapes, matured for at least two years following the harvest with at least 18 months of slow bottle refermentation on the lees. Franciacorta is also labeled *VSQPRD* (quality sparkling wines produced in specific regions), which designates the highest level of sparkling wines and refers to fermentation in autoclave or in the bottle for a set minimum period. Still white and red wines are also produced, under the denomination "Terre di Franciacorta DOC."

Riso Arborio *& Co*

RICE (RISO) HAS ALWAYS PLAYED AN IMPORTANT ROLE IN LOMBARDY'S COOKING. Almost every city has its own special risotto – with saffron, with pumpkin, with Botticino wine. Risotto alla pilota derives its name from the rice-paddy workers responsible for the husking (pilatura) the rice grains. Rice is produced in the provinces of Pavia and Mantua, and the main varieties are Arborio and Carnaroli. Particularly prized rices such as Balilla, Ambra and Volano are also cultivated.

Panettone *milanese*

THE ORIGINS OF MILAN'S PANETTONE LIE SHROUDED IN MYTH AND TWO LEGENDS, both involving a character called Toni and set in the Renaissance Milan of Ludovico Sforza, one of Italy's most powerful princes. In one version Toni is a baker who invents a sweet bread made with butter, sugar, raisins and candied fruit in order to make enough money to pay his daughter's dowry. Milan goes crazy for the cake, and he becomes rich. In the other, Toni is a scullery boy in the Sforza kitchens, and after the head chef ruins the dessert for a banquet, Toni saves him from Ludovico's ire by inventing a new dessert called panettone.

Bagòss, *il Grana* bresciano

A COW'S MILK CHEESE WITH A STRONG BUT NOT SHARP FLAVOR FROM THE VALLEYS AROUND BRESCIA: Val Camonica, Val Trompia, Valle del Caffaro and Val Sabbia. In local dialect, "Bagòss" means someone from Bagolino. The best versions of the cheese are made in Alpine huts in the spring and summer, when the cows are grazing on mountain meadows of sweet grass and aromatic herbs. Bagòss has a smooth, slightly hard rind with a brownish ochre color. During aging the surface is rubbed with raw linseed oil to maintain its elasticity and to prevent the formation of unpleasant molds.

Formaggi caprini

IN BOSCASSO, IN THE PROVINCE OF PAVIA, THE PRODUCTION OF FORMAGGI CAPRINI, goat's milk cheeses, is an ancient art. Produced using natural methods, the caprini have a soft, white paste, an intense milky fragrance and a delicate flavor. Sometimes they are wrapped in walnut and chestnut leaves, giving them even more complex aromas. They can be sold fresh or aged for a few weeks, during which the distinctive goat's milk flavors becomes even stronger.

Salame *di Milano*

ONE OF THE BEST-KNOWN ITALIAN CURED MEATS, once made only around Codogno and San Colombano al Lambro, but now found throughout Brianza and around Lake Como. The salami is made from a mix of pork and lean beef with some pancetta, ground finely so the white fat looks like grains of rice. Salt and crushed peppercorns are added for flavor, and sometimes a strained infusion of crushed garlic and white wine. Of notable size, salami di Milano can weigh three to four kilos and are aged for three to six months in airy, dry cellars, or a minimum of two weeks in artificially ventilated rooms. The color is always bright red, the flavor delicately mild, and it is traditionally eaten in a michetta, a typical Milanese bread roll. A similar cured meat is also made around Milan and Lodi, the salamella dei Morti, traditionally eaten around All Souls' Day.

Gorgonzola *(o stracchino verde)*

THE PRINCE OF ITALIAN BLUES, GORGONZOLA IS MADE FROM WHOLE MILK FROM ONE OR TWO MILKINGS. Creamy with a sharp flavor or firmer with a milder aroma, Gorgonzola is a soft cheese which apparently arose out of a fortuitous mistake. Legend goes that a careless cheesemaker forgot to clean the copper cauldrons, leading to the flowering of a greenish mold. But some say that the cheese was first made in Valsassina, whose natural caves provide the humidity and constant temperature perfect for the proliferation of penicillin molds. Others claim that it was created in the town of Gorgonzola, where an innkeeper sold a batch of Stracchino cheese gone moldy as a delicious local specialty. Whatever the true story, the cheese has a long history. While the town of the same name is the most famous site, over time production has spread into Piedmont, particularly the province of Novara.

Bresaola *Valtellinese*

A CURED MEAT WHICH HAS BEEN MADE SINCE THE LATE MIDDLE AGES, BRESAOLA COMES FROM THE BACK LEG OF COWS, from different cuts which give different shapes and textures and aged between two and four years. The meat is thoroughly trimmed of fat, then rubbed with salt, black and white pepper, juniper, bay, garlic and red wine before being brined for 20 days, then packed in a casing and aged for between 6 to 8 weeks. Valtellina's bresaola has an IGP (Indication of Protected Origin) guarantee, used exclusively by producers in the province of Sondrio.

Lumache trifolate
Parsley Snails

Serves 4-6

2 ¼ lb (1 kg) whole snails, purged
5 ½ Tbsps (3 oz or 80 g) butter
2 garlic cloves, sliced
2 bunches of parsley, minced
2/3 cup (150 ml) white wine
salt
sliced cooked polenta, fried or grilled (optional)

Preparation time **20 minutes**
Cooking time **50 minutes**
Level **easy**
Wine **Colli Morenici del Garda Rosato**

Clean the snails and remove and discard the shells. Chop the meat into small pieces.

Melt 3 ½ tablespoons (2 oz or 50 g) of butter in a frying pan and sauté the garlic and half the parsley. Add the snails, brown and then pour over the wine. Cover and cook for 40 minutes over low heat. Remove the cover and raise the heat to thicken the sauce, then add salt and the remaining butter and parsley.

Serve hot, accompanied by slices of fried or grilled polenta.

Nervetti alla salvia
Pig's Feet with Sage

Serves 4-6

6 pig's feet, cleaned and scraped
salt
1 onion - 1 celery stalk
1/2 bunch of parsley, chopped
1 carrot - 2 thyme sprigs
1 bay leaf - 1 pat of butter
1/2 cup (3 ½ oz or 100 g) cooked butter beans
2 sage leaves
salt and pepper
3 Tbsps heavy cream
3 Tbsps grated Parmesan cheese
grated nutmeg

Preparation time **30 minutes**
Cooking time **3 hours 20 minutes**
Level **medium**
Wine **Valcalepio Rosso**

Place the pig's feet in a large pan and cover with salted water. Add the onion, celery, parsley, carrot, thyme and bay leaf. Bring to a boil and cook for 3 hours.

As soon as the feet are soft, remove them from the cooking liquid with a slotted spoon. Remove the meat from the bone and cut it into pieces. Melt the butter in a frying pan and add the meat. Brown for 10 minutes, then add some of the cooking liquid.

Meanwhile put the beans in another frying pan with some sage leaves, let cook for 5 minutes, season with salt and pepper, then add the cream, Parmesan and a grating of nutmeg. Mix the beans with the meat and serve hot.

Involtini di verza
Stuffed Cabbage

Serves 4-6

14 oz (400 g) pork
20 Savoy cabbage leaves
salt and pepper
3 Tbsps grated Parmesan cheese
2 eggs
3 Tbsps breadcrumbs
1 garlic clove, minced
3 Tbsps minced parsley
1 pat of butter
1 small onion, minced
1 sage leaf
2 Tbsps ready-made tomato sauce
2 Tbsps vegetable broth

Preparation time **20 minutes**
Cooking time **1 hour 40 minutes**
Level **easy**
Wine **Cellatica**

Boil the pork for about an hour, then drain
and finely chop in a food processor. Blanch
the cabbage leaves in boiling salted water
until just tender, then drain and lay out
on a work surface.

Mix the chopped pork with the Parmesan,
eggs, breadcrumbs, garlic, parsley and salt.
Place small piles of the mixture in the center
of each cabbage leaf, then roll them up into
little parcels and tie with kitchen string.

Melt the butter in a large frying pan and
sauté the onion, sage, salt and pepper, then
add the cabbage rolls. Mix the tomato sauce
and broth together and add to the pan, then
cook over low heat for about 30 minutes.

Nervetti alla salvia

Involtini di verza

Risotto alla certosina
Monk's Risotto

Serves 4

salt - 1 celery stalk - 1 carrot
2 onions (1 whole and 1 minced) - 1 bay leaf
10 ½ oz (300 g) small shrimps
10 ½ oz (300 g) frog legs - 1/2 tsp fennel seeds
2 cups (9 oz or 250 g) peas
2 Tbsps extra-virgin olive oil
3/4 cup (180 ml) white wine
5 Tbsps (2 ½ oz or 70 g) butter
1 ½ cups (10 ½ oz or 300 g) Carnaroli rice

Preparation time **30 minutes**
Cooking time **50 minutes**
Level **medium**
Wine **Oltrepò Pavese Cortese**

Bring a pot of salted water to a boil and add
the celery, carrot, whole onion, bay, shrimp, frog
legs and fennel seeds. Cook for 5 minutes then
remove the shrimp and frog legs, reserving the
water with the vegetables. Separately, boil the
peas for 10 minutes, then drain. Remove the frog
meat from the bones and shell the shrimp. Add
the shrimp shells to the vegetables and cook for
15 minutes, then strain. Heat the olive oil in a
saucepan and sauté half the minced onion until
golden. Add the shrimp and frog meat and sauté.

Add the wine, then the peas and salt and cook
for about 5 minutes, adding some shrimp and frog
broth. In another saucepan melt half the butter
and sauté the remaining onion until golden.

Add the rice and toast, then continue cooking,
adding broth little by little unti the rice is done.
Stir in the remaining butter. Serve hot, topped
with the frog legs, peas and shrimp.

Tortelli di zucca
Squash Tortelli

Serves 4

2 ¼ lb (1 kg) yellow-fleshed squash or pumpkin,
peeled, deseeded and cut into wedges
3 ½ oz (100 g) amaretti cookies, crumbled
3 ½ oz (100 g) Mantuan mostarda
(spicy preserved fruit), finely chopped
3/4 cup (3 oz or 80 g) grated Parmesan cheese,
plus extra for topping
grated nutmeg - salt and pepper
2 ⅓ cups plus 1 Tbsp (10 ½ oz or 300 g)
all-purpose flour
3 eggs - 2 Tbsps milk
7 Tbsps (3 ½ oz or 100 g) butter, melted

Preparation time **50 minutes**
Cooking time **20 minutes**
Level **medium**
Wine **Colli Morenici Mantovani del Garda Bianco**

Preheat the oven to 350°F (180°C or Gas
Mark 4). Roast the squash in the oven until soft,
then puree in a food processor. Stir in the amaretti, mostarda, Parmesan and a pinch of nutmeg
and season with salt and pepper to taste. Stir
well, then cover and refrigerate for 1 hour.

Meanwhile mix together the flour, eggs and
milk to make a dough. Roll the dough out thinly
and place small spoonfuls of the squash mixture
evenly spaced around half the sheet. Fold over
the other half and cut out rectangles around
the filling. Press well with the fingers around
the edges to seal.

Bring a large pot of salted water to a boil and
cook the tortelli for a few minutes. Drain and
toss with melted butter and extra Parmesan.

Pizzoccheri
Buckwheat Pasta

Serves 4

3 cups (9 oz or 350 g) black buckwheat flour
3/4 cup plus 1 Tbsp (3 ½ oz or 100 g) all-purpose flour
salt
1 lb (500 g) Swiss chard, chopped
9 Tbsps grated Grana Padano cheese
14 oz (400 g) unaged Valtellina Casera cheese, sliced
3 Tbsps (1 ½ oz or 40 g) butter
3 garlic cloves, crushed

Preparation time **20 minutes**
Cooking time **20 minutes**
Level **easy**
Wine **Valtellina Superiore Valgella**

Mix the buckwheat and all-purpose flours and mound on a work surface. Form a well in the center and pour in enough water to obtain a smooth dough. Mix well, let rest for a few minutes then roll out a thin sheet. Cut first into rectangles 2 ¾ inches (7 cm) wide and then into 1/5-inch (1/2 cm) thick noodles. Bring a pot of salted water to a boil. Add the chard, cook for about 5 minutes, then add the pasta. When it is cooked (about 7 minutes), use a slotted spoon to drain some of the pasta and chard and place in a baking dish. Top with a layer of grated Grana and Casera cheese slices, then add some more pasta and chard and continue making layers, finishing with a thin layer of cheese. Melt the butter with the garlic cloves, remove the garlic and pour the butter over the pasta. Serve hot.

Tortelli di zucca

Pizzoccheri

risotto allo zafferano
saffron risotto

Serves 4

7 Tbsps (3 ½ oz or 100 g) butter
1 onion, minced
2 cups (14 oz or 400 g) Carnaroli rice
6 cups (1 ½ l) beef broth
1 large pinch of saffron
4 Tbsps grated Parmesan cheese,
plus extra for sprinkling
salt and pepper

Preparation time **5 minutes**
Cooking time **20 minutes**
Level **easy**
Wine **Oltrepò Pavese Barbera**

Melt half the butter in a saucepan and sauté half the onion.
Stir with a wooden spoon, and as soon as the onion is golden,
add the rice and toast, stirring constantly, for 1 minute.
   Add a ladleful of broth and continue cooking, adding broth
when necessary, until the rice is done.
   Dissolve the saffron in a spoonful of broth and add to the
cooked rice. Stir in the Parmesan and remaining butter
and season with salt and pepper. Stir well, cover for a few
minutes, then serve hot, sprinkled with extra Parmesan.

Note *The classic recipes uses 2-3 oz (50-100 g) beef marrow,
melted with the butter at the beginning. The better the quality
of saffron used, the better the risotto will be. This risotto is
the traditional accompaniment to ossobuco, another typical
local dish.*

Traditional recipe

Risotto alla pilota
Rice-Huskers' Risotto

Serves 4

2 cups (14 oz or 400 g) Vialone Nano rice
5 oz (140 g) salamelle mantovane or other small
salami, remove the casings and crumble the meat
1 cup (3 ½ oz or 100 g) grated
Grana Padano cheese
5 Tbsps (2 ½ oz or 70 g) butter
salt

Preparation time **10 minutes**
Cooking time **20 minutes**
Level **easy**
Wine **Lambrusco Mantovano**

Bring a pot of lightly salted water to a boil.

Twist a piece of parchment paper into a cone
with a hole at the bottom and pour the rice
into the cone. Add the rice to the water, letting
it pass through the bottom of the cone.

The rice will form a pyramid formation with
the top sticking out of the water. During the
cooking, shake the pan so that the rice falls
completely to the bottom of the pan and cook
for another 10 minutes. Remove from the heat
and cover the pot with a cloth. Let sit for
15 minutes.

Meanwhile melt the butter in a frying pan and
brown the salami meat. Drain the rice and mix
with the meat and half the grated Grana Padano
cheese. Serve hot, sprinkled with the remaining
cheese.

Urgiada (Zuppa d'orzo)
Barley Soup

Serves 4

2 oz (60 g) lardo (cured lard), chopped
1 onion, chopped
2 leeks, chopped
1 celery stalk, chopped
3/4 cup (5 oz or 140 g) pearl barley
3/4 cup (5 ½ oz or 150 g) fresh beans
(such as cranberry)
1 medium potato (about 7 oz or 200 g),
peeled and chopped
3/4 cup (180 ml) warm milk
salt and pepper
extra-virgin olive oil (optional)
bread, sliced and grilled (optional)

Preparation time **20 minutes**
Cooking time **1 hour 30 minutes**
Level **easy**
Wine **Valcalepio Rosso**

Soak the barley in cold water for 12 hours.

Sauté the lardo, onion, leeks and celery in a
saucepan until browned. Add the soaked and
drained barley and cover with water. Cook for
30 minutes, then add the beans and potato.

Add the warm milk and cook over low heat
for about 1 hour, stirring often to avoid sticking.
Season with salt and pepper.

Serve hot, if desired with a drizzle of olive oil,
a sprinkling of black pepper and grilled slices
of bread.

Casoncelli camuni
Camonica-Style Casoncelli

Serves 4-6

1 celery stalk, chopped - 1 carrot, chopped
7 oz (200 g) Swiss chard
7 Tbsps (3 ½ oz or 100 g) butter
2 garlic cloves, minced - 1 onion, minced
7 oz (200 g) roast beef, finely chopped
2 oz (50 g) prosciutto, finely chopped
2 oz (50 g) mortadella, finely chopped
4 eggs - 1/4 cup (1 oz or 30 g) breadcrumbs
3 Tbsps grated Parmesan cheese,
plus extra for sprinkling
1 pinch of ground cinnamon
grated nutmeg - salt and pepper
4 cups (1 lb 2 oz or 500 g) all-purpose flour
2 Tbsps extra-virgin olive oil - 10 sage leaves

Preparation time **40 minutes**
Cooking time **10 minutes**
Level **medium**
Wine **Valcalepio Rosso**

Boil the celery, carrot and chard until
tender, then puree in a food processor. Melt
a little butter in a frying pan and sauté the
garlic and onion until soft, then add the
vegetables. Sauté briefly then add the roast
beef, prosciutto and mortadella. Add 1 egg,
breadcrumbs, Parmesan, cinnamon, nutmeg,
salt and pepper. Mix the flour, 3 eggs and olive
oil into a dough. Roll out and place spoonfuls
of the meat mixture around half the sheet.
Fold over and cut out triangles around the
filling. Melt the remaining butter with the
sage. Bring a pot of salted water to a boil and
cook the casoncelli. Drain and toss with the
sage butter and extra Parmesan.

Casoncelli camuni

Baccalà alla mantovana
Mantuan-Style Salt Cod

Serves 6

2 ¼ lb (1 kg) pre-soaked salt cod
1/2 stick (2 oz or 60 g) butter
2 garlic cloves, minced
juice of 2 lemons
1 Tbsp minced parsley
freshly ground black pepper

Preparation time **20 minutes**
Cooking time **20 minutes**
Level **easy**
Wine **Colli Morenici Mantovani del Garda Rosato**

Wash the salt cod well under cold running water. Cut into small pieces.

Melt half the butter in a heavy-bottomed aluminum pan, then add the salt cod. Sprinkle over the garlic, parsley and lemon juice and cook over low heat, stirring often.

After about 10 minutes, sprinkle with freshly ground black pepper, add the remaining butter and continue cooking for another 10 minutes, stirring occasionally. Serve hot.

Ossibuchi in umido
Braised Veal Ossobuco

Serves 4

3 ½ Tbsps (2 oz or 50 g) butter
2 Tbsps extra-virgin olive oil
1/2 onion, minced - 2 garlic cloves
3 sage leaves, minced
4 ossobuco steaks (veal shank steaks)
3 Tbsps all-purpose flour
1/2 cup (120 ml) white wine
1/2 cup (120 ml) vegetable broth
1 bunch of parsley, plus extra for sprinkling
1 rosemary sprig
grated zest of 1 organic lemon
salt and pepper

Preparation time **20 minutes**
Cooking time **1 hour 20 minutes**
Level **easy**
Wine **Valtellina Rosso**

Sauté the onion, one garlic clove and the sage in the butter and olive oil in a saucepan until the onion is transparent. Lightly dust the shanks with flour and add them to the saucepan, turning until evenly browned on all sides.

Pour over the white wine, let it reduce, lower the flame and cook, covered, for about an hour, adding a little broth when necessary. Mince the parsley, remaining garlic clove, rosemary and the lemon zest together to make the gremolada.

As soon as the meat starts to pull away from the bone, season with salt, pepper and the gremolada. Let the flavors absorb for a few minutes then serve the steaks hot, sprinkled with minced parsley.

Polenta taragna
Buckwheat Polenta

Serves 6

16 cups (4 l) water
salt
4 cups (1 lb 2 oz or 500 g) buckwheat flour
3 cups (1 lb 2 oz or 500 g) polenta cornmeal
(not instant polenta)
2 ½ sticks plus 1 Tbsp (10 ½ oz or 300 g)
butter, chopped
1 ¼ lb (600 g) Casera cheese, diced,
plus extra for topping

Preparation time **20 minutes**
Cooking time **1 hour**
Level **easy**
Wine **Valtellina**

Bring the water to a boil in a large saucepan
and add salt. Mix together the buckwheat flour
and polenta, and sprinkle the mixture into
the water little by little, whisking constantly
to avoid lumps forming. When the mixture
thickens, switch to stirring with a wooden
spoon. Continue cooking until a crust forms
on the bottom and sides of the pan and the
polenta comes away easily from the sides, at
least 45 minutes. Add the butter and cheese
and cook for another 5 minutes.

Pour the polenta onto a wooden cutting
board and serve hot, topped with more cheese.

Note *The name "taragna" comes from
the taratura (adjustment) necessary during
cooking to make sure the polenta doesn't stick
to the bottom of the pan. The dish is so rich
that it can be served on its own, or accompanied
by sausages.*

Ossibuchi in umido

Polenta taragna

Lingua di vitello al Botticino
Tongue with Botticino Wine

Serves 4-6

1 veal or beef tongue
2 Tbsps all-purpose flour
2 Tbsps extra-virgin olive oil
2 onions, thinly sliced - 1 garlic clove
1 cup (7 oz or 200 g) crushed tomatoes
4 cups (1 l) Botticino wine - 5 cloves
2 bay leaves
1 cinnamon stick
2 cups (500 ml) veal or beef broth
all-purpose flour for thickening - salt

Preparation time **30 minutes**
Cooking time **3 hours 30 minutes**
Level **medium**
Wine **Botticino**

Boil the tongue in water for about 1 hour 30 minutes. Drain, peel, dry and lightly dust with flour. Heat the olive oil in a saucepan and sauté the onions and whole peeled garlic clove until golden. Add the tongue, brown, then add the tomatoes and wine. When the liquid comes to a boil lower the heat and continue cooking.

Place the bay leaves, cinnamon and cloves in a piece of cheese cloth or fabric and tie closed with kitchen string. Add to the saucepan. Continue cooking the tongue, adding broth when necessary. After 2 hours remove the tongue, discard the bag of spices and puree the rest of the cooking liquid with an immersion blender. Continue cooking until thickened, adding a little flour if necessary. Season with salt and serve with thick slices of tongue.

Costolette alla milanese
Milanese-Style Veal Cutlets

Serves 4

4 veal cutlets
5 Tbsps breadcrumbs
2 eggs
salt
grated nutmeg (optional)
3 Tbsps (1 ½ oz or 40 g) butter
fried potatoes (optional)

Preparation time **15 minutes**
Cooking time **20 minutes**
Level **easy**
Wine **San Colombano**

Pound out the cutlets with a meat tenderizer until thin and make small cuts around the edges with a sharp knife.

Spread the breadcrumbs on a work surface. Beat the eggs in a bowl with salt and a pinch of nutmeg, if desired.

Dip the cutlets in the egg mixture and then the breadcrumbs, coating well on both sides. Melt the butter in a frying pan and fry the breaded cutlets, turning often so they cook evenly and brown on both sides. Remove from the pan and dry on paper towels.

Serve hot, seasoned with a pinch of salt, and accompanied by fried potatoes, if desired.

Note *A famous variation is called orecchia d'elefante (elephant's ear), made using very large and thin slices of meat which curl up during cooking to resemble an elephant's ear.*

Cassoeula
Pork Rib Stew

Serves 4

1 large Savoy cabbage
10 ½ oz (300 g) pork rind
1 pat of butter
2 onions, minced
3 Tbsps extra-virgin olive oil
1 ¼ lb (600 g) pork ribs - salt
3/4 cup (180 ml) white wine
2 carrots, minced
2 celery stalks, minced
4 salamini (small salami)
cooked polenta (optional)

Preparation time **30 minutes**
Cooking time **2 hours**
Level **medium**
Wine **Terre di Franciacorta Rosso**

Remove the tougher external leaves from the cabbage and roughly chop the rest. Boil for 20 minutes, then drain and squeeze out excess water. Boil the pork rind in water for 10 minutes, then drain.

Heat the butter and olive oil together in a large saucepan and sauté the onion until golden. Add the ribs and brown. Season with salt and add the white wine. Add the pork rind, carrot and celery.

Cover and cook over low heat, stirring often with a wooden spoon, for about an hour, adding water when necessary. Add the salamini and cook for another 30 minutes, then add the cabbage. Cook for a few more minutes. Serve hot, with polenta if desired.

Costolette alla milanese

Cassoeula

Sbrisolona
Almond Cornmeal Cake

Serves 8

2 cups (9 oz or 250 g) all-purpose flour,
plus extra for flouring

1 cup plus 3 Tbsps (5 ½ oz or 150 g)
finely ground cornmeal

1 cup (7 oz or 200 g) sugar, plus extra for sprinkling

15 ½ Tbsps (7 ½ oz or 220 g) butter at room
temperature, chopped, plus extra for buttering

2 egg yolks

grated zest of 1 organic lemon

1 Tbsp aniseed liqueur

salt

1 ½ cups (7 oz or 200 g) blanched almonds,
coarsely chopped

Preparation time **30 minutes**
Cooking time **50 minutes**
Level **easy**
Wine **Oltrepò Pavese**
Moscato Spumante Dolce

Preheat the oven to 350°F (180°C or Gas Mark 4).

Mix together the flour and cornmeal and sift them onto a wooden pastry board. Add the sugar, butter, egg yolks, lemon zest, aniseed liqueur and a pinch of salt. Mix well with the hands to obtain and smooth and uniform dough.

Butter and flour a baking dish. Press the dough into it and sprinkle with the almonds. Bake for about 50 minutes, until golden.

Remove from the oven and let cool. Serve sprinkled with sugar.

Note *This is a typical dessert from Mantua, and its name comes from the word sbriciolare, meaning "to crumble," because of its crumbly texture. It is usually broken into pieces and eaten by hand.*

Panadèl
Sweet Apple Pancake

Serves 4

5 Tbsps sugar
1/4 cup (60 ml) grappa
1 tsp grated zest of 1 organic lemon
4 apples, cored and sliced
3 Tbsps all-purpose flour
1 tsp baking powder
2 Tbsps raisins
salt
1/2 cup (120 ml) milk
2 egg whites
1 pat of butter
2 Tbsps extra-virgin olive oil
confectioners' sugar for dusting

Preparation time **10 minutes**
Cooking time **5 minutes**
Level **easy**
Wine **Asti Moscato Spumante**

Sprinkle 2 tablespoons of sugar, the grappa and lemon zest over the apples and toss to coat.

Mix together the flour, remaining sugar, baking powder, raisins, a pinch of salt and enough milk to make a thick batter. Stir the apples into the batter. Beat the egg whites to soft peaks and fold them into the batter.

Heat the olive oil in a frying pan and pour in the batter. Cook like an omelet, adding the butter to the pan when flipping. Serve hot, sprinkled with confectioners' sugar.

Miascia
Apple and Pear Cake

Serves 4

1 lb (500 g) stale bread
1 handful of amaretti cookies, crumbled
2 cups (500 ml) milk
2 eggs
1/3 cup (2 oz or 50 g) raisins
2 apples, cored and thinly sliced
2 pears, cored and thinly sliced
2 ½ Tbsps pine nuts
4 Tbsps sugar
1/4 cup (60 ml) Disaronno amaretto liqueur
grated zest of 1 organic lemon
1 pat of butter
1 Tbsp all-purpose flour

Preparation time **20 minutes**
Cooking time **1 hour**
Level **easy**
Wine **Moscato Passito Valcalepio**

Soak the bread and amaretti in the milk for about an hour, until the liquid has been completely absorbed. Preheat the oven to 400°F (200°C or Gas Mark 6).

Puree the bread mixture in a food processor. Mix it with the eggs, raisins, apples, pears, pine nuts, sugar, liqueur and lemon zest. Stir well, then pour into a buttered and floured baking dish.

Level off the top and bake for 15 minutes, then turn down the oven to 325°F (170°C or Gas Mark 3) and bake for another 45 minutes. Serve warm.

Pan de mei
Elderflower Cookies

Serves 4-6

2 ½ tsps active dry yeast

2 ⅓ cups plus 1 Tbsp (10 ½ oz or 300 g)
finely ground cornmeal

1 cup plus 3 Tbsps (5 ½ oz or 150 g)
all-purpose flour

3 eggs

salt - milk

1 cup (7 oz or 200 g) sugar,
plus extra for sprinkling

1 stick plus 1 Tbsp (4 ½ oz or 125 g) butter
at room temperature, chopped,
plus extra for buttering

2 oz (50 g) elderflowers,
plus extra for sprinkling

Preparation time **30 minutes**
Cooking time **30 minutes**
Level **easy**
Wine **San Colombano**

Mix the yeast with a little warm water.
Sift the cornmeal and flour together onto
a wooden pastry board. Add the eggs, sugar,
butter, a pinch of salt, elderflowers and the
yeast mixture. Mix together, adding milk
as necessary, to form a smooth dough. Form
into a ball, cover with a clean kitchen towel
and let rest for 30 minutes. Preheat the oven
to 350°F (180°C or Gas Mark 4).
Divide the dough into many small
portions, about 2 oz (50 g) each, and arrange
them on a lightly buttered baking sheet.
Sprinkle with sugar and elderflowers.
Bake for 30 minutes, until golden-brown.

Miascia

Pan de mei

Trentino-Alto Adige

Beautiful snow-covered peaks, painted fiery colors by the sunset.

Alpine meadows filled with flowers. A region for skiing and hiking, for ancient mountain huts and simple yet delicious *cheeses*, for impregnable castles and an agriculture known for its exceptional *wines*, *meat*, *fruit* and *speck*. Discover the characteristic dishes and tempting desserts of this northern region.

TRENTINO-ALTO ADIGE
local products

Mela *Golden*

THE REGION'S AGRICULTURE IS DOMINATED BY FRUIT FARMING. The apple (*mela*) has been grown here for centuries, as recorded by both historical documents and place names: Malé, in Val di Non, derives from the Latin *Maletum*, "place of the apples." Renette and Golden Delicious apples are the major varieties cultivated in the Non and Sole valleys in the province of Trento in Alto Adige, while Stark Delicious, Morgenduft, Gloster, Royal Gala and others are also harvested in the Venosta, Bassa Atesina and Isarco valleys. The texture and flavor of Renette apples varies depending on when they are picked, and can be crisp and acidic or soft and sweet, but always marked by the distinctive Renette fragrance. Golden Delicious is a versatile variety of American origin, introduced to Trentino-Alto Adige's valleys in the 1960s. Golden Delicious apples have crunchy, juicy flesh and an unusual sweet-tart flavor, and in just a few years have become the stars of the Non and Sole valleys. Val di Non apples were the first to obtain a DOP (Denomination of Protected Origin) recognition, followed by several other varieties.

Trentin *grana*

A CHEESE BELONGING TO THE GRANA FAMILY, IDENTIFIED BY THE WORD "TRENTINO" ON THE RIND. Cow's milk from two milkings is used, the surface skimmed and the heated milk curdled using a whey starter and veal rennet. The curd is broken up and then reheated and cooked. After draining off the whey, the curd is pressed into wooden molds. After a long brine bath, the forms are aged for 18 to 24 months. Each cheese weighs between 65 to 85 pounds (30-38 kg).

Speck dell'*Alto Adige*

SPECK IS MADE FROM THE BEST-QUALITY PORK LEGS, lightly salted and seasoned with pepper, pimento, garlic, juniper and sugar, then cold-smoked over aromatic wood for about three weeks, during which the meat takes on a characteristic smoky flavor. The speck is then dried at temperatures no higher than 68°F (20°C) and aged for between 20 and 24 weeks. Speck from Alto Adige is produced throughout the province of Bolzano.

Fragoline di *bosco*

BERRIES (*FRUTTI DI BOSCO*) ARE A VALUABLE RESOURCE FOR TRENTINO. Smaller than domesticated strawberries but very sweet, wild strawberries are picked in July and August. Blueberries and lingonberries are harvested between July and October and are renowned for their high vitamin C and A content. Raspberries, collected between July and August, can be ruby red or golden yellow. They can be eaten fresh, but they also freeze well.

Strauben

THESE DELICIOUS FRITTERS are usually eaten during village festivals or family festivities. The name comes from the verb *strauben*, meaning "to curl." The batter is made from milk, eggs, flour, beer and Trentino grappa and is funneled in spirals into the hot oil. The fritters are sprinkled with sugar and often served with applesauce or blueberry jam.

Gewürztraminer

AN AROMATIC WHITE WINE made from Traminer grapes and produced in different municipalities of the province of Bolzano. It has a characteristic fruity fragrance and is dry, flavorful and distinctive. It pairs well with meat or fish appetizers and medium-aged cheeses.

Puzzone di Moena

THE AROMA AND FLAVOR OF THIS CHEESE are as unusual as its name, which means "smelly." Made from full-fat milk from Bruno Alpina cows, it has a mild flavor with a pleasantly sharp aftertaste. The cylindrical forms weigh 17-22 pounds (8-10 kg) and are aged between 2 months and a year.

Smacafam
Hearty Focaccia

Serves 6

1 cup plus 3 Tbsps (5 ½ oz or 150 g)
all-purpose flour, plus extra for flouring
1 cup plus 3 Tbsps (5 ½ oz or 150 g)
buckwheat flour
2 cups (500 ml) warm milk
salt
1 Tbsp extra-virgin olive oil
2 oz (50 g) lardo (cured lard), diced
2 oz (50 g) pancetta, diced
7 oz (200 g) luganega sausage, sliced
1 pat of butter

Preparation time **20 minutes**
Cooking time **30 minutes**
Level **easy**
Wine **Teroldego Rotaliano**

Preheat the oven to 350°F (180°C or Gas
Mark 4). In a bowl, mix together the two
flours, milk and salt to form a smooth,
soft dough.

   Fry the lardo and pancetta in the olive oil,
and add to the dough, together with half
the luganega.

   Lightly butter and flour a baking sheet and
spread the dough out on it, using a spatula to
make an even layer. Sprinkle over the rest of
the luganega and bake for about 30 minutes.
Serve hot.

Note *This kind of focaccia is typically prepared
during carnival. Its name literally means
"hunger-killer."*

Canederli allo speck
Speck Dumplings

Serves 4

2 Tbsps extra-virgin olive oil
1/2 onion, minced
5 ½ oz (150 g) speck, diced
12 ½ oz (350 g) stale crusty bread
with crusts removed, cubed
3/4 cup plus 1 Tbsp (200 ml) milk
3 Tbsps all-purpose flour
3 eggs
salt
2 Tbsps minced parsley, plus extra for garnish
2 Tbsps minced chives
10 cups (2 ½ l) beef broth

Preparation time **30 minutes**
Cooking time **15 minutes**
Level **medium**
Wine **Lago di Caldaro Schiava**

Heat the olive oil in a frying pan and sauté
the onion until golden.

   Add the speck and let brown for a few
minutes. Soak the bread in the milk until soft.

   Add the speck mixture, flour, eggs, salt,
parsley and chives. Stir well, then use damp
hands to form the mixture into small balls.

   Bring a large pot of broth to a boil and cook
the dumplings for 15 minutes. Serve them hot
in the broth, garnished with minced parsley.

Canederli allo speck

Gnocchi in brodo
Semolina Dumplings in Broth

Serves 4

2 cups (500 ml) milk
1 cup (5 ½ oz or 150 g) semolina flour
2 Tbsps extra-virgin olive oil
8 cups (2 l) beef broth

Preparation time **15 minutes**
Cooking time **20 minutes**
Level **easy**
Wine **Trentino Müller Thurgau**

Bring the milk to a boil in a large saucepan. Sprinkle in the semolina and cook for 15 minutes, whisking continuously to avoid lumps forming.

Pour the mixture into an oiled baking dish and smooth off the top with a spatula. Let cool until firm. Use a teaspoon to form small semolina dumplings about the size of a hazelnut.

Bring the broth to a boil and cook the dumplings for about 5 minutes. Serve with the broth.

Note *This dish is originally Austrian, but is very common in Trentino and Friuli. A variation adds yeast to the semolina.*

Strozzapreti alle erbette
Ricotta and Chard Strozzapreti

Serves 4-6

1 ½ lb (700 g) Swiss chard
14 oz (400 g) ricotta
4 eggs
2 ⅓ cups plus 1 Tbsp (10 ½ oz or 300 g) all-purpose flour
grated nutmeg
salt
3 ½ Tbsps (2 oz or 50 g) butter, melted
1/2 cup (2 oz or 50 g) grated Parmesan cheese

Preparation time **25 minutes**
Cooking time **20 minutes**
Level **easy**
Wine **Alto Adige Sauvignon**

Boil the chard until tender, then drain, trim off the white stalks and finely chop the green leaves. Place the ricotta in a bowl and add the chard leaves, eggs, flour and a grating of nutmeg. Mix well to form a smooth, soft dough.

Form the dough into long ropes and then break the ropes into 1-inch (2 cm) lengths.

Bring a large pot of salted water to a boil and add the strozzapreti. A few minutes after the water comes to a boil, drain them. Serve tossed with melted butter and grated Parmesan.

Ravioli alle rape rosse
Beet Ravioli

Serves 4

1 ⅔ cups (7 oz or 200 g) buckwheat flour
2 ⅓ cups plus 1 Tbsp (10 ½ oz or 300 g)
all-purpose flour
3 eggs - 1 Tbsp extra-virgin olive oil
salt and pepper - 1 carrot, chopped
1 potato, peeled and chopped
3 beets (about 8 oz or 250 g in total)
breadcrumbs
3 Tbsps (1 ½ oz or 40 g) butter, melted
4 Tbsps grated Trentingrana cheese
2 Tbsps poppy seeds

Preparation time **40 minutes**
Cooking time **30 minutes**
Level **medium**
Wine **Alto Adige Lagrein Dunkel**

Mix together the two flours, eggs, olive oil
and salt to make a dough. Form into a ball,
wrap in plastic wrap and let rest.

Meanwhile, boil the carrot and potato until
tender, then drain. Boil the beets until tender,
then peel and puree in a food processor with
the carrot and potato. Season with salt and
pepper. If the mixture seems too thin, stir in some
breadcrumbs. Roll the dough out thinly and use
a rolling cutter to cut squares. Place a spoonful of
the beet mixture in the center of each square and
fold over to close, pressing firmly around the edges
with the fingertips. Bring a pot of salted water
to a boil and cook the ravioli for 10 minutes.

Drain and toss with melted butter and sprinkle
with Trentingrana cheese and poppy seeds.

Strozzapreti alle erbette

Ravioli alle rape rosse

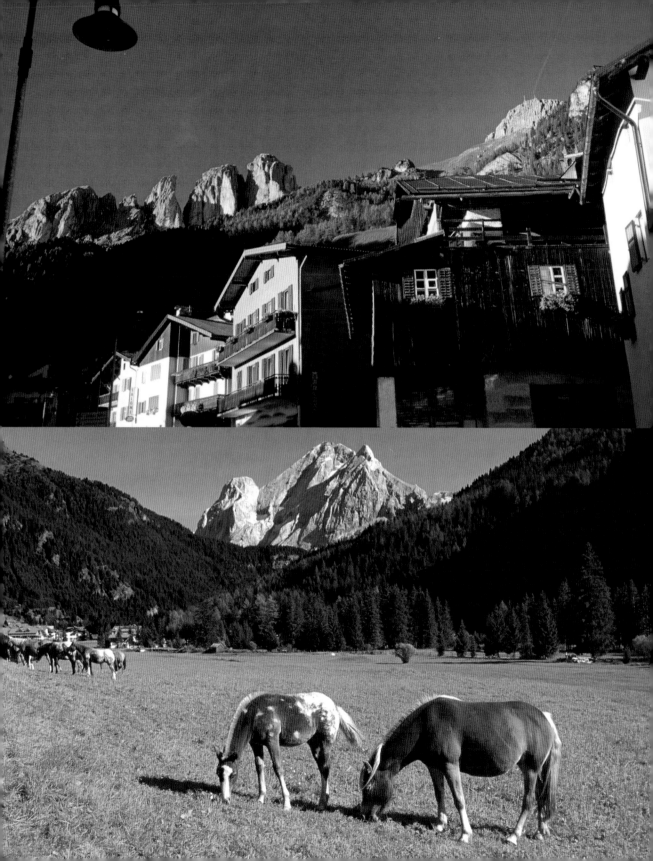

Rosticciata di carne
Beef and Potato Sauté

Serves 4

3 ½ lb (1 ½ kg) potatoes, peeled
11 Tbsps (5 ½ oz or 160 g) butter
1 onion, minced
1 ¼ lb (600 g) beef or veal, cut into strips
2 bay leaves
1 marjoram sprig
salt and pepper
1 bunch of parsley, minced

Preparation time **25 minutes**
Cooking time **40 minutes**
Level **easy**
Wine **Alto Adige Lagrein Dunkel**

Boil the potatoes until tender, drain and slice. In another frying pan melt half the butter and sauté the sliced potatoes until browned.

Melt the rest of the butter in another large frying pan and sauté the onion until golden. Add the beef and brown over high heat.

Add the potatoes, bay leaves, marjoram, salt and pepper and sauté together for a few more minutes, until the meat is cooked through.

Sprinkle with parsley and serve hot.

Note *This is a very typical dish in Trentino, and many variations exist. One of the most popular is with potatoes, chanterelle mushrooms and speck.*

Gulasch
Goulash

Serves 4-6

4 Tbsps extra-virgin olive oil
5 onions, minced
1 garlic clove, minced
1 ¼ lb (600 g) beef, diced
2 Tbsps all-purpose flour
1 tsp paprika
3/4 cup (180 ml) red wine
1 Tbsp tomato paste
grated zest of 1 organic lemon
1/2 tsp ground cumin
1 rosemary sprig
2 bay leaves
1 marjoram sprig
salt and pepper

Preparation time **20 minutes**
Cooking time **1 hour 40 minutes**
Level **medium**
Wine **Alto Adige Lagrein Dunkel**

Heat the olive oil in a large saucepan and sauté the onions and garlic until golden. Add the beef and brown for a few minutes, stirring with a wooden spoon.

Mix the flour and paprika with a little water and add to the saucepan together with the wine, tomato paste, lemon zest, cumin, rosemary, bay leaves, marjoram, salt and pepper.

Add a little water and cook, covered, for 1 hour 30 minutes over medium heat, adding water if necessary. Serve hot.

Pulenta carbonera
Polenta with Cheese

Serves 6-8

6 cups (2 lb 3 oz or 1 kg) coarsely ground
polenta cornmeal (not instant polenta)

14 Tbsps (7 oz or 200 g) butter

1 onion, minced

1 lb (500 g) salami, casing removed,
meat chopped

9 oz (250 g) aged Valchiese cheese, chopped

9 oz (250 g) soft Valchiese cheese, chopped

salt and pepper

1 cup (3 ½ oz or 100 g) grated
Trentingrana cheese

Preparation time **5 minutes**
Cooking time **40 minutes**
Level **easy**
Wine **Teroldego Rotaliano**

Bring a large pot of water to a boil
and sprinkle in the cornmeal, whisking
constantly. Cook for about 30 minutes,
stirring with a wooden spoon. Meanwhile
melt half the butter in another saucepan
and sauté the onion until golden. Add
the salami and brown for a few minutes.

As soon as the polenta is done, stir in
the two cheeses and the rest of the butter.

Season to taste with salt and pepper, and
serve topped with the salami and grated
Trentingrana. Serve immediately.

Note *Valchiese is a cheese made in the Valle
delle Chiese, and comes in two versions, one
made from November to March, and a summer
one which is a kind of local version of Brescian
Bagòss.*

Gulasch

Pulenta carbonera

Spezzatino di capriolo
Venison Stew

Serves 6

1 celery stalk, minced - 1 onion, minced
3 carrots, minced - 2 ¼ lb (1 kg) venison, cubed
2 bottles (1 ½ l) red wine - 5 sage leaves
5 juniper berries - 2 cloves - 3-4 peppercorns
1 cinnamon stick - 1/2 bunch of chives
2 sprigs each of rosemary, thyme and marjoram
3 salted anchovies, chopped
3 ½ oz (100 g) pork liver, finely minced
2 oz (50 g) lardo (cured lard), finely minced
1 piece of organic lemon rind
3 ½ Tbsps (2 oz or 50 g) butter
4 Tbsps extra-virgin olive oil - salt

Preparation time **30 minutes**
Cooking time **2 hours**
Level **easy**
Wine **Refosco dal Peduncolo Rosso**

Mix together the celery, onion and carrots. Place the venison in a large bowl. Add the wine, half the vegetable mixture, the sage, juniper, cloves, peppercorns, cinnamon, chives, rosemary, thyme and marjoram. Let marinate for 48 hours. Refrigerate the remaining celery, onion and carrots.

Once the venison has marinated, mix the reserved celery, onion and carrots with the anchovies, pork liver, lardo and lemon rind. Heat half the butter and half the olive oil in a saucepan and sauté the mixture until the vegetables are soft. Remove the lemon rind.

Drain the venison, strain and reserve the marinade. Heat the rest of the butter and olive oil in another saucepan and brown the venison. Add the sautéed vegetable mixture, marinade and salt. Cook for about 3 hours, adding extra wine if necessary. Serve hot, with polenta if desired.

Sella di cerbiatto ai mirtilli
Venison with Blueberry Sauce

Serves 4

1 ¾ lb (800 g) venison saddle
3 Tbsps extra-virgin olive oil
1 onion, sliced - 1 carrot, sliced
1 celery stalk, sliced
3 ⅓ cups (800 ml) vegetable broth
5 peppercorns - 5 juniper berries
2 bay leaves - 2 thyme sprigs
1 pat of butter - 2 ½ Tbsps blueberry jam

Preparation time **15 minutes**
Cooking time **1 hour 30 minutes**
Level **medium**
Wine **Alto Adige Schiava**

Trim and debone the venison saddle, reserving the bones and trimmings. Heat 1 tablespoon olive oil in a saucepan and brown the venison bones and trimmings. Add the onion, carrot and celery. Cover with vegetable broth and simmer for about 1 hour.

Preheat the oven to 350°F (180°C or Gas Mark 4). Tie the venison saddle with kitchen string. Heat the remaining 2 tablespoons of olive oil in a frying pan and brown the venison on all sides. Remove the string. Wrap the venison in a large piece of parchment paper together with the peppercorns, juniper, bay leaves and thyme. Bake in the oven for 15 minutes.

Strain the broth and cook down until reduced by half. Stir in the butter and blueberry jam. Remove the venison from the oven, unwrap and slice. Serve with the blueberry sauce.

Note *If desired, the venison can be accompanied by polenta and sautéed wild mushrooms.*

Sella di cerbiatto ai mirtilli

Torta di grano saraceno
Buckwheat Cake

Serves 6-8

2 ½ sticks plus 1 Tbsp (10 ½ oz or 300 g) butter, softened
1 ½ cups (10 ½ oz or 300 g) sugar
6 eggs, separated
2 tsps vanilla extract
2 ½ cups (10 ½ oz or 300 g) buckwheat flour
3 Tbsps all-purpose flour
2 tsps baking powder
1 jar lingonberry or blueberry jam
confectioners' sugar for dusting

Preparation time **40 minutes**
Cooking time **45 minutes**
Level **medium**
Wine **Alto Adige Moscato Giallo**

Preheat the oven to 350°F (180°C or Gas Mark 4). Cream the butter and sugar.

Add the egg yolks one at a time and then the vanilla and mix until creamy. Sift in the flours and baking powder.

Beat the egg whites to stiff peaks and fold into the batter. Butter and flour a cake pan and pour in the batter. Bake for 45 minutes. Remove from the oven and let cool.

Cut the cake in half horizontally to form 2 rounds.

Spread the jam over one round and top with the remaining round. Dust with confectioners' sugar and serve.

Strudel di mele
Apple Strudel

Serves 4-6

2 ¾ cups (12 ½ oz or 350 g) all-purpose flour
2 egg yolks - 1 egg - 2 Tbsps raisins - salt
6 ½ Tbsps (3 ½ oz or 90 g) butter, melted
6 acidic apples (Grafensteiner or Renette)
3 Tbsps rum - 3 Tbsps sugar
1/2 tsp ground cinnamon - 2 Tbsps breadcrumbs
confectioners' sugar for dusting

Preparation time **1 hour**
Cooking time **1 hour**
Level **medium**
Wine **Alto Adige Moscato Rosa**

Mix 2 1/3 cups plus 1 tablespoon (10 ½ oz or 300 g) all-purpose flour, 1 egg yolk, the egg, 3 ½ tablespoons (2 oz or 50 g) of melted butter and salt with enough warm water to form an elastic dough. Let rest for 1 hour. Preheat the oven to 400°F (200°C or Gas Mark 6). Soak the raisins in warm water, drain and squeeze out. Peel, core and slice the apples, then toss with rum, raisins, sugar and cinnamon. Roll the dough out on a clean kitchen towel into a thin oval.

Brush with melted butter, sprinkle with breadcrumbs and spread over the apples, leaving a border of 1-inch (2 ½ cm) around the edges. Lift up the edges of the towel and roll up. Press down around the edges of the dough and transfer to a buttered baking sheet.

Mix together the remaining egg yolk and melted butter and brush the surface of the strudel. Bake for 15 minutes, then lower the temperature to 350°F (180°C or Gas Mark 4) and bake for another 45 minutes, until golden-brown. Serve hot, dusted with confectioners' sugar.

Omelette al mirtillo
Blueberry Crêpes

Serves 4

2 ⅓ cups plus 1 Tbsp (10 ½ oz or 300 g)
all-purpose flour
3 eggs
2 cups (500 ml) milk
salt
sunflower oil for sautéeing crêpes
1/2 cup (5 ½ oz or 150 g) blueberry jam
confectioners' sugar for sprinkling

Preparation time **30 minutes**
Cooking time **20 minutes**
Level **medium**
Wine **Alto Adige Gewürztraminer
Vendemmia Tardiva**

Sift the flour into a bowl. Add the
eggs, milk and a pinch of salt and
whisk to obtain a smooth batter.

Heat a little sunflower oil in a large
cast-iron frying pan. Ladle in enough
batter to cover the surface. Brown
on both sides, then remove from the
pan. Continue making crêpes until
the batter is finished.

Spread a layer of jam on each crêpe,
then fold or roll up. Serve sprinkled
with confectioners' sugar.

Strudel di mele

Omelette al mirtillo

frittelle di mele
apple fritters

Serves 4-6

1/4 cup (60 ml) grappa
6 Tbsps sugar
1 tsp ground cinnamon
5 apples, peeled, cored and thinly sliced
2 eggs, separated
1/4 cup (60 ml) milk
salt
1 cup (4 ½ oz or 130 g) all-purpose flour
2 tsps baking powder
sunflower oil for frying
confectioners' sugar for sprinkling

Preparation time **40 minutes**
Cooking time **20 minutes**
Level **medium**
Wine **Trentino Moscato Rosa**

Mix half the grappa, the sugar and cinnamon together
and toss with the apples. Beat the egg yolks with the milk,
remaining grappa and a pinch of salt.

Sift the flour and baking powder together into the mixture
and stir well, making sure there are no lumps. Beat the egg
whites to soft peaks and fold into the batter. Stir in the apple
slices.

Heat sunflower oil until very hot, then start frying the apple
slices in batches. Fry until golden on both sides, then drain
and sprinkle with confectioners' sugar before serving.

Traditional recipe

Veneto

A *special atmosphere envelops* magical and unique cities

like Venice, Verona and Treviso, where
a romantic air pervades every building.
Waterways from sea and river, wide plains
and rolling hills that disappear into the
hazy blue horizon. Every little corner of
the region has its own specialties, whether
flavorful *cheeses*, *moleche* lagoon crabs,
creamy *polenta*, *rice* for risottos,
red-and-white *radicchio*, artisanal
salumi or vintage *wines*.

VENETO
local products

Ciliegia di *Marostica*

MAROSTICA LIES NEAR VICENZA, AND IS KNOWN FOR ITS FAMOUS CHERRIES (CILIEGIE), PROTECTED BY AN **IGP** (INDICATION OF PROTECTED ORIGIN). The legend goes that the first cherry trees were planted by the governor in 1454 for his daughter's wedding, to produce a fruit as red as love. The first cherry market goes back to the late 19th century, and since then fruit production has reached the highest quality levels. Integrated pest management techniques are used to protect the flowering trees from parasites. The Marostica cherries, which today include a number of different varieties, are harvested by hand, and if they are not sold within 48 hours, they will be chilled and used for preserves like jam and syrups.

Fagiolo di *Lamon*

THE LAMON BEANS (FAGIOLI) IGP INCLUDES FOUR DIFFERENT VARIETIES: Spagnol, with an oval shape, red streaks and aromatic qualities that made it ideal for salads; Spagnolet, smaller and rounder, with a very thin skin also streaked with red; Calonega, the biggest, with an elongated shape and a chestnut flavor, good for soups and purees; and Canalino, with an intense flavor and thick external skin.

Formaggi *veneti*

WHILE MANY CHEESES (*FORMAGGI*) ARE PRODUCED IN THE VENETO REGION, some merit special mention. The most important cheese from the area around Belluno is Piave DOP (Denomination of Protected Origin), made from semi-skimmed milk from Alpine pastures. It comes in three varieties: "Fresco" is aged 20 to 60 days, "Mezzano" 61 to 120 days and "Vecchio" for more than 120 days.

From the province of Treviso comes Imbriago, with a hard, violet-colored rind and a mildly sharp flavor. The cheeses are aged the pomace left after crushing Cabernet, Merlot and Raboso grapes, and continuously sprinkled with pressed wine for 35-50 hours.

The Asiago plateau is home to the cheese of the same name, made from cow's milk and with a semi-cooked curd. Its production area also extends to the neighboring provinces of Trento, Padua and Treviso. Asiago can be aged or fresh, with a soft, creamy texture and a mild aroma. Morlacco, once called the cheese of the poor, is an Alpine cheese produced only in the summer, using artisanal methods, and is hard to find because very few are produced. The soft, white paste with small holes is covered by a yellow rind, and has an intense fragrance and very salty flavor. This cheese pairs well with polenta, cut into thick slices and served with soppressa, or melted as a filling for gnocchi or ravioli.

Radicchi *veneti*

RED RADICCHIO IS INDISSOLUBLY LINKED TO THE TERRITORY OF THE VENETO.
The winter vegetable's origins go back to the second half of the nineteenth century, when the original plant underwent forcing, removing its roots and leaves and leaving it in the dark under a layer of peat. There are several varieties of radicchio. There are two types of Treviso radicchio, one early and one late. The former has a dark red head, elongated (around 7-10 inches or 18-25 cm), with tightly closed leaves and a thick white stalk.

Late Treviso radicchio is harvested a month later (from early November) and has narrower, reddish leaves with a brilliant white veining. Verona radicchio has bright red leaves, not as long as Treviso, and with a rounder head. Chioggia radicchio is very popular and the most cultivated: dark red leaves and a round head with branching white veins. Radicchio has an unmistakable bitter flavor. Traditional Veneto cuisine uses the vegetable in many dishes, cooked in frittatas, fried in batter, as a sauce for lasagna, to top bruschetta or raw as an accompaniment to saor.

Pandoro di *Verona*

A SYMBOL OF CHRISTMAS FESTIVITIES, THIS CAKE IS MADE OF JUST A FEW SIMPLE INGREDIENTS, but to make it properly requires following a long, complex procedure, with three phases of kneading and rising. Opinions vary about pandoro's links to the city of Verona: it might be a variant of a Veronese Christmas dessert in the shape of a star called *nadalin*, or, more probably, it derives from *pane di Vienna* (Vienna bread), imported by the Hapsburg pastry cooks who were employed in the late 19th century in Verona's best bakeries. It's likely that the ingredients and cooking technique come from the Hapsburgs, while the star shape comes from the traditional Veronese nadalin.

Amarone della *Valpolicella*

AMONG THE BEST RED WINES IN ITALY, Amarone is produced around Valpolicella in the province of Verona from Corvina, Rondella and Monilara varieties and other local grapes. Ruby-red with garnet tinges, it has a bouquet of great complexity recalling flowers, ripe red and black fruits and spices. The densely concentrated flavor makes it one of the country's most original wines. The production technique contributes to this strong personality: According to regulation, the wine is aged in oak barrels and then barriques for two years, but usually is sold only after at least four years. If stored well it can last for up to 10 to 15 years, developing pleasantly surprising characteristics. Structured, full-bodied, but soft and elegant, it pairs with hearty meat stews, roast game and aged cheeses.

Gratin polesano
Polesine-Style Potato Gratin

Serves 4

2/3 cup (150 ml) vegetable broth
1 large pat of butter
1 ¾ lb (800 g) potatoes, peeled and thinly sliced
salt and pepper
10 ½ oz (300 g) Fontina cheese, sliced
5 ½ oz (150 g) pancetta, sliced

Preparation time **15 minutes**
Cooking time **30 minutes**
Level **easy**
Wine **Colli Euganei Merlot**

Preheat the oven to 350°F (180°C or Gas Mark 4). Bring the vegetable broth to a boil in a saucepan. Butter a baking dish.

Arrange half the potato slices in a layer in the baking dish. Pour over the boiling broth. Season with salt and pepper and bake until the broth has been completely absorbed.

Remove from the oven and cover with half the Fontina and half the pancetta. Top with the remaining potatoes and then the rest of the Fontina and pancetta.

Bake for about 20 minutes, until the top is browned. Serve hot.

Crocchette di baccalà
Salt Cod Croquettes

Serves 4

2 potatoes (about 10 ½ oz or 300 g), peeled and cubed
5 ½ oz (150 g) pre-soaked salt cod
1 egg
1 bunch of parsley, minced
1 garlic clove, minced
salt
sunflower oil for frying

Preparation time **20 minutes**
Cooking time **40 minutes**
Level **easy**
Wine **Breganze Bianco**

Boil the potatoes in salted water for about 20 minutes. Drain and pass through a food mill or potato ricer to obtain a smooth puree.

Boil the salt cod in water for about 20 minutes. Drain and crumble into small pieces, then mix with the potatoes.

Stir the egg, parsley and garlic into the salt cod mixture. Season to taste with salt and mix well. Form the mixture into small balls about the size of a walnut.

Heat sunflower oil until very hot, then fry the balls until golden. Drain with a slotted spoon, dry on paper towels and serve immediately.

Frittelle di fiori di zucca
Squash Blossom Fritters

Serves 4-6

30 squash blossoms - 1 egg yolk
6 Tbsps sugar
1 cup plus 3 Tbsps (5 ½ oz or 150 g)
all-purpose flour
1 pinch of active dry yeast
grated zest of 1 organic lemon - salt
1 Tbsp extra-virgin olive oil
1/4 cup (60 ml) dry Marsala wine
1 Tbsp grappa - milk
sunflower oil for frying
1 tsp ground cinnamon

Preparation time **20 minutes**
Cooking time **25 minutes**
Level **easy**
Wine **Prosecco di Conegliano
e Valdobbiadene Brut**

Open the squash blossoms, remove the pistils
and wash the flowers under cold running
water. Dry on paper towels.

Beat the egg yolk with 4 tablespoons of
sugar, then add the flour, yeast, lemon zest
and salt. Let sit for a few minutes and then
stir with a wooden spoon. Mix in the olive
oil, Marsala, grappa and enough milk to form
a smooth batter. Stir well to eliminate any
lumps. Heat sunflower oil. Dip the squash
blossoms in the batter and fry them in the hot
oil in batches. Turn them frequently while
frying, and once golden drain with a slotted
spoon and dry on paper towels. Mix together
the remaining sugar with the cinnamon and
sprinkle on the blossoms before serving.

Crocchette di baccalà

Frittelle di fiori di zucca

Risotto con gli asparagi
White Asparagus Risotto

Serves 4

1 bunch of white asparagus (about 1 lb or 500 g)
3 ½ Tbsps (2 oz or 50 g) butter
2 Tbsps extra-virgin olive oil
1/2 onion, minced
1/2 celery stalk, minced
6 cups (1 ½ l) vegetable broth
1 ½ cups (10 ½ oz or 300 g) Vialone Nano rice
1/2 cup (120 ml) white wine
5 Tbsps grated Parmesan cheese
2 Tbsps heavy cream
ground white pepper

Preparation time **10 minutes**
Cooking time **30 minutes**
Level **easy**
Wine **Colli Berici Sauvignon**

Peel the asparagus stalks and cut them into 3/4-inch (1-2 cm) pieces. Set aside the tips.

Melt half the butter with the olive oil in a saucepan and sauté the onion and celery until soft. Add the asparagus stalks and sauté for about 10 minutes, stirring with a wooden spoon.

Bring the broth to a boil and keep hot. Add the rice to the asparagus, toast for a few minutes and then add the wine. Continue cooking, adding ladlefuls of hot broth when necessary and stirring frequently. Half-way through the cooking add the asparagus tips.

When the rice is cooked through, stir in the remaining butter, the cream and the Parmesan. Season with white pepper and serve immediately.

Zuppa alla veneta
Venetian-Style Soup

Serves 4

1 cup (7 oz or 200 g) dried cranberry beans
1/4 cup (2 oz or 50 g) dried black-eyed peas
1/4 cup (2 oz or 50 g) pearl barley
3 Tbsps extra-virgin olive oil, plus extra for drizzling
1/2 onion, minced - 1 celery stalk, minced
1 carrot, minced - salt
1/4 cup (2 oz or 50 g) sweetcorn - 1 potato, cubed
4 slices of bread, toasted (optional)

Preparation time **20 minutes**
Cooking time **1 hour 40 minutes**
Level **easy**
Wine **Bardolino Classico**

Soak the beans, barley and black-eyed peas separately overnight. Drain and rinse.

Boil the barley for about 40 minutes, then drain. Meanwhile heat the olive oil in a saucepan and sauté the onion, celery and carrot until soft. Add the beans, water and salt and bring to a boil. Cook, covered, for about 1 hour over medium heat. Meanwhile cook the black-eyed peas in salted water for about 45 minutes, then add the corn and potato and cook for another 15 minutes.

Pass about half of the cooked beans through a food mill or puree in a food processor. Drain the black-eyed peas, corn and potatoes and mix with the whole and pureed beans. Add the barley. Cook for a few minutes, stirring with a wooden spoon. Serve the soup hot, drizzled with extra-virgin olive oil and accompanied by toasted bread, if desired.

Zuppa alla veneta

Bigoli in salsa
Bigoli with Sardines

Serves 4

8 ½ oz (240 g) salted sardines
1/2 cup (120 ml) extra-virgin olive oil
2 onions, minced
salt and pepper
12 ½ oz (360 g) bigoli, bucatini or thick spaghetti

Preparation time **5 minutes**
Cooking time **20 minutes**
Level **easy**
Wine **Colli Berici Tocai Italico**

Rinse the sardines under cold running water to remove the salt and debone them.

Heat the olive oil in a large saucepan and sauté the onions. Add the sardines and a pinch of pepper and cook for about 15 minutes over medium heat, stirring every so often with a wooden spoon.

Bring a large pot of salted water to a boil and cook the pasta until al dente. Drain and add to the saucepan with the sardines. Stir well and serve immediately.

Note *This dish is traditionally prepared the night before a religious holiday or on Fridays during Lent.*

Risi e bisi
Rice and Peas

Serves 4

1 ¾ lb (800 g) peas in pods
4 cups (1 l) vegetable broth
3 ½ Tbsps (2 oz or 50 g) butter
1/2 onion, minced
2 oz (50 g) pancetta, minced
1 bunch of parsley, minced
1 ¼ cups (9 oz or 250 g) Vialone Nano rice
1/2 cup (2 oz or 50 g) grated Parmesan cheese

Preparation time **20 minutes**
Cooking time **1 hour 10 minutes**
Level **easy**
Wine **Colli Berici Garganega**

Shell the peas, reserving a handful of empty pods. Boil the reserved pods in salted water for about 30 minutes.

Bring the broth to a boil in a separate saucepan and keep hot. Melt a large pat of butter in a separate saucepan and sauté the onion and pancetta. When the onion is golden and the pancetta transparent, add the peas and half the parsley. Pour over 1 ladleful of hot broth, cover and cook for 10 minutes.

Meanwhile puree the cooked pea pods with a few spoonfuls of their cooking liquid in a food processor. Strain the puree and add to the hot broth. Add the mixture to the pan with the peas and bring back to a boil. Stir well and add the rice. Cook until the rice is tender, stirring often. Stir in the rest of the butter and the Parmesan. Serve sprinkled with the remaining parsley.

Risi e bisi

Risotto con il radicchio
Radicchio Risotto

Serves 6

1 lb (500 g) Treviso radicchio
7 Tbsps (3 ½ oz or 100 g) butter
2 oz (60 g) pancetta, cubed
2 onions, minced
1 garlic clove, minced
salt and pepper
2 ¾ cups (1 ¼ lb or 550 g) Carnaroli rice
1/2 cup (120 ml) red wine
4 cups (1 l) vegetable broth
6 Tbsps grated Parmesan cheese,
plus extra for sprinkling

Preparation time **25 minutes**
Cooking time **25 minutes**
Level **easy**
Wine **Gambellara**

Remove any external wilted leaves from
the radicchio and cut the rest into thin strips.

Melt 3 tablespoons butter in a large saucepan,
brown the pancetta, then sauté the onions
and garlic.

As soon as they are golden add the radicchio,
let wilt and season with salt and pepper. Cook,
covered, for 10 minutes over moderate heat.

Add the rice and toast for 1 minute. Add the
wine and as soon as it evaporates add the broth
little by little, stirring frequently, until the rice
is cooked. Stir in the remaining butter and
Parmesan.

Serve hot, topped with more Parmesan.

Casunzièi di zucca
Winter Squash Ravioli

Serves 4

4 cups (1 lb 2 oz or 500 g) all-purpose flour
7 egg yolks - 1 Tbsp extra-virgin olive oil
7 Tbsps (3 ½ oz or 100 g) butter,
plus extra for topping
1/4 onion, minced
1 ¼ lb (600 g) winter squash, peeled and chopped
3 Tbsps grated Parmesan cheese
1/2 tsp ground cinnamon - 1 tsp sugar
1 Tbsp poppy seeds

Preparation time **30 minutes**
Cooking time **40 minutes**
Level **medium**
Wine **Lison-Pramaggiore Sauvignon**

Mound the flour on a work surface and make
a well in the center. Add two egg yolks and the
olive oil to the well. Mix to form a smooth and
uniform dough, adding water as necessary.
Cover and let rest for 30 minutes. Melt the butter
in a frying pan. Add the onion and sauté until it
begins to brown. Add the squash and cook until
soft, stirring occasionally. Add water if necessary.

Puree the squash mixture and add 5 egg yolks,
the Parmesan cheese, cinnamon and sugar. Using
a pasta machine roll the rested pasta dough out
into long sheets. Cut into rounds and place
1 teaspoon of filling on each round. Fold the pasta
over and press down around the edges to seal.

Bring a large pot of salted water to a boil
and cook the ravioli for a few minutes. Drain.
Meanwhile melt some butter in a saucepan. Pour
the melted butter over the ravioli and sprinkle
with poppy seeds. Serve immediately.

Risotto con il tastasal
Pork Risotto

Serves 4

4 cups (1 l) beef broth
3 ½ Tbsps (2 oz or 50 g) butter
1 onion, minced
1 garlic clove, smashed
3/4 cup (180 ml) white wine
10 ½ oz (300 g) tastasal (see below)
1 ½ cups (10 ½ oz or 300 g) Vialone Nano rice
5 Tbsps grated Parmesan cheese
1 pinch of ground cinnamon
1 pinch of ground cloves - pepper

Preparation time **5 minutes**
Cooking time **25 minutes**
Level **easy**
Wine **Lison-Pramaggiore Cabernet Franc**

Bring the broth to a boil and keep hot.
   Melt the butter in a saucepan and sauté
the onion and garlic until golden.
Add the wine and let evaporate. Add
the tastasal and rice and cook for a few
minutes, stirring constantly.
   Add a ladleful of hot broth and continue
cooking, adding broth when necessary,
until the rice is tender. Stir in the Parmesan,
cinnamon, cloves and pepper. Serve hot.

Note *Tastasal is a mix of seasoned ground pork
used to make salami. Its name comes from* tastare
la salatura *(test the salting), and this recipe was
used to check the quality of the meat before filling
the casings for the salami. It can be replaced here
by a fatty mix of ground pork seasoned with salt
and pepper, or the meat from mild Italian sausages.*

Risotto con il tastasal

Baccalà alla vicentina
Vicenza-Style Salt Cod

Serves 4

1 onion, minced
1 bunch of parsley, minced
2 oz (50 g) anchovies in oil or salt,
rinsed and minced
7 Tbsps grated Parmesan cheese
1 lb 11 oz (750 g) pre-soaked salt cod
6 ½ Tbsps all-purpose flour
salt and pepper
1/2 cup (120 ml) extra-virgin olive oil
7 Tbsps (3 ½ oz or 100 g) butter, chopped
1/2 cup (120 ml) milk

Preparation time **30 minutes**
Cooking time **4 hours 10 minutes**
Level **easy**
Wine **Breganze Bianco Superiore**

Mix together the onion, parsley, anchovies and
Parmesan. Remove any bones from the salt cod.
Rinse it, dry well and cut into pieces about
6 inches (15 cm) long.

Dust the pieces with flour and make a single
layer of cod pieces in a heavy-bottomed saucepan.
Season with salt and pepper and sprinkle over
a little of the onion mixture.

Drizzle over 1 tablespoon of olive oil and add
a few pieces of butter, then continue making
layers until the ingredients are used. Heat the
milk. Cook the salt cod over medium heat for
about 10 minutes, then add the hot milk and
the remaining olive oil. Simmer very gently
for 4 hours without covering.

Serve the salt cod with its cooking liquid.

Sarde in saor
Sardines in White Wine Sauce

Serves 4

14 oz (400 g) large fresh sardines
2/3 cup (3 oz or 80 g) all-purpose flour
1 ½ cups (360 ml) sunflower oil
1 ¾ lb (800 g) onions, thinly sliced
3/4 cup plus 1 Tbsp (200 ml) white wine vinegar
1/3 cup (80 ml) white wine
5 Tbsps raisins
5 Tbsps pine nuts

Preparation time **30 minutes**
Cooking time **15 minutes**
Level **easy**
Wine not recommended

Descale the sardines, remove the head and
wash well under running water. Lightly dust
with flour.

Heat the sunflower oil until very hot and
fry the sardines until almost cooked, about
5 minutes. Remove from the pan, leaving the
oil, and set aside. Pour off most of the sunflower
oil. Use the remaining part to sauté the onions
until soft. Add the vinegar and wine and reduce.
Add the raisins and pine nuts and stir well.

Arrange a layer of fried sardines in a container
and top with the still-hot onion mixture, so that
the fish continues cooking. Continue forming
more layers of sardines and onions, until the
ingredients are used up. Cover with plastic
wrap and let marinate in the refrigerator
for 2 days before serving.

Sarde in saor

Fegato alla veneziana
Venetian-Style Liver

Serves 4

4 Tbsps extra-virgin olive oil
3 Tbsps (1 ½ oz or 40 g) butter
4 onions, sliced
14 oz (400 g) calves' liver,
thinly sliced and trimmed
salt and pepper
lemon wedges for serving
cooked polenta (optional)

Preparation time **15 minutes**
Cooking time **10 minutes**
Level **easy**
Wine **Valpolicella Classico**

Heat the olive oil and butter in a saucepan
and gently sauté the onions until soft and
transparent, about 20 minutes.

Add the liver and sauté for a few minutes
over high heat until it becomes firm, leaving
the center pinkish. Season with salt and pepper
and serve the liver and onions with lemon
wedges and soft cooked polenta, if desired.

Anguilla chioggiotta
Chioggia-Style Eel

Serves 4

1 ¾ lb (800 g) eel
salt and pepper
1/2 cup (5 ½ oz or 150 g) canned
tomato sauce
1 red onion, minced
3 sage leaves, minced
2 bay leaves
1 rosemary sprig, minced
1 ½ cups (360 ml) white wine
1/4 cup (60 ml) grappa

Preparation time **20 minutes**
Cooking time **40 minutes**
Level **easy**
Wine **Bardolino Chiaretto**

Clean the eel, rub it with salt and cut into
pieces. Place in a heavy-bottomed saucepan
with the tomato sauce and cook over low heat
for a few minutes.

Add the onion, sage, bay leaves and rosemary,
season with salt and
pepper and cook for 20 minutes over low heat.

Add the wine, raise the heat and let it
evaporate, then lower the heat and continue
cooking for another 20 minutes. Add the grappa
and remove from the heat.

Stir, then cover the pan and let sit for a few
minutes before serving.

Anguilla chioggiotta

Scampi alla bùsara

Scampi alla bùsara
Sautéed Shrimp

Serves 4

16 shrimp
2 Tbsps extra-virgin olive oil
1 onion, minced
1 garlic clove, minced
2 ½ Tbsps brandy
2 tomatoes (about 7 oz or 200 g),
blanched, peeled and chopped
1/2 cup (120 ml) white wine
salt and pepper
3 Tbsps (1 ½ oz or 40 g) butter
1 Tbsp all-purpose flour
1/2 bunch of parsley, minced
cooked polenta (optional)

Preparation time **20 minutes**
Cooking time **20 minutes**
Level **easy**
Wine **Lison-Pramaggiore Pinot
Bianco Spumante**

Wash the shrimp and make an incision along their backs. Heat the olive oil in a large frying pan and sauté the onion and garlic.

Add the shrimp and brown for a few minutes. Add the brandy and flame it. Add the tomatoes, wine, salt and pepper and cook for a few more minutes.

Remove the shrimp from the pan and arrange them on a serving dish. Keep warm. Mix together the butter and flour and whisk into the tomato mixture. Cook for a few minutes until thickened. Pour the sauce over the shrimp, sprinkle with parsley and serve, accompanied by polenta if desired.

torta di patate dolci
sweet potato cake

Serves 4

4 sweet potatoes
2/3 cup (3 ½ oz or 100 g) raisins
1 cup (4 oz or 120 g) all-purpose flour
4 apples, peeled, cored and chopped
2/3 cup (3 ½ oz or 100 g) dried figs, chopped
3/4 cup plus 1 Tbsp (200 ml) milk
4 Tbsps sugar
1 tsp honey
2 eggs
salt
1/4 cup (60 ml) aniseed liqueur (optional)
2 Tbsps breadcrumbs

Preparation time **25 minutes**
Cooking time **1 hour**
Level **medium**
Wine **Gambellara Recioto Vin Santo**

Preheat the oven to 350°F (180°C or Gas Mark 4).
   Boil the potatoes until tender. Drain, peel and mash the flesh into a smooth puree. Transfer to a bowl.
   Soak the raisins in a little warm water until soft, then drain and squeeze out excess liquid.
   Sift the flour into the bowl with the potatoes, then add the apples, figs, milk, raisins, sugar, honey, eggs and salt. Mix well and add the aniseed liqueur if desired.
   Sprinkle a baking dish with breadcrumbs and pour in the cake batter. Bake for about 1 hour. Serve warm or room temperature.

Traditional recipe

Amaretti veneziani
Almond Cookies

Serves 8

4 egg whites
3 ½ cups (1 lb 3 oz or 500 g) blanched almonds
1/3 cup (2 oz or 50 g) bitter almonds, peeled
2 ½ cups (1 lb 2 oz or 500 g) sugar
grated zest of 2 organic lemons
1 Tbsp ground cinnamon
salt
1 large pat of butter

Preparation time **30 minutes**
Cooking time **20 minutes**
Level **easy**
Wine **Torcolato di Breganze**

Preheat the oven to 350°F (180°C or Gas Mark 4). Beat the egg whites to stiff peaks.

Chop the almonds very finely in a food processor and place in a large bowl. Stir in the sugar, lemon zest, cinnamon and a pinch of salt, then fold in the egg whites. Mix until smooth.

Butter a baking sheet and place spoonfuls of the batter around the sheet. Lightly flatten each spoonful and then bake them for 20 minutes or until golden.

Note *The name of these cookies comes from the slightly bitter (*amarognolo*) flavor they get from the small quantity of bitter almonds. Ideally they should be crunchy outside and soft inside.*

Siarese marostegane a la pana
Cherries and Cream

Serves 4

1 ½ lb (700 g) cherries, plus extra for garnish
1/2 cup (3 ½ oz or 100 g) sugar
1 clove
grated zest of 1/2 organic lemon
3/4 cup (180 ml) red wine
1/2 cup (120 ml) whipping cream

Preparation time **40 minutes**
Cooking time **25 minutes**
Level **easy**
Wine not recommended

Pit the cherries, reserving the stones. Wrap the cherry stones in a clean piece of cheesecloth and tie tightly closed with kitchen string.

Place the cherries and pits in a saucepan with the sugar, clove and lemon zest. Pour over the wine and cook for 30 minutes. Let cool and refrigerate until chilled.

About 30 minutes before serving, whip the cream. Drain the cherries, reserving the liquid, and divide them between four serving dishes or glasses. Return to the refrigerator for 20 minutes.

Add 1 tablespoon of the cooking liquid to each portion, then garnish with whipped cream and serve, garnished with fresh cherries.

Zaleti
Raisin Cookies

Serves 4

2 tsps active dry yeast
2 Tbsps warm milk
1 cup (5 ½ oz or 150 g) raisins
1 ⅔ cups (7 oz or 200 g) all-purpose flour
1 ½ cups (9 oz or 250 g)
finely ground cornmeal
1 stick (4 oz or 120 g) softened butter
1 egg
grated zest of 1 organic lemon
3 Tbsps grappa

Preparation time **25 minutes**
Cooking time **15 minutes**
Level **easy**
Wine **Vin Santo di Gambellara**

Preheat the oven to 350°F (180°C or Gas Mark 4).

Dissolve the yeast in the warm milk. Soak the raisins in warm water until soft, then drain and squeeze out excess liquid. Mix together the flour, cornmeal, 7 tablespoons (3 ½ oz or 100 g) of softened butter and the yeast mixture.

Stir in the egg, lemon zest, grappa and raisins and mix to form a soft dough. If it seems too firm, add some more milk.

Butter a baking sheet and place spoonfuls of the dough around it, leaving space around each one. Bake for 15 minutes. Serve the cookies warm or at room temperature.

Siarese marostegane a la pana

Zaleti

Friuli-Venezia Giulia

A region of borders, a meeting **point**

between the Latin, Germanic and Slavic worlds. A complex landscape, marked by a Roman past and a Hapsburg empire, held between mountains and plains, the sea and lagoons. Here gastronomic tradition ranges from the fresh *fish* of the Adriatic to boiled *pork* with horseradish, from rustic *cheese*-based dishes to excellent *cured meats* and great *wines*.

FRIULI-VENEZIA GIULIA
local products

Montasio Dop

USING FULL-FAT MILK FROM FRISONA-BREED COWS, Montasio cheese is made by breaking up the curd, cooking it to 111°F (44°C), purging it of the whey and then removing it with a jute cloth and pressing it into moulds. After salting in brine and drying, the forms are aged for anywhere between two months and a year. Fresh Montasio has a soft paste with scattered holes and a delicate, aromatic flavor. The aged version has a firmer, crumblier and slightly grainy texture, with an even stronger, sharper flavor. These characteristics become more pronounced in the extra-aged (*stravecchio*) cheese, matured for over a year, which is excellent for grating.

Polenta *di* mais

CORN POLENTA (*POLENTA DI MAIS*) CAN PLAY MANY ROLES IN AN ITALIAN MEAL, AS A FIRST COURSE, A SIDE DISH or the main attraction. An indispensable element in traditional Friulian cuisine, polenta is made of cornmeal cooked in water to form a kind of porridge. According to tradition, the first step in preparing polenta is to draw the sign of the cross in the boiling water with a wooden spoon. Once cooked, ideally in a copper cauldron, it is turned out onto a wooden board and divided using a cotton thread. Polenta can also be made from buckwheat, chestnut, millet, spelt or farro flour.

Miti enologici *friulani*

THE REGION IS KNOWN FOR ITS EXCELLENT WINES (*VINI*), THANKS TO A FAVORABLE CLIMATE AND SOIL COMPOSITION. There are many outstanding wine-making zones such as Colli Orientali, where Verduzzo, Ribolla, Pinot Bianco and Pinot Grigio whites and Refosco and Merlot reds are made. The difficult task of cultivating grapes in the Collio zone is rewarded by excellent wines: Collio, Traminer and Riesling Italico among the whites and Pinot Nero and Cabernet Franc among the reds. Other areas worth mentioning are Grave, between Udine and Pordenone, as well as Aquileia and the small Latisana zone.

Prosciutto *di* San Daniele

A RAW HAM FROM SAN DANIELE WITH AN INSTANTLY RECOGNIZABLE APPEARANCE AND FLAVOR, this prosciutto is closely linked to its place of origin. Its secret lies not just in the quality of the raw materials and the production process, but also the unique microclimate of this magical place in the province of Udine. The pink, lean meat has a mild fragrance and delicate taste, with a soft texture. The prosciutto is made from the legs of pigs primarily from farms in Lombardy, Emilia-Romagna, Veneto and Piedmont, which are trimmed, salted and pressed into the classic guitar shape. After three months the legs are rinsed and then treated with lard, salt, pepper and grain flours rubbed over the surface. The ham is then aged for a year, in an optimal climate with cool air from the Alpine foothills meeting the mild breezes from the Adriatic Sea.

Frittata alle erbe
Vegetable Frittata

Serves 4

10 ½ oz (300 g) mixed Swiss chard,
spinach and leeks, chopped
salt and pepper
2 Tbsps extra-virgin olive oil
1 onion, minced
4 basil leaves
2 sage leaves
6 eggs

Preparation time **15 minutes**
Cooking time **25 minutes**
Level **easy**
Wine **Friuli Aquileia Chardonnay**

Boil the leeks in boiling salted water for
15 minutes, then add the chard and spinach.
Cook for a few more minutes, then drain.

Squeeze out excess water. Heat the olive
oil in a frying pan and sauté the cooked
vegetables for a few minutes.

Add the onion, basil and sage and
continue cooking. Beat the eggs in a bowl
and season with salt and pepper. Add to the
pan with the vegetables and stir with
a wooden spoon to combine thoroughly.

Cook over medium heat and once
browned underneath, flip the frittata
and continue cooking until firm. Serve
hot or warm.

Salviade
Sage-Leaf Fritters

Serves 4

1 egg, separated
salt
3 Tbsps all-purpose flour
milk
20 sage leaves
sunflower oil for frying

Preparation time **15 minutes**
Cooking time **10 minutes**
Level **easy**
Wine **Grave del Friuli Verduzzo Frizzante**

Whisk the egg yolk with a pinch of salt.
Add the flour and whisk in enough milk
to form a smooth, liquid batter. Let rest
for 1 hour.

Beat the egg whites to soft peaks and then
fold into the rested batter with a wooden
spoon. Wash the sage leaves under cold
running water, then pat dry and stir into
the batter.

Heat sunflower oil and then fry the battered
sage leaves, in batches if necessary, until golden.
Drain with a slotted spoon, dry on paper towels
and serve immediately.

Salviade

Riso e fagioli alla friuliana
Friulian-Style Rice and Beans

Serves 4

2/3 cup (5 ½ oz or 150 g) dried beans

3 ½ oz (100 g) lardo (cured lard), minced

1 onion, minced

1 celery stalk, minced

2 bay leaves

2 potatoes (about 10 ½ oz or 300 g),
peeled and cubed

6 cups (1 ½ l) vegetable broth

1 cup (7 oz or 200 g) Carnaroli rice

salt

Preparation time **10 minutes**
Cooking time **2 hours**
Level **easy**
Wine **Grave del Friuli Refosco
dal Peduncolo Rosso**

Soak the beans in warm water overnight,
then drain. Sauté the lardo, onion and celery
in a large saucepan.

Add the beans, bay leaves, potatoes and
broth and cook for 1 hour 40 minutes.

Add the rice and continue cooking for
another 20 minutes, until tender, then
season with salt and serve immediately.

Fasoi e farro
Farro Soup

Serves 6

1 cup (9 oz or 250 g) dried cranberry beans

2 ¼ cups (16 oz or 450 g) pearled farro
(also known as spelt or emmer)

3 ½ oz (100 g) lardo (cured lard), minced

3 parsley sprigs, minced

4 potatoes, peeled and diced

5 Tbsps extra-virgin olive oil

salt and pepper

3 Tbsps grated Parmesan cheese (optional)

Preparation time **15 minutes**
Cooking time **3 hours**
Level **easy**
Wine **Friuli Aquileia Cabernet Franc**

Soak the beans overnight. Drain and transfer
to a saucepan. Add the farro and lardo and
cover with water. Bring to a boil and simmer
for 1 hour 30 minutes.

Add the parsley, potatoes, olive oil, salt and
pepper, then continue cooking for another
1 hour 30 minutes.

Before serving, mash the potatoes with a fork.
Serve sprinkled with grated Parmesan, if desired.

Tagliatelle con cacciagione
Tagliatelle with Wild Boar

Serves 4

14 oz (400 g) wild boar, cubed
1 onion, minced - 1 celery stalk, minced
1 carrot, minced - 1 garlic clove, minced
3 juniper berries, crushed
1 rosemary sprig - 2 sage leaves
5 peppercorns - 2 ½ cups (620 ml) red wine
2 Tbsps extra-virgin olive oil - salt
1 lb (500 g) canned plum tomatoes
9 oz (250 g) tagliatelle
1/2 cup (2 oz or 50 g) grated Pecorino cheese

Preparation time **20 minutes**
Cooking time **2 hours 20 minutes**
Level **medium**
Wine **Latisana Cabernet**

Mix together the wild boar, half the onion, the celery, carrot, garlic, juniper berries, rosemary, sage, peppercorns and 2 cups (500 ml) of red wine. Marinate for 8 hours.

Drain the meat and vegetables, reserving the liquid. Discard the peppercorns, juniper berries, rosemary and sage.

Heat the olive oil in a saucepan and sauté the remaining onion until golden. Add the wild boar and brown briefly. Season with salt and add the remaining 1/2 cup (120 ml) of wine. Once it has cooked off, add the marinated vegetables, then the marinade and tomatoes. Cook over low heat until thickened. Cook the tagliatelle in salted water. Drain and toss with the sauce. Sprinkle with pecorino and serve.

Fasoi e farro

Tagliatelle con cacciagione

Jota
Bean and Brovade Soup

Serves 4

3/4 cup (7 oz or 200 g) dried beans
2 oz (50 g) lardo (cured lard), finely chopped
1/2 onion, minced - 2 sage leaves, minced
1/2 bunch of parsley, minced
1 garlic clove, minced - salt
2 Tbsps extra-virgin olive oil
1 Tbsp all-purpose flour - 1 cup (250 ml) milk
7 oz (200 g) mixed radicchio, lettuce and celery
7 oz (200 g) brovade (see below), cut into strips
3/4 cup (3 ½ oz or 100 g) finely ground cornmeal

Preparation time **20 minutes**
Cooking time **1 hour**
Level **easy**
Wine **Isonzo Cabernet Sauvignon**

Soak the beans overnight. Drain the beans and soak in warm water for a few minutes.

Drain and boil for 30 minutes. Drain, reserving the cooking water. Mix together the lardo, onion, sage, parsley and garlic.

Heat the olive oil in a saucepan. Add the flour and cook for a minute, stirring. Add the beans and three-quarters of their cooking liquid, the milk, mixed radicchio, lettuce and celery, chopped, and the brovade. Bring to a boil and then stir in the cornmeal and lardo mixture. Season with salt and cook for 30 minutes. Stir well before serving.

Note *Brovade is a Friulian specialty of sliced turnips fermented in grape pomace for a month. It can be replaced in this recipe by sauerkraut.*

Gnocchi di zucca
Squash Dumplings

Serves 4

1 lb (500 g) yellow-fleshed squash, such as pumpkin, peeled and cubed
1 ⅔ cups (7 oz or 200 g) all-purpose flour
1 egg
7 Tbsps (3 ½ oz or 100 g) butter
6 sage leaves
salt
grated aged ricotta (optional)

Preparation time **30 minutes**
Cooking time **20 minutes**
Level **medium**
Wine **Friuli Aquileia Riesling Renano**

Boil the squash until tender. Alternatively roast in the oven. Pass the cooked squash through a sieve to obtain a puree and let cool in a bowl.

Add the flour and egg to the squash and stir energetically to obtain a smooth, thick batter. Melt the butter in a frying pan and add the sage leaves.

Bring a large pot of lightly salted water to a boil. Make small spoonfuls of the squash mixture and drop them to the water. As soon as they float to the surface, drain them with a slotted spoon and transfer to the frying pan with the butter. Toss to coat and serve sprinkled with grated aged ricotta if desired.

Gnocchi di zucca

Frico
Cheese Crisp

Serves 4

7 Tbsps (3 ½ oz or 100 g) butter
1 onion, thinly sliced
7 oz (200 g) hard cheese, thinly sliced
3 ½ oz (100 g) aged Montasio cheese, thinly sliced
salt and pepper

Preparation time **5 minutes**
Cooking time **20 minutes**
Level **easy**
Wine **Grave del Friuli Cabernet Franc**

Heat the butter in a large frying pan. Add the sliced onion and sauté until it begins to brown.

Add the cheese slices and mix. Continue cooking until the cheese melts, forming a uniform layer. Add salt and pepper to taste. When the cheese forms a golden crust on the bottom, flip it over.

Cook until both sides have formed a golden-brown crust. Remove from the pan and place on paper towels to absorb excess oil. Slice into wedges and serve immediately.

Note *Frico is usually served with the ubiquitous polenta. There are richer versions which incorporate eggs, vegetables or speck.*

Lepre in salsa
Hare with Red Wine

Serves 4-6

2 cups (500 ml) red wine
3/4 cup (180 ml) red wine vinegar
2 carrots, chopped - 1 celery stalk, chopped
1 hare or rabbit, cut into pieces
3 peppercorns - 5 sage leaves - 3 bay leaves
1 pinch of dried oregano - 1 rosemary sprig
7 Tbsps (3 ½ oz or 100 g) butter
2 Tbsps extra-virgin olive oil - 2 onions, sliced
1 garlic clove, smashed - 1 Tbsp all-purpose flour
3/4 cup (180 ml) white wine - salt and pepper

Preparation time **20 minutes**
Cooking time **1 hour 30 minutes**
Level **easy**
Wine **Grave del Friuli Refosco dal Peduncolo Rosso**

Bring the red wine, vinegar, carrots, celery, peppercorns, sage, bay leaves, oregano and rosemary to a boil and simmer for 15 minutes, then let cool. Pour the cooled wine mixture over the hare or rabbit and marinate for about 12 hours. Drain the meat, straining and reserving the marinade. Melt 5 ½ tablespoons (3 oz or 80 g) of the butter with the olive oil and brown the hare or rabbit pieces. Once browned, add the onions and garlic. Add the white wine and a little of the strained marinade. Season with salt and pepper and continue cooking for 1 hour 30 minutes, adding more marinade as necessary. Remove the hare or rabbit from the sauce and keep warm. Melt the remaining butter and stir in the flour.

Cook for a few minutes, then whisk the mixture into the sauce to thicken. Serve the hare or rabbit hot with the sauce.

Gulash triestino
Triestian-Style Goulash

Serves 4-6

2 marjoram sprigs
1 rosemary sprig
2 bay leaves
3 ½ oz (100 g) lardo (cured lard), minced
1 ¼ lb (600 g) onions, thinly sliced
1 ½ lb (700 g) beef, cubed
salt
1 large pinch of paprika
5 Tbsps ready-made tomato sauce

Preparation time **10 minutes**
Cooking time **50 minutes**
Level **easy**
Wine **Colli Orientali del Friuli Cabernet Franc**

Make a bouquet garni by tying the marjoram, rosemary and bay leaves in a piece of cheesecloth. Sauté the lardo in a saucepan.

Add the onions and sauté until golden. Add the beef, salt, paprika and bouquet garni. Cook for 20 minutes, then add the tomato sauce and a little water.

Continue cooking over medium heat until the beef is cooked through and the sauce has thickened. Remove the bouquet garni and serve hot.

Lepre in salsa

Gulasch triestino

presnitz
raisin and nut strudel

Serves 6

4 cups (1 lb 2 oz or 500 g) all-purpose flour,
plus extra for flouring

2 ½ sticks (10 oz or 280 g) butter, melted,
plus extra for buttering

7 ½ Tbsps sugar

2 Tbsps rum - salt - 4 eggs - 1/2 cup (2 oz or 60 g) raisins

1/2 cup (2 oz or 60 g) finely chopped walnuts

1/2 cup (2 oz or 60 g) finely chopped hazelnuts

1/3 cup (2 oz or 50 g) finely chopped candied citrus

3 ½ Tbsps pine nuts

Preparation time **45 minutes**
Cooking time **45 minutes**
Level **medium**
Wine **Collio Goriziano Traminer Vendemmia Tardiva**

Preheat the oven to 350°F (180°C or Gas Mark 4). Place the flour, 2 sticks (8 ½ oz or 240 g) of melted butter, sugar, rum and a pinch of salt in a mixing bowl. Mix together, then add 3 eggs, one at a time.

Form the dough into a ball and cover with plastic wrap. Let rest in a warm place. Soak the raisins in warm water until soft, then drain and squeeze out excess liquid. Dust the raisins with 1 tablespoon of flour. Mix with the walnuts, hazelnuts, candied citrus, pine nuts and the remaining melted butter. Beat the remaining egg. Roll the dough out into a sheet about 1/2 inch (1 cm) thick. Sprinkle the raisin and nut mixture over the dough, then roll it up in a cylinder. Lay it on a well-buttered and floured baking sheet and roll up into a spiral. Brush the surface with beaten egg. Bake for about 1 hour. Serve warm.

Traditional recipe

Chifeletti
Sweet Fritters

Serves 6

1 lb 3 oz (500 g) potatoes
3 ½ Tbsps sugar
1 cup plus 3 Tbsps (5 1/2 oz or 150 g)
all-purpose flour
1 large pat of butter, softened
1 egg
1 pinch of ground cinnamon
salt
sunflower oil for frying
confectioners' sugar for sprinkling

Preparation time **30 minutes**
Cooking time **20 minutes**
Level **easy**
Wine **Cesanese di Olevano Romano**

Boil the potatoes until tender, then drain
and peel. Mash in a large bowl. Stir in the
sugar, flour, butter, egg, cinnamon and salt.
Mix well to obtain a soft dough with no
lumps.

Break off small pieces of the dough
and form them into half-moon shapes.

Heat the sunflower oil until very hot
and fry the half-moons until golden. Drain
and dry on paper towels.

Serve sprinkled with confectioners' sugar.

Kugelhupf
Bundt Cake

Serves 8-10

3 ½ tsps active dry yeast
2 ⅓ cups plus 1 Tbsp (10 ½ oz or 300 g)
all-purpose flour
5 Tbsps sugar
2 eggs - 2 egg yolks
grated zest of 1 organic lemon
2 Tbsps rum
1/2 cup (2 oz or 60 g) raisins
1 large pat of butter
2 Tbsps breadcrumbs
1/3 cup (2 oz or 50 g) blanched almonds
confectioners' sugar for dusting

Preparation time **30 minutes**
Cooking time **1 hour**
Level **medium**
Wine **Colli Orientali del Friuli Picolit**

Dissolve the yeast in a little warm water.

Mix the flour with the sugar, yeast mixture,
eggs, egg yolks, lemon zest and rum to form a
smooth, firm dough. Cover with a cloth and
let rise for about 1 hour. Soak the raisins in
a little warm water until soft, then drain and
squeeze out excess liquid. Stir the raisins into
the dough. Butter a Bundt mold and sprinkle
with breadcrumbs.

Arrange the almonds around the bottom
of the mold, then fill with the dough. Cover
and let rise for another 30 minutes.

Preheat the oven to 350°F (180°C or Gas
Mark 4). Bake for about an hour, until golden.
Serve dusted with confectioners' sugar.

Kugelhupf

Emilia-Romagna

A land of art, pleasure and hospitality along the Po River.

Exceptional typical products that have found worldwide fame such as *Parmigiano* cheese, *prosciutto* and *balsamic vinegar*, along a taste itinerary that crosses valleys and plains, through castles and dairies, cellars and magnificent piazzas. A region rich in culture and gastronomic traditions.

EMILIA-ROMAGNA
local products

Culatello di **Zibello** Dop

THE PINNACLE OF CURED MEATS FROM THE **BASSA PARMENSE, CULATELLO DI ZIBELLO DOP** (Denomination of Protected Origin) must be made in one of eight municipalities (Zibello, Busseto, Polesine Parmense, Soragna, Roccabianca, San Secondo, Sissa and Colorno) from the best-quality pigs born and reared in Emilia and Lombardy. The secret lies in the unique microclimate found in these villages along the Po River, essential for the aging process. The combination of hot summers, foggy autumns and freezing winters is an integral part of the maturation that gives culatello its uniquely intense fragrance and flavor. The *massalen*, the butchers who make culatello, follow traditional techniques, with the meat prepared according to ancient customs. The back leg of the pig is skinned and deboned and the external part, with the best meat, is removed. This piece is salted and massaged before being tied with four pieces of string. The culatello is then trimmed again, rubbed with more salt, left to rest for a week, tightly sewn into a pig's bladder and tied into a pear shape. After more aging, the culatello is ready to be trimmed of its external fat, thinly sliced and eaten.

Mortadella **Bologna**

AUTHENTIC MORTADELLA, AN **IGP** (INDICATION OF PROTECTED ORIGIN) SINCE 1998, COMES FROM BOLOGNA. It is one of the cooked cured meats most used in cooking, in tortellini fillings, flans or to stuff meat. Mortadella is made from pork, prepared following a method regulated by a European production protocol: The meat is finely minced in three different phases, then mixed with cubes of fat from the pig's neck and black peppercorns, enclosed in a natural casing and cooked. Mortadella has a delicate, lightly spiced and savory flavor.

Squacquerone **di Romagna**

THIS SOFT CHEESE HAS NO CRUST AND IS BRIGHT WHITE IN COLOR, with a sweetish, lightly acidic, milky flavor. Squacquerone's quality comes from a genuine, natural raw material: full-fat cow's milk from locally raised grass-fed cattle. Production techniques have remained unchanged for centuries, resulting in a truly excellent cheese, with a minimum water content and high fat percentage.

Formaggio **di Fossa**

THIS CHEESE (FORMAGGIO) MADE FROM UNCOOKED COWS OR SHEEP'S MILK is originally from Sogliano al Rubicone but is now also made in the provinces of Forlì-Cesena, Rimini and Pesaro-Urbino. Its namecomes from the traditional *fosse*, or pits, dug into the tuff rock. In August, after 30 days of aging, the cheeses are closed inside cloth bags and place in the underground straw-lined pits. The pits are sealed up and the cheeses are left for three months, during which they acquire their unique aroma and flavor.

Parmigiano *Reggiano*

PERHAPS ITALY'S MOST FAMOUS CHEESE, TRUE PARMIGIANO, OR PARMESAN, can only be produced around Parma, Reggio Emilia, Modena and Bologna. Rightly known as the king of cheeses, it is made from milk obtained only from cows raised locally and fed a natural diet. Whey and rennet are added to the milk and it is carefully cooked in large copper cauldrons. The curd is shaped into forms weighing around 200 lb (90 kg), which are then aged for two years to obtain real Parmigiano Reggiano. The resulting cheese has a hard consistency, with an unmistakable fragrance and flavor. Extremely versatile, it is one of the most-used cheeses in cooking, flavoring pasta dishes, rice, meat stuffings, vegetables and savory pies. Many attempts have been made to imitate the cheese, but the authentic version is recognizable from the name, dairy code, year of production and number of the form branded onto the cheese's rind. After aging, a selection brand is also burned onto the rind.

Aceto **balsamico** *tradizionale*

THERE ARE ONLY TWO KINDS OF TRADITIONAL BALSAMIC VINEGAR, MADE EITHER IN MODENA OR REGGIO EMILIA, both DOP designated. Cooked grape must is fermented and then aged for at least 12 years, passing through barrels of different sizes made of different woods. Each one imparts its own unique flavor to the vinegar. Dark in color with a dense consistency, on the palate it is sweet and acidic at the same time. The longer the vinegar is aged, the higher its prestige and cost. Real balsamic vinegar is sold only in glass bottles in a traditional upside-down tulip shape.

Prosciutto crudo **di Parma**

PROSCIUTTO DI PARMA, OR PARMA HAM, IS THE RESULT OF TRADITIONAL PRODUCTION METHODS, passed down through the generations. The climatic conditions in the province of Parma also contribute to the ham's high quality, and its uniqueness has been recognized by the DOP branding. Legs from heavy pigs are not cooked, but

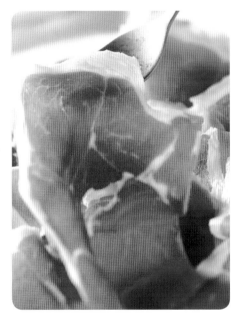

aged for at least a year. They have a typical pear shape and must weigh more than 15 lb (7 kg). The cut meat has a rosy color, delicate fragrance and soft, sweet flavor. Prosciutto di Parma can be eaten on its own, and also pairs well with melon and figs.

Fungo *di Borgotaro*

THIS MUSHROOM (FUNGO), A TYPE OF PORCINI, IS ONE OF THE MOST FAMOUS AND PRIZED IN ITALY, and since 1993 its nobility and prestige have been recognized by the European IGP protection. The inhabitants of the Taro Valley in the province of Parma are by now accustomed to spending from August to the start of the fall in search of this wild mushroom. It is the star of the local cuisine, eaten fresh as soon as it is picked, or dried.

Torta fritta di Parma
Parma-Style Savory Fritters

Serves 4-6

4 cups (1 lb 2 oz or 500 g) all-purpose flour
3 Tbsps extra-virgin olive oil
salt
lard for frying

Preparation time **15 minutes**
Cooking time **5 minutes**
Level **easy**
Wine **Colli di Parma Rosso**

Mound the flour on a work surface and make a well in the middle. Add the olive oil and salt and mix in enough hot water to form a smooth, soft dough.

Roll the dough out very thinly and cut into small diamond-shaped pieces. Melt the lard over high heat, and as soon as it starts to boil, start frying the pieces of dough in batches, turning them so they cook on both sides. Once golden, drain and dry on paper towels. Serve immediately.

Note *These fritters have different names in different parts of Emilia – in Bologna they are* crescentine, *in Modena,* gnocchi fritti, *always using the same basic ingredients of water, salt, flour and lard. They are traditionally served as an accompaniment to local cured meats.*

Tigelle modenesi
Modena-Style Flatbreads

Serves 4

6 ½ tsps dry active yeast
4 ¾ cups plus 1 Tbsp (1 lb 5 oz or 600 g) all-purpose flour
4 Tbsps lard - salt
3/4 cup plus 1 Tbsp (200 ml) heavy cream
7 oz (200 g) lardo (cured lard), minced
1 garlic clove, minced - 1 rosemary sprig, minced
2 Tbsps grated Parmesan cheese - pepper

Preparation time **25 minutes**
Cooking time **15 minutes**
Level **easy**
Wine **Lambrusco Salamino di Santa Croce**

Dissolve the yeast in a little warm water.

Mix the flour with the yeast, lard and a pinch of salt, then add the cream and knead to create a smooth and uniform dough. Leave to rest for 1 hour. Once the dough has rested, form ropes about 1-inch (2 ½ cm) in diameter then tear off pieces of the same length. Form them into balls, then flatten them, creating a hollow on one side. Let them rest for 30 minutes on a clean kitchen towel.

Preheat the oven to 350°F (180°C or Gas Mark 4). Once the tigelle have rested, press them out to form circles 4 inches (10 cm) in diameter and 1/5-inch (1/2 cm) thick. Bake in the oven until golden. Meanwhile grind the lardo with the garlic, rosemary, Parmesan and a pinch of pepper in a mortar and pestle.

Serve the tigelle hot, opened and filled with the lardo mixture.

Erbazzone reggiano
Reggio-Style Savory Tart

Serves 6

2 ¼ lb (1 kg) Swiss chard - salt - 1 garlic clove
3/4 cup plus 1 Tbsp (3 ½ oz or 100 g)
all-purpose flour
2 ½ oz (70 g) lard - 2 ½ Tbsps warm milk
1 pat of butter - 2 oz (60 g) pancetta, minced
1 onion, minced - 1/2 bunch of parsley, minced
2 cups (7 oz or 200 g) grated Parmesan cheese
1/2 cup (2 oz or 60 g) breadcrumbs - 4 eggs
2 oz (60 g) lardo (cured lard), thinly sliced

Preparation time **20 minutes**
Cooking time **45 minutes**
Level **easy**
Wine **Ortrugo**

Preheat the oven to 300°F (150°C or Gas Mark 2). Cook the Swiss chard in boiling salted water until tender, then drain, squeeze out excess water and chop finely. Mix the flour with the lard and enough warm milk to form a dough. Cover and let rest for a few minutes. Melt the butter and sauté the pancetta, onion, parsley and whole peeled garlic clove. Once the onion is soft, add the chard and cook for 15 minutes.

Transfer the mixture to a bowl and stir in the Parmesan, breadcrumbs, eggs and a pinch of salt. Remove and discard the garlic. Line a baking dish with half of the lardo slices. Roll the dough out into two thin sheets. Lay one sheet in the baking dish on top of the lardo. Cover with the chard mixture. Lay the other dough sheet on top. Poke holes in the dough with a fork and cover with the rest of the lardo. Bake for about 30 minutes, until golden. Serve cut into slices, warm or at room temperature.

Tigelle modenesi

Erbazzone reggiano

Lasagne alla bolognese
Bolognese-Style Lasagna

Serves 6

12 ½ oz (250 g) spinach
4 ¾ cups plus 1 Tbsp (1 lb 5 oz or 600 g)
all-purpose flour
3 eggs - 3 Tbsps extra-virgin olive oil
7 Tbsps (3 ½ oz or 100 g) butter
4 cups (1 l) milk - grated nutmeg - salt and pepper
Bolognese-Style Ragù (see recipe on the right)
1/2 cup (2 oz or 50 g) grated Parmesan cheese

Preparation time **1 hour**
Cooking time **40 minutes**
Level **medium**
Wine **Colli di Parma Rosso**

Boil the spinach until tender, drain, squeeze out
excess liquid and finely chop. Mix together 4 cups
(1 lb 2 oz or 500 g) of the flour with the eggs,
1 tablespoon olive oil and the spinach. Cover
and let rest for 30 minutes. Preheat the oven to
350°F (180°C or Gas Mark 4). Roll out the dough
and cut into rectangles. Bring a large pot of salted
water to a boil and add the remaining olive oil.

Cook the pasta sheets, drain and let cool on
a kitchen towel. Melt the butter and stir in the
remaining 3/4 cup (3 ½ oz or 100 g) of flour. Cook,
stirring constantly, for a few minutes, then whisk in
the milk and continue cooking until the béchamel
sauce thickens. Season to taste with nutmeg, salt
and pepper. Butter a baking dish and start with a
layer of pasta sheets. Top with some béchamel, the
ragù and a sprinkling of Parmesan. Make another
layer of pasta and continue, making a total of 4
to 6 layers. Finish with ragù mixed with béchamel,
Parmesan and a rectangle of pasta. Bake for about
30 minutes. Serve hot, cut into squares.

Ragù alla bolognese
Bolognese-Style Ragù

Serves 6

3 ½ Tbsps (2 oz or 50 g) butter
1 onion, minced
1 carrot, minced
1 celery stalk, minced
4 oz (110 g) pancetta, diced
10 ½ oz (300 g) ground beef
(or a mix of ground pork and veal)
2-3 cloves
3/4 cup (180 ml) beef broth
1 Tbsp tomato paste
salt and pepper
1/2 cup (120 ml) heavy cream

Preparation time **20 minutes**
Cooking time **2 hours**
Level **easy**
Wine **Colli di Parma Rosso**

Melt the butter in a large saucepan and sauté
the onion, carrot, celery and pancetta for
a few minutes.

Add the meat and cloves and briefly brown
over high heat. Add the broth, tomato paste,
salt and pepper.

Cover the meat with water and continue
cooking over low heat until all the liquid has
been absorbed. Stir in the cream. Remove
the cloves before serving.

Note *This ragù can be served as a sauce
for dried or fresh egg pasta, and is particularly
suited to tagliatelle.*

Passatelli in brodo
Passatelli Soup

Serves 4

3 eggs
grated nutmeg
salt
1 cup (5 ½ oz or 150 g) breadcrumbs
2 cups (7 oz or 200 g) grated
Parmesan cheese, plus extra for garnish
10 cups (2 ½ l) beef broth

Preparation time **15 minutes**
Cooking time **10 minutes**
Level **easy**
Wine **Lambrusco di Sorbara**

Beat the eggs, nutmeg and salt in a mixing
bowl. Add the breadcrumbs and mix.
Add Parmesan cheese and stir to combine.
The mixture should be smooth but firm.
Add some broth or more breadcrumbs if
necessary. Pass the mixture through a potato
ricer to form long ropes of pasta. Bring the
beef broth to a boil, add the pasta and boil.
The passatelli are cooked when they rise
to the surface. Serve in soup bowls with
grated Parmesan cheese.

Ragù alla bolognese

Passatelli in brodo

Risotto alla parmigiana
Parma-Style Risotto

Serves 4-6

2 Tbsps extra-virgin olive oil
7 Tbsps (3 ½ oz or 100 g) butter
1 onion, minced
2 cups (14 oz or 400 g) Carnaroli rice
4 cups (1 l) beef broth
1 cup (3 ½ oz or 100 g) grated Parmesan cheese
salt

Preparation time **15 minutes**
Cooking time **20 minutes**
Level **easy**
Wine **Colli di Parma Rosso**

Heat the olive oil and about half the butter in a saucepan and sauté the onion until golden.

Add the rice and toast for a few minutes, stirring constantly. Start adding the broth and continue cooking, adding broth when necessary, until the rice is almost done.

Stir in half the remaining butter, a little Parmesan and salt to taste and continue cooking for 5 more minutes, until the rice is tender. Stir in the remaining butter and Parmesan cheese and serve immediately.

Maltagliati con i fagioli
Maltagliati with Beans

Serves 6

2 ⅓ cups plus 1 Tbsp (10 ½ oz or 300 g) all-purpose flour
1/4 cup (60 ml) extra-virgin olive oil - 3 eggs
1 garlic clove, minced - 1/2 onion, minced
1 carrot, minced - 1 celery stalk, minced
8 cups (2 l) water - 1 rosemary sprig, minced
1 ¾ lb (800 g) fresh beans (such as cranberry)
salt and freshly ground black pepper
4 Tbsps grated Parmesan cheese

Preparation time **30 minutes**
Cooking time **50 minutes**
Level **medium**
Wine **Colli Bolognesi Merlot**

Mound the flour on a wooden pastry board and make a well in the center. Break the eggs into the hollow. Mix to form a dough then knead until smooth and uniform. Roll the dough out thinly with a rolling pin, then roll it up and slice the roll into thick tagliatelle. Using a serrated rolling cutter, cut the tagliatelle into uneven pieces. Dust with flour and lay out on a tray covered by a clean kitchen towel. Let rest in a dry place for 2 hours.

Meanwhile heat the olive oil in a frying pan and sauté the garlic. Add the onion, carrot and celery and sauté until softened. Add the water, beans and rosemary. Cook over medium heat, adding extra water if necessary, until the beans are tender. Adjust the salt. Bring a large pot of salted water to a boil and cook the maltagliati until al dente. Drain and add to the beans. Serve with a grinding of black pepper and a sprinkling of grated Parmesan.

Bomba di riso
Rice Timbale with Squab Ragù

Serves 4

2 Tbsps extra-virgin olive oil
1 celery stalk, minced - 1 carrot, minced
1 onion, minced - 2 squabs, cut into pieces
3 ½ oz (100 g) chicken giblets (liver, kidneys)
3/4 cup (180 ml) white wine
1 Tbsp tomato paste - 2 cups (500 ml) beef broth
2 ½ cups (1 lb 3 oz or 500 g) Carnaroli rice
3 eggs - grated zest of 1/2 organic lemon
salt - 1 ¼ cups (5 ½ oz or 150 g) peas
5 Tbsps (2 ½ oz or 70 g) butter, chopped
4 Tbsps breadcrumbs

Preparation time **40 minutes**
Cooking time **1 hour**
Level **medium**
Wine **Colli di Parma Rosso**

Preheat the oven to 350°F (180°C or Gas Mark 4). Sauté the celery, carrot and onion in the olive oil. Add the squab and giblets and sauté until browned. Add the white wine, and then the tomato paste and a ladleful of broth. Cook until the squab is cooked through, adding extra broth if necessary.

Debone the squab and return the meat to the sauce. Cook the rice until al dente. Mix the cooked rice, eggs and lemon zest and salt to taste. Boil the peas in salted water until tender, then drain. Butter a hemispherical mold and sprinkle with half the breadcrumbs. Fill with three-quarters of the rice. Place the squab ragù and peas in the center, then top with the rest of the rice.

Sprinkle with breadcrumbs and pieces of butter. Bake for 30 minutes. Unmold and serve.

Tortelli d'erbette
Chard and Ricotta Tortelli

Serves 4-6

1 ½ lb (700 g) Swiss chard
10 ½ oz (300 g) ricotta
5 ½ Tbsps (3 oz or 80 g) butter, melted
5 eggs
2 cups (7 oz or 200 g)
grated Parmesan cheese
grated nutmeg
salt
4 cups (1 lb 2 oz or 500 g) all-purpose flour

Preparation time **45 minutes**
Cooking time **25 minutes**
Level **easy**
Wine **Colli di Parma Sauvignon**

Remove the white stalk from the Swiss chard. Boil the chard in salted water for 15 minutes, drain, squeeze out excess liquid and finely chop.

Mix together the ricotta, chard, 2 tablespoons of melted butter, 1 egg and a handful of Parmesan until smooth. Season with freshly grated nutmeg and salt. Mound the flour on a work surface and make a well in the middle. Add 4 eggs and add a pinch of salt. Mix into a firm dough, adding water as necessary. Knead until smooth. Roll the dough into a thin sheet and cut into 4-inch (10 cm) wide strips. Place spoonfuls of filling along one edge of the strips, about 2 inches (5 cm) apart, then fold over the strip to cover the filling. Press around the filling with the fingers to expel any air. Cut the tortelli into rectangles with a rolling cutter.

Boil the tortelli in salted water for 10 minutes, then drain. Make layers in a serving dish of tortelli, melted butter and grated Parmesan. Serve hot.

cappelletti o anolini
stuffed anolini pasta in broth

Serves 6

7 Tbsps (3 ½ oz or 100 g) butter - 1 onion, minced

1 carrot, minced - 1 celery stalk, minced

14 oz (400 g) beef in 1 piece

2 cloves - salt and pepper - 2 cups (500 ml) beef broth

1 ½ cups (360 ml) red wine - 1 Tbsp ready-made tomato sauce

9 eggs - grated nutmeg

6 cups (1 ½ l) beef and chicken broth

4 ½ cups plus 1 Tbsp (1 lb 5 oz or 600 g) all-purpose flour

1 ⅔ cups (5 ½ oz or 160 g) grated Parmesan cheese, plus extra for sprinkling

1 ½ cups (6 ½ oz or 180 g) breadcrumbs

Preparation time **1 hour**
Cooking time **10 hours**
Level **medium**
Wine **Colli di Parma Rosso**

Melt the butter in a saucepan and sauté the onion, carrot and celery until soft. Add the meat, cloves and pepper. Brown for a few minutes, then cover with beef broth. Cook over low heat for 8-10 hours, adding the red wine little by little. About 6-7 hours after the start of cooking, add the tomato sauce. When the meat is falling apart and the sauce is very thick, remove from the heat.

Once the meat has cooled, chop it finely. Remove and discard the cloves. Mix together the meat, cooking liquid, breadcrumbs, Parmesan, 4 eggs, a pinch of grated nutmeg, salt and pepper.

Mix together the flour, 5 eggs, salt and enough water to obtain a smooth dough. Roll the dough out with a rolling pin, and cut into strips about 4-inches (9 cm) wide. Place spoonfuls of the filling along one edge of the strips, about 2-inches (5 cm) apart. Fold over the long edges of the strips, pressing around the filling with the fingertips to expel any air. Use an anolino mold to cut out little circles, or use a shot glass. Lightly dust the anolini with flour.

Bring the broth to a boil and cook the anolini. Serve very hot in the broth, sprinkled with extra Parmesan cheese.

Traditional recipe

Faraona ripiena al forno
Roast Guinea Hen

Serves 4-6

1 large guinea hen, deboned
3 thick slices of ham
salt and pepper
4 slices of Fontina cheese
2 Tbsps grated Parmesan cheese
1 egg - 14 oz (400 g) ground rabbit meat
5 baby artichokes preserved in oil, drained
1 rosemary sprig, minced
2 sage leaves, minced
5 slices of pancetta
6 Tbsps extra-virgin olive oil

Preparation time **20 minutes**
Cooking time **1 hour**
Level **medium**
Wine **Colli Piacentini Barbera**

Preheat the oven to 400°F (200°C or Gas Mark 6). Lay the guinea hen out on a cutting board and salt it inside. Roll up a slice of ham and a slice of Fontina and insert into one leg, then repeat with the other leg. Mix together the Parmesan, egg, rabbit, salt and pepper in a bowl. Spread the mixture over the guinea hen, then add the artichokes and cover with the remaining slices of ham and Fontina.

Thread a wooden skewer through the bird from the head to the tail and close it up, sewing it closed with kitchen string. Season with salt and cover with the rosemary and sage.

Lay the pancetta over the top and drizzle with olive oil. Roast in the oven for about 1 hour, then let cool slightly before serving.

Zampone modenese
Modena-Style Zampone

Serves 4-6

1 zampone (pig's foot stuffed with seasoned mincemeat)
2 ½ cups (1 lb 3 oz or 500 g) lentils
1 large pat of butter
2 Tbsps extra-virgin olive oil
1 onion, minced
2 carrots, minced
1 celery stalk, minced
4 cups (1 l) beef broth
1 Tbsp canned tomato sauce
salt and pepper

Preparation time **30 minutes**
Cooking time **5 hours**
Level **easy**
Wine **Lambrusco di Sorbara**

Separately soak the zampone and the lentils overnight. Poke holes in the zampone with a fork, wrap in a clean cloth and boil for about 3 hours.

Meanwhile heat the butter and olive oil in a saucepan and sauté the onion, carrot and celery until golden.

Add the drained lentils and cover with beef broth. Cook for 2 hours. Add the tomato sauce and extra broth if necessary, season with salt and pepper and continue cooking until the lentils are tender. Serve the zampone sliced, accompanied by the lentils.

Melanzane alla parmigiana
Emilia-Style Eggplant Parmesan

Serves 10

10 small eggplants
salt
5 Tbsps all-purpose flour
sunflower oil for frying
7 oz (200 g) mozzarella cheese, sliced
1 bunch of basil
1 cup (3 ½ oz or 100 g) grated
Parmesan cheese
3 Tbsps (1 ½ oz or 40 g) butter, chopped

Preparation time **20 minutes**
Cooking time **20 minutes**
Level **easy**
Wine **Colli di Parma Sauvignon**

Preheat the oven to 350°F (180°C or Gas
Mark 4). Peel the eggplants and cut them
lengthwise into 1/2-inch (1 cm) thick slices.
Arrange them on a plate, sprinkle with salt
and let sit for 15 minutes to give off water.

   Pat the eggplant slices dry and dust with
flour. Heat sunflower oil and fry the slices
for a few minutes, working in batches if
necessary. Drain with a slotted spoon and
dry on paper towels.

   Butter a large baking dish. Make a layer
of eggplant slices, topped with mozzarella
slices, basil leaves and Parmesan, and repeat.
Continue until the ingredients are finished.
Top with more Parmesan and pieces of butter.

   Bake in a water bath for 15 minutes, and
serve hot.

Zampone modenese

Melanzane alla parmigiana

Trippa in brodo
Tripe Soup

Serves 4-6

1 ¼ lb (600 g) tripe
salt and pepper
1 Tbsp extra-virgin olive oil
5 Tbsps (2 ½ oz or 70 g) butter
1 carrot, sliced
1 onion, sliced
1 celery stalk, sliced
1 garlic clove, minced
1/2 bunch of parsley, minced
3/4 cup (180 ml) tomato passata
(pureed tomatoes)
2 cups (500 ml) beef broth
2 medium potatoes, peeled and diced
1/2 cup (2 oz or 50 g)
grated Grana Padano cheese

Preparation time **30 minutes**
Cooking time **3 hours 20 minutes**
Level **easy**
Wine **Gutturnio Classico Superiore**

Wash the tripe and blanch it for 1 minute
in boiling salted water. Slice into strips
and let drain in a colander. Heat the
olive oil and half the butter and sauté
the carrot, onion and celery until soft,
then add the garlic and parsley.

Add the tripe, tomato passata, broth, salt
and pepper and cook over low heat for
1 hour 40 minutes. Add the potatoes and
cook for another 20 minutes. Serve the soup
hot, with the remaining butter and
the grated cheese.

Fagiano ripieno di pere
Pheasant with Pears

Serves 4

3 cups (700 ml) water
1 cup (7 oz or 200 g) sugar
zest and juice of 1 organic lemon
2 Williams pears
1 pheasant (around 2.2 lb or 1 kg)
3 tbsps sunflower oil
salt and white pepper
3½ tbsps butter - 1 onion, sliced
3/4 cup (180 ml) white wine
3/4 cup (180 ml) Port wine
1 tsp corn flour

Preparation time **25 minutes**
Cooking time **25 minutes**
Level **medium**
Wine **Nebbiolo d'Alba**

Bring the water to a boil with the sugar and lemon
zest. Peel the pears, cut in half and remove the core.
Poach in the boiling water for 10 minutes. Drain
and set aside. Cut the pheasant into pieces. Heat the
sunflower oil in a frying pan and brown the pheasant
evenly on all sides. Season with salt and pepper.

Remove the pheasant from the pan and pour off the
fat. Add the butter and sauté the onion, then return
the pheasant to the pan and cook for 2 minutes.

Add the wines, cook for a few minutes then cover
and cook for 12 minutes. Add the lemon juice and
cook for another 3 minutes. Arrange the pheasant
on a serving plate, together with the pears. Mix the
corn flour in a little water, then add it to the sauce
left in the pan and stir well, cooking over high heat
until thickened. Pour the sauce over the meat and
serve immediately.

Fagiano ripieno di pere

Bomboloni dolci
Sweet Doughnuts

Serves 6

6 tsps active dry yeast - 3 cups (750 ml) milk
4 cups (1 lb 2 oz or 500 g) plus 6 ½ Tbsps
all-purpose flour
2/3 cup (4 oz or 125 g) plus 5 Tbsps sugar,
plus extra for sprinkling
1/2 stick (2 oz or 60 g) butter, melted
7 egg yolks - 2 Tbsps rum - salt
1 vanilla bean, sliced lengthwise
sunflower oil for frying

Preparation time **30 minutes**
Cooking time **15 minutes**
Level **medium**
Wine **Colli di Parma Malvasia Dolce Spumante**

Dissolve the yeast in the 1 cup (250 ml) milk
and mix with 4 cups (1 lb 2 oz or 500 g) flour
and 5 tablespoons of sugar. Let rise for 10 minutes,
then mix in the melted butter, 3 egg yolks, rum
and a pinch of salt. Let rest for 20 minutes.

Roll the dough out with a rolling pin and cut
out 1-inch (3 cm) diameter circles. Cover with
a damp cloth and let rise until doubled in volume.

Meanwhile make the pastry cream: Heat the
remaining 2 cups (500 ml) milk and vanilla bean
in a saucepan. Beat the remaining 4 egg yolks
and remaining 2/3 cup (4 oz or 125 g) sugar until
thick and sift in the remaining 6 ½ tablespoons of
flour. Whisk in the hot milk, removing the vanilla
bean, and return the mixture to the saucepan.
Cook over low heat until the cream coats the
back of a spoon.

Heat the sunflower oil until very hot and fry the
dough circles. Drain and dry on paper towels. Fill
with the pastry cream and sprinkle with sugar.

Ciambella
Ring Cake

Serves 4

8 cups (2 lb 3 oz or 1 kg) all-purpose flour
1 cup (7 oz or 200 g) sugar
3/4 cup plus 1 Tbsp (200 ml) milk
3 ½ sticks (14 oz or 400 g) butter,
melted and cooled
grated zest of 1 organic lemon
4 eggs, beaten
salt
2 tsps baking powder

Preparation time **20 minutes**
Cooking time **30 minutes**
Level **easy**
Wine **Colli di Parma Malvasia Dolce**

Stir together the flour, milk, sugar, melted
butter, lemon zest, beaten eggs and a pinch
of salt. Mix well and add the baking powder.
Butter a ring mold and pour in the batter.
Let rise for around 1 hour.

Preheat the oven to 350°F (180°C or Gas
Mark 4). Bake the cake for about 30 minutes.

Note *This cake can be found throughout Emilia
with minor variations, sometimes without milk or
without lemon zest, sprinkled with confectioners'
sugar, sugar grains or sugar crystals. It also has
different names in different local dialects; for
example in Ferrara it is called* brazadela.

Ciambella

Spongata
Fruit and Nut Cakes

Serves 6-8

5 cups (1 lb 5 oz or 600 g) finely chopped walnuts
3/4 cup (3 ½ oz or 100 g) finely chopped almonds
2 cups (10 ½ oz or 300 g) finely chopped candied fruit
2 cups (10 ½ oz or 300 g) raisins
2 ¼ cups (10 ½ oz or 300 g) pine nuts
3 cloves - 1 pinch of grated nutmeg
1 tsp ground cinnamon - 2 tsps vanilla extract
3 cups (2 lb 3 oz or 1 kg) honey
2 cups (9 oz or 250 g) breadcrumbs - 2 Tbsps rum
3 cups (1 lb 5 oz or 600 g) sugar
1 cup (250 ml) white wine
8 cups (2 lb 3 oz or 1 kg) all-purpose flour
2 ½ sticks plus 1 Tbsp (10 ½ oz or 300 g) butter

Preparation time **40 minutes**
Cooking time **30 minutes**
Level **medium**
Wine **Colli di Parma Malvasia Dolce**

Mix together the walnuts, almonds, candied fruit, raisins, pine nuts, cloves, nutmeg and cinnamon.

Heat the honey in a large saucepan and as soon as it starts to boil, add the nut mixture, breadcrumbs and rum. Stir the mixture, remove from the heat and let cool. In a bowl, mix together the sugar and wine, then add the flour, softened butter and vanilla. Mix to form a dough.

Roll out the dough and cut into 16 circles. Divide the honey and nut mixture between 8 of the circles, then top with the remaining 8. Cover with a kitchen towel and let rest for 24 hours. Preheat the oven to 350°F (180°C or Gas Mark 4). Arrange the cakes on an oiled baking sheet and bake for 30 minutes. Serve sprinkled with confectioners' sugar, if desired.

Albicocche sciroppate
Apricots in Syrup

Serves 4-6

4 cups (1 ¾ lb or 800 g) sugar
1 ¾ cups (400 ml) water
2 bottles (1 ½ l) Albana Dolce or other sweet wine
4 cloves
1 cinnamon stick
rind of 1 organic lemon
6 ½ lb (3 kg) apricots, halved and pitted

Preparation time **20 minutes**
Cooking time **15 minutes**
Level **medium**
Wine not recommended

Mix the sugar and water in a saucepan and bring to a boil. Remove from the heat and add the wine, cloves, cinnamon and lemon rind. Let cool, then remove the lemon rind.

Arrange the apricots in glass jars and pour over the syrup. Close the jars, sterilize in a bain-marie and keep in a cool, dark place for at least 3 months before consuming.

Note *Peaches are also well-adapted to this preserving method. The fruit can be eaten as a dessert or snack.*

Chiacchiere
Carnival Fritters

Serves 6

4 cups (1 lb 2 oz or 500 g) all-purpose flour
salt
2 Tbsps malt extract
1 Tbsp corn oil
1/4 cup (60 ml) grappa
1 egg - juice of 1/2 orange
3 Tbsps sweet white wine
sunflower oil for frying
confectioners' sugar for sprinkling

Preparation time **20 minutes**
Cooking time **5 minutes**
Level **easy**
Wine **Asti Moscato Spumante**

Sift the flour with a pinch of salt. Stir in the malt extract, corn oil, grappa, egg and orange juice. Add enough white wine to make a soft, elastic dough. Roll the dough into thin sheets and cut out strips using a fluted rolling cutter.

   Heat the sunflower oil until very hot and fry the dough strips in batches. When golden, drain with a slotted spoon and dry on paper towels. Serve sprinkled with confectioners' sugar.

Note *This is a typical carnival-period sweet and can be found all over Italy under different names: in Bologna they are* spappole, sprell *in Parma,* chiacchiere di monaca *in Busseto,* intrigòun *in Reggio Emilia,* cenci *in Tuscany,* goulami *in Veneto,* bugie *in Piedmont, as well as* zeppole, frangette, fiocchi...

Chiacchiere

Torta duchessa
Duchess Cake

Serves 6

Cake

1 cup plus 1 tbsp (5 ½ oz or 150 g)
hazelnuts, toasted and finely chopped
1 cup (5 ½ oz or 150 g) almonds, finely chopped
2 cups (9 oz or 250 g) confectioners' sugar
1 cup plus 2 tbsps (9 oz or 250 g) butter
2 cups plus 2 tbsps (10 ½ oz or 300 g) cake flour

Sabayon

4 egg yolks
4 tbsps sugar
1/3 cup (80 ml) dry Marsala
3 ½ tbsps (50 ml) white wine

Chocolate Cream

4 egg yolks
4 tbsps sugar
2 tbsps all-purpose flour
½ cup plus 1 tsp (125 ml) milk
5 ½ oz (150 g) dark chocolate, chopped

Garnish

confectioners' sugar
candied cherries

Preparation time **30 minutes**
Cooking time **40 minutes**
Level **medium**
Wine **Colli di Parma Malvasia Passita**

Mix together the chopped nuts with the sugar, add the butter and stir until smooth. Add the flour and stir to obtain an even dough. Refrigerate for 2-3 hours. Preheat the oven to 400°F (200°C or Gas Mark 6). Roll out the dough and cut out three rounds. Transfer the rounds to a buttered baking sheet and bake for 5 minutes.

Meanwhile, prepare the sabayon. Beat the egg yolks with the sugar until creamy and add the Marsala and white wine. Cook over a double boiler over medium heat, whisking constantly, until the mixture is creamy and has doubled in volume.

Prepare the chocolate cream: beat the egg yolks with the sugar until thick and creamy. Sift in the flour and beat until smooth. Bring the milk to a boil and remove from heat. Drizzle the milk into the egg mixture, whisking constantly.

Return the mixture to the saucepan and cook over low heat until thick. Remove from heat, add the chocolate and stir until smooth.

Refrigerate until cool. Place one cake round on a serving plate and spread over a layer of chocolate cream. Top with the second layer of cake and spread over the sabayon. Place the remaining cake layer on top and frost with the remaining chocolate cream. Decorate the cake with confectioners' sugar and candied cherries.

Liguria

Narrow winding lanes, a generous sea

rich in fish, hills rising steeply from the coastline, olive trees feeding on the fresh breezes to produce a delicately fruity *oil*, perfect for drizzling on simple *focaccia* or blending with basil for the world-famous *pesto*. Asparagus, *artichokes*, *Taggiasca olives* and the sweet *Sciacchetrà* wine to be discovered along spectacular coastal paths winding along the cliffs and beaches.

LIGURIA
local products

Basilico genovese

THE CLIMATE AND TERRAIN OF THE
TYRRHENIAN COASTLINE give basil (*basilico*)
grown here unique characteristics. Genoan
basil, recently awarded a DOP (Denomination
of Protected Origin) recognition, has an
intense aroma and small, oval leaves.
It is sold fresh in bunches of 3-10 plants and
is the essential ingredient in Genoan pesto.

Oliva *taggiasca*

LIGURIAN OLIVE OIL IS RENOWNED AROUND ITALY, THANKS TO THE
QUALITY OF THE REGION'S OLIVES. The fruits are excellent not only
for pressing but also for eating whole, preserved in olive oil or brine.
The best-known variety is Taggiasca, cultivated primarily in the
province of Imperia. It is small, with a dark flesh and a strong perfume.
It is harvested during the winter, and from November nets are placed
under the trees to catch all the fruit that fall naturally. The olives
are used in many meat and fish dishes, particularly stews.

Asparago *violetto* d'Albenga

THIS PRIZED VEGETABLE COMES FROM AROUND THE TOWN OF ALBENGA in the province of Savona. Purple Albenga asparagus is sweeter and has a more buttery, less fibrous texture than normal asparagus. The Albenga plateau has a unique microclimate and sandy soil perfect for the cultivation of this variety.

Formaggio *di* Triora

NAMED AFTER THE TOWN OF TRIORA, in the province of Imperia, this cheese (*formaggio*) is made from raw cow's milk, heated with the addition of liquid rennet to obtain a rapid curdling. The rind varies in shade, while the paste is golden-yellow with small holes. The cheese is made all year round, but the summer version is the highest quality.

Olio *di* oliva *extravergine*

ONE OF THE PRODUCTS FOR WHICH LIGURIA IS FAMOUS IS ITS DOP (PROTECTED DENOMINATION OF ORIGIN) EXTRA-VIRGIN OLIVE OIL (OLIO DI OLIVA EXTRAVERGINE), produced along the Riviera. The delicate flavor and palatability of DOP Riviere Ligure extra-virgin olive oil come from the olive varieties used (Taggiasca, Lavagnina, Pignola and other local cultivars of the Frantoio variety) which have had centuries to adapt to the Ligurian terrain and climate. The resulting oil is low in acidity, with a gentle fruitiness and mildness that enhances foods without dominating them.

Antipasto "a scabeggio"
Moneglia-Style Marinated Fish

Serves 4

sunflower oil for frying
1 lb (500 g) fish fillets
3/4 cup (3 ½ oz or 100 g) all-purpose flour
1 onion, thinly sliced
1 organic lemon, thinly sliced
2 garlic cloves
3 sage leaves, plus extra for garnish
1/4 cup (60 ml) white wine vinegar
1/4 cup (60 ml) white wine

Preparation time **20 minutes**
Cooking time **10 minutes**
Level **easy**
Wine **Riviera Ligure di Ponente Vermentino**

Heat the sunflower oil until very hot. Dip the fish fillets in flour and then fry them until golden. Drain and cool.

Layer the fish in a baking dish with the onion, lemon, whole garlic cloves and sage leaves and pour over the vinegar and wine. Let sit for at least 1 hour, then serve together with the marinade. Garnish with sage leaves.

Note *This recipe comes from the town of Moneglia near Genoa, where the marinating technique is known as a scabeggio and is used for mackerel, eel and anchovies. It is similar to Lombardy's "carpione."*

Capponadda
Tuna and Bread Salad

Serves 6

1/2 loaf of stale bread
4 ripe tomatoes, chopped,
plus tomato slices for garnish
12 salted anchovies, rinsed, deboned and halved
11 ½ oz (320 g) tuna in olive oil, drained and crumbled
30 pitted Taggiasca olives
2 Tbsps capers
1 garlic clove, minced
3 parsley sprigs, minced
1 pinch of minced fresh oregano
salt
extra-virgin olive oil for dressing
4 eggs

Preparation time **20 minutes**
Cooking time **8 minutes**
Level **easy**
Wine **Riviera Ligure di Ponente Pigato**

Break up the bread and sprinkle with a little water to soften it. Place in a bowl and mix with the tomatoes, anchovies, tuna, olives, capers, garlic, parsley, oregano and salt and dress with extra-virgin olive oil to taste.

Boil the eggs, drain and cool. Peel and slice into wedges. Serve the salad garnished with egg wedges and sliced tomatoes.

Capponadda

Frittelle (frisciö)
Savory Fritters

Serves 6-8

4 cups (1 lb 2 oz or 500 g) all-purpose flour
2 tsps baking powder
2 egg yolks
salt
extra-virgin olive oil for frying

Preparation time 15 **minutes**
Cooking time **5 minutes**
Level **easy**
Wine **Colli di Luni Bianco**

Mix the flour with enough water to make a fluid batter. Mix well and let rest for 2 hours.

Stir the baking powder, egg yolks and a pinch of salt into the batter. Mix well.

Heat the olive oil until very hot, and then drop in spoonfuls of the batter. Working in batches, fry until golden then drain with a slotted spoon and dry on paper towels. Serve hot.

Note *These fritters are a Ligurian classic, and there are many variations on the basic recipe. Minced parsley and garlic might be added, sometimes the yeast is left out, and sometimes bianchetti (whitebait) are stirred into the batter before frying.*

Focaccia alla genovese
Genoan-Style Focaccia

Serves 4

2 potatoes
2 ½ tsps active dry yeast
3/4 cup (180 ml) warm milk
3 cups plus 3 Tbsps (14 oz or 400 g) all-purpose flour
salt
6 Tbsps extra-virgin olive oil
coarse salt

Preparation time **30 minutes**
Cooking time **30 minutes**
Level **medium**
Wine **Cinqueterre**

Peel the potatoes, boil until tender and mash into a puree. Dissolve the yeast in the warm milk. Mound the flour on a work surface.

Mix in the yeast and milk, regular salt, potato puree and 2 tablespoons of olive oil. Knead the ingredients well to obtain a soft and smooth dough, adding warm water if necessary. Cover with a clean kitchen towel and let rest for at least 45 minutes.

Preheat the oven to 400°F (200°C or Gas Mark 6). Roll the dough out on a lightly oiled baking tray. Form deep dimples in the dough with fingertips. Sprinkle over coarse salt, drizzle with olive oil and bake until the surface is golden-brown.

Salsa di noci
Walnut Sauce

Serves 4

2 ½ cups (250 g) walnuts - 2 bread rolls
2 garlic cloves - 6 Tbsps pine nuts
1 marjoram sprig - salt
1 ½ Tbsps heavy cream
3 Tbsps extra-virgin olive oil

Preparation time **25 minutes**
Level **easy**

Blanch the walnuts in boiling water for
a few minutes. Drain and rub with a kitchen
cloth to remove the skins.

Scoop out the crumb from the bread rolls
and soak in water for a few minutes, then
drain and squeeze out excess liquid.

In a food processor or mortar and pestle,
grind together the walnuts, garlic, pine nuts,
soaked bread, marjoram and a pinch of salt.
When smooth, transfer to a bowl and stir in
the cream and olive oil.

Note *This is an ancient recipe that is often
adapted according to taste, leaving out the pine
nuts or replacing the marjoram with parsley,
for example. The sauce is excellent with pasta,
particularly traditional chard-filled pansoti
(see p. 179), and also chestnut-flour gnocchi.
This is an ancient recipe that is often adapted
according to taste, leaving out the pine nuts
or replacing the marjoram with parsley, for
example. The sauce is excellent with pasta,
particularly traditional chard-filled pansoti,
and also chestnut-flour gnocchi.*

Focaccia alla genovese

Salsa di noci

Zuppa di pesce
Fish Soup

Serves 6

3 tomatoes
4 ½ lb (2 kg) mixed fish (halibut, turbot,
cod and pollock)
8 cups (2 l) water
6 Tbsps extra-virgin olive oil
1 onion, minced - 1 celery stalk, minced
1 carrot, minced
1 bunch of parsley, minced
1 garlic clove
3/4 cup (180 ml) white wine
salt and pepper
1 baguette, sliced and toasted

Preparation time **40 minutes**
Cooking time **1 hour 30 minutes**
Level **medium**
Wine **Riviera Ligure di Ponente Pigato**

Blanch the tomatoes in boiling water
for a few minutes, then drain, peel, deseed
and chop. Wash the fish in cold water,
descale them and cut into large pieces.
Bring the water to a boil in a saucepan.

Heat the olive oil in another large
saucepan and sauté the onion, celery, carrot,
parsley and whole garlic clove until golden.
Add the wine and let evaporate.

Add the tomatoes and boiling water and
cook for 20 minutes. Add the fish, starting
with the pieces that need the most time to
cook. Adjust salt and pepper and cook for
about 1 hour, then pass the soup through
a sieve. Serve hot with the toasted bread.

Minestrone alla genovese
Genoan-Style Minestrone

Serves 4

8 cups (2 l) water - salt
1 cup (7 oz or 200 g) fresh beans,
such as cranberry
2 tomatoes, blanched, peeled and chopped
2 potatoes, peeled
1 cup (5 ½ oz or 150 g) peas
1 small onion, minced
1 garlic clove, minced
1 celery stalk, diced - 2 carrots, diced
4 zucchini, diced
4 Swiss chard leaves, finely chopped
1 large handful of green beans, chopped
4 Tbsps extra-virgin olive oil
5 ½ oz (150 g) spaghetti,
broken into smaller pieces
1 Tbsp pesto
2 Tbsps grated Parmesan cheese

Preparation time **40 minutes**
Cooking time **2 hours 30 minutes**
Level **medium**
Wine **Cinqueterre**

Bring the water to a boil in a large saucepan
and add salt. Add the beans, tomatoes, whole
potatoes, peas, onion, garlic, celery, carrots,
zucchini, Swiss chard and green beans.
Add the olive oil and cook for 2 hours.

Remove the potatoes, mash them with a fork
and return to the soup. Add the spaghetti
to the soup and continue cooking until
the spaghetti is done. Dilute the pesto
in a little of the broth and stir into the soup.
Serve hot, sprinkled with Parmesan.

Pansoti con salsa di noci
Pansoti with Walnut Sauce

Minestrone alla genovese

Pansoti con salsa di noci

Serves 6

4 cups (1 lb 2 oz or 500 g) all-purpose flour
6 eggs - 2 Tbsps extra-virgin olive oil - salt
3 Tbsps white wine
10 ½ oz (300 g) mixed Swiss chard and borage
6 Tbsps grated Pecorino cheese
3 ½ oz (100 g) Quagliata
or other fresh, soft cheese
Walnut Sauce (see recipe on p. 177)
4 Tbsps grated Parmesan cheese (optional)

Preparation time **40 minutes**
Cooking time **20 minutes**
Level **medium**
Wine **Riviera di Ponente Ormeasco**

Mound the flour on a work surface and
mix in 3 eggs, 1 tablespoon of olive oil and
a pinch of salt. Work into a dough, adding
white wine as necessary, until smooth and
uniform. Form into a ball, cover with plastic
wrap and set aside. Boil the Swiss chard and
borage in water. Drain, squeeze out excess
water and chop finely. Beat the remaining
3 eggs and mix with the chard, borage,
Pecorino, Quagliata and salt. Roll the dough
out thinly and cut out squares of 4 inches
(10 cm) each side.

   Place 1 tablespoon of filling in the center of
every piece then fold from corner to corner to
create a triangle and press firmly around the
edges to seal. Bring a large pot of salted water
to the boil and cook the pansoti, adding a
tablespoon of olive oil to the water to avoid
sticking. Drain and serve with the walnut
sauce and grated Parmesan if desired.

trofie di Recco
Recco-style trofie with pesto

Serves 4

3 cups (750 ml) water
4 cups (1 lb 2 oz or 500 g) durum-wheat flour
salt - 40 basil leaves
2 Tbsps pine nuts
1 garlic clove - salt
6 Tbsps extra-virgin olive oil
1 Tbsp grated Pecorino cheese
4 Tbsps grated Parmesan cheese,
plus extra for sprinkling

Preparation time **50 minutes**
Cooking time **10 minutes**
Level **medium**
Wine **Riviera Ligure di Ponente Vermentino**

Bring the water to a boil. Mound the flour on a work surface, add a pinch of salt and just enough of the boiling water to make a medium-consistency dough, stirring first with a spoon and then kneading by hand once the temperature has cooled. Once smooth and uniform, divide the dough into small pieces about the size of a bean. Rub each piece in the palm of the hand to obtain little curls.

Place the basil in a food processor with the pine nuts, garlic, a pinch of salt and a tablespoon of olive oil. Puree briefly, then add the two cheeses and mix again until smooth. Transfer to a bowl and stir in 4 tablespoons of olive oil.

Bring a large pot of salted water to a boil and add a tablespoon of olive oil. Cook the trofie until al dente, then drain and toss with the pesto. Serve hot, sprinkled with more Parmesan.

Pizza dell'Andrea
Anchovy Pizza

Serves 6

4 ¾ cups (1 lb 5 oz or 600 g) all-purpose flour
4 tsps active dry yeast - salt - 2 onions, sliced
10 Tbsps extra-virgin olive oil,
plus extra for drizzling
5 ripe tomatoes (about 1 lb or 500 g),
peeled, deseeded and chopped
3 ½ oz (100 g) salted anchovies,
cleaned and minced
2 basil leaves
10 black olives in brine, drained
2 garlic cloves, sliced

Preparation time **30 minutes**
Cooking time **1 hour**
Level **easy**
Birra **Chiara alla Spina**

Mix together the flour, yeast, 4 tablespoons
of olive oil, a pinch of salt and enough warm
water to make a smooth dough. Cover with
a clean kitchen towel and leave to rise in
a warm place for at least 2 hours. Preheat the
oven to 475°F (240°C or Gas Mark 9).

Heat the remaining 6 tablespoons of olive oil
in a frying pan and sauté the onions until they
just start to brown. Add the tomatoes and cook
until the sauce has thickened. Add the anchovies
and cook for a few more minutes.

Spread the dough out on an oiled baking sheet.
Press it out with oiled fingers to about 1/2-inch
(1 cm) thick. Spread the tomato sauce over the
top and add the basil, olives, garlic and a drizzle
of olive oil. Bake for 30 minutes, until the crust
is golden and crunchy.

Moscardini in umido
Stewed Baby Octopus

Serves 4-6

2 Tbsps extra-virgin olive oil
1 onion, minced
1 garlic clove
1 rosemary sprig
3 Tbsps minced parsley, plus sprigs for garnish
1 cup (9 oz or 250 g) canned tomato sauce
salt and pepper
4 ½ lb (2 kg) baby octopus (moscardini), cleaned
8 slices of stale bread, toasted

Preparation time **20 minutes**
Cooking time **1 hour**
Level **easy**
Wine **Riviera Ligure di Ponente Pigato**

Heat the olive oil in a saucepan and sauté the
onion, garlic clove, rosemary and parsley until
the onion is soft. Add the tomato sauce and
adjust the salt and pepper.

Cook for 15 minutes, adding hot water if
necessary. Add the baby octopus, cover and cook
for 45 minutes over low heat.

Arrange the toasted bread on serving plates
and serve the stew over the bread. Garnish with
parsley sprigs and serve.

Stecchi ripieni
Liver and Sweetbread Skewers

Serves 6

1 pat of butter - 1 small black truffle
7 oz (200 g) chicken livers, roughly chopped
7 oz (200 g) sweetbreads, roughly chopped
3 cups (10 ½ oz or 300 g) mushrooms,
roughly chopped
3/4 cup (180 ml) béchamel sauce
5 Tbsps grated Parmesan cheese
2 oz (50 g) prosciutto, minced
2 Tbsps minced parsley - 2 egg yolks
1 Tbsp all-purpose flour - 1 egg, beaten
breadcrumbs for breading
sunflower oil for frying - salt

Preparation time **20 minutes**
Cooking time **20 minutes**
Level **easy**
Wine **Rossese di Dolceacqua**

Heat the butter in a saucepan. Sauté the
chicken livers until cooked through and
remove. Sauté the sweetbreads until cooked
through and remove. Sauté the mushrooms
until cooked through and remove.

Thread alternating chicken liver, sweetbread
and mushroom pieces on wooden skewers. Use
a mandoline to thinly slice the truffle.

Mix the béchamel, Parmesan, prosciutto,
parsley and egg yolks in a bowl and add the
truffle shavings. Dip the skewers in the sauce
so that they are well coated, then lay them
carefully on a work surface.

When they are cool, dip each into flour,
then beaten egg, then breadcrumbs. Heat the
sunflower oil and fry the skewers. Drain, dry
on paper towels, salt to taste and serve.

Moscardini in umido

Stecchi ripieni

Cappon magro
Seafood Salad

Serves 4

1 cauliflower, cut into florets
2 large handfuls of green beans
1 celery stalk, chopped - 4 carrots, sliced
1 large potato (about 7 oz or 200 g), cubed
1 bunch of dandelion greens, chopped
1 bunch of asparagus, chopped
2 small artichokes, trimmed and quartered
2 Tbsps extra-virgin olive oil
14 oz (400 g) gurnard or sea bass fillet, cubed
8 slices of slightly stale bread - salsa verde
1/2 cup (120 ml) white wine vinegar - 8 shrimps
1 lb (500 g) mixed shellfish (mussels and clams)

Preparation time **30 minutes**
Cooking time **30 minutes**
Level **medium**
Wine **Riviera Ligure di Ponente Pigato**

Boil the cauliflower until tender and drain with
a slotted spoon. Return the water to a boil and add
the green beans. Cook until tender, then repeat
with the celery and carrots. In a separate pot boil the
potato, dandelion greens, asparagus and artichokes
individually. Sauté the fish in the olive oil until cooked
through. Place a slice of bread in the bottom of
4 glass containers. Layer the vegetables and fish in each
glass. Dip the remaining 4 slices of bread in vinegar
and place over the vegetables and fish. Cover with
plastic wrap and place a small weight on top of each
container. Refrigerate overnight. Just before serving,
boil the shrimp until cooked through and cook the
mussels and clams in a covered frying pan until they
open. Unmold the cappon magro and garnish with
the shrimp, mussels, clams and salsa verde.

Buridda
Ligurian Fish Soup

Serves 6

6 Tbsps extra-virgin olive oil
1 garlic clove, peeled
1 onion, minced
3 tomatoes, sliced
2 anchovies in oil, drained
4 Tbsps minced parsley
3/4 cup (180 ml) white wine
3 ½ lb (1 ½ kg) monkfish, cut into pieces
1 bay leaf
salt
4 slices of crusty bread

Preparation time **15 minutes**
Cooking time **30 minutes**
Level **easy**
Wine **Colli di Luni Vermentino**

Heat the olive oil in a large saucepan and sauté
the whole peeled garlic clove and onion until
they begin to soften.

Remove the garlic and discard. Add the sliced
tomatoes, anchovies and minced parsley. Add
the white wine and let reduce slightly, then
add the monkfish, and bay leaf and season with
a pinch of salt. Cook, uncovered, over low heat
for 20 minutes.

Meanwhile, slice the bread and toast under
the broiler until golden-brown. Serve the
buridda with the toasted bread.

Buridda

Pandolce genovese
Genoan-Style Fruitcake

Serves 4

1 cup (5 ½ oz or 150 g) sultanas
6 ½ tsps active dry yeast
1/4 cup (60 ml) milk
8 cups (2 lb 3 oz or 1 kg) all-purpose flour,
plus extra for flouring
1 pat of butter, melted, plus extra for buttering
2 Tbsps orange-flower water - 6 Tbsps sugar
3/4 cup (3 ½ oz or 100 g) pine nuts
2/3 cup (3 ½ oz or 100 g) Zibibbo raisins
1/3 cup (2 oz or 50 g) diced candied pumpkin
1/3 cup (2 oz or 50 g) diced candied citron

Preparation time **50 minutes**
Cooking time **1 hour**
Level **medium**
Wine **Riviera di Ponente Ormeasco Sciacchetrà**

Soak the sultanas in warm water until soft, the
drain and squeeze out excess liquid. Dissolve the
yeast in the milk. Mound the flour on a wooden
pastry board and make a well in the center. Pour
in the milk, melted butter, orange-flower water
and sugar. Mix together energetically, adding
warm water if necessary, to obtain a soft dough.

Knead the pine nuts, sultanas, Zibibbo raisins
and candied pumpkin and citron and continue
kneading for at least 30 minutes. Form the dough
into a ball. Cover with a kitchen cloth and leave
to rise in a warm place for at least 12 hours.

Preheat the oven to 350°F (180°C or Gas
Mark 4). Butter and flour a baking sheet and
place the ball of dough in the middle. Make
3 cuts in the surface in the shape of a triangle
and then bake for about 1 hour.

Frittelle dolci
Raisin Fritters

Serves 4

4 cups (1 lb 2 oz or 500 g) all-purpose flour
2 tsps baking powder
1/2 cup (3 ½ oz or 100 g) sugar
1 cup (250 ml) milk
grated zest of 1 organic lemon
1 ⅓ cups (7 oz or 200 g) raisins
sunflower oil for frying
dark chocolate shavings for garnish

Preparation time **15 minutes**
Cooking time **20 minutes**
Level **easy**
Wine **Cinque Terre Sciacchetrà**

Sift the flour and baking powder together
into a large mixing bowl. Add the sugar, milk
and lemon zest and stir until smooth and free
of lumps. Cover the bowl and let rise for 1 hour.

Soak the raisins in warm water until soft, then
drain, squeeze out excess liquid and pat dry with
paper towels. Stir the raisins into the batter.

Heat the sunflower oil in a deep frying pan
and fry spoonfuls of the batter in batches. When
golden on both sides, drain with a slotted spoon
and dry on paper towels. Serve garnished with
chocolate shavings.

Canestrelli
Butter Cookies

Serves 6

4 cups (1 lb 2 oz or 500 g) all-purpose flour
3/4 cup (5 ½ oz or 150 g) sugar
2 ½ sticks plus 1 Tbsp (10 ½ oz or 300 g)
butter, softened, plus extra for buttering
2 eggs
1 pinch baking soda
1/2 cup (125 ml) milk
confectioners' sugar for sprinkling

Preparation time **20 minutes**
Cooking time **15 minutes**
Level **easy**
Wine **Riviera di Ponente**
Ormeasco Sciacchetrà

Preheat the oven to 350°F (180°C or Gas
Mark 4). Mix together the flour, sugar,
softened butter, eggs and baking soda to
form a dough. Let rest for 30 minutes.

Roll or press the dough into a thick sheet
and use a fluted cookie cutter to cut out rings
of the dough.

Brush them with milk and arrange on
a buttered baking sheet. Bake for about
15 minutes. Remove from the oven, let cool
and sprinkle with confectioners' sugar.

Note *The name canestrelli means "little baskets."*

Frittelle dolci

Canestrelli

Tuscany

Known for its rich artistic history and beautiful rolling

vineyard-covered hills, Tuscany is filled with typical products such as fennel-spiced *finocchiona* salami, *Chianina*-beef, spicy *extra-virgin olive oil* and world-renowned wines like Chianti Classico. The hills, fields, farms, castles, medieval hill towns and splendid Renaissance cities hold a wealth of gastronomic treasures and traditional dishes.

TUSCANY
local *products*

Olio *d'oliva* extravergine

TUSCAN EXTRA-VIRGIN OLIVE OIL (*olio d'oliva extravergine*) dominates Italian cuisine, thanks to its high quality standards rather than the quantity, as production is quite limited. Leccino, Frantoio and Moraiolo are the three best-known cultivars, and they produce a green oil, with an intense flavor and spicy aftertaste. There are other types of Tuscan oil with different characteristics: Lucca DOP (Denomination of Protected Origin), for example, has a delicate, fruity taste. There are many varieties of oil available, from the most common to newer, more original styles, such as the oil from the Maremma around Livorno and Grosseto. Tuscany recently obtained an IGP (Indication of Protected Origin) classification for its extra-virgin olive oil, and the region is already home to DOP-designated extra-virgin olive oils such as Chianti Classico, Colline di Firenze, Terre di Siena, Colline Pisane and Seggiano.

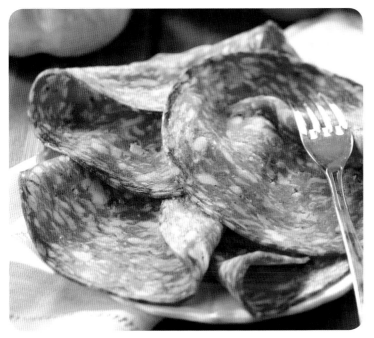

Finocchiona

THIS LEGENDARY SALAMI IS ONE OF THE PINNACLES OF TUSCAN CURED MEATS. It is made from finely ground pork (though some versions include some beef as well) seasoned with garlic, salt, pepper and the fennel seeds (*semi di finocchio*) which give it its name. The result is a large salami with a very distinctive flavor.

Vin Santo *Toscano*

THE NAME MEANS "HOLY WINE" BECAUSE OF ITS ASSOCIATIONS with the catholic mass, and in fact in some areas Vin Santo is still used for communion. This dessert wine is the result of a slow, laborious production process. After the grapes are harvested, they are semi-dried before being pressed. The must is then fermented and matured in small, sealed barrels for at least three years before being bottled. The wine has a golden color, and the flavor can range from sweet to decidedly dry. It is the classic accompaniment to Prato biscotti (right).

Grandi rossi
toscani

THE CULTURE OF TUSCAN WINEMAKING BOASTS
A LONG AND RICH HISTORY. The Etruscans
were the first to cultivate grapes here in the
8th century B.C., but it was during the Roman
Empire that the wines from this region began to
acquire a fame that has endured to the present.
The red wines (*vini rossi*) are particularly
celebrated, starting with *Chianti*, produced in
seven specific zones from Sangiovese, Canaiolo
and Trebbiano grapes, with the best wines
coming from the hills of Rufina and Chianti
Classico. *Brunello di Montalcino* is made in
the village of Montalcino from Sangiovese
grapes, and has today become synonymous with
exclusive quality. With intense bouquets and
dry yet soft flavors, the wines can
be sold after an obligatory aging
of five years, but they can last for
up to half a century. Not far from
Montalcino lies the area known
for another great red, *Nobile di
Montepulciano*, also made from
Sangiovese but with the addition
of Caniolo Nero and other varietals.
These important reds pair well
with red meats and game.
Despite the fame of Tuscan reds,
the whites should not be overlooked,
particularly the famous Vernaccia
di San Gimignano DOCG
(Denomination of Controlled
Protected Origin), Elba Bianco and
Bianco di Pitigliano.

Chianina

CONSIDERED ONE OF THE HIGHEST-QUALITY BEEFS IN THE WORLD, meat from the Chianina breed of cattle is lean and bright red with a thin veining of fat. The native breed is raised in Val di Chiana, in the provinces of Arezzo and Siena. The Maremmano breed from around the Maremma also produces highly prized meat. Both breeds have obtained IGP status.

Lardo di Colonnata

THE MOUNTAIN VILLAGE OF COLONNATA PRODUCES THIS CURED LARD, OR LARDO. The area is known for marble quarrying, and the lardo is actually aged in conche, large marble tubs, for anywhere from six months to a year. The thick slices of fat are layered with coarse sea salt, pepper, garlic, spices, sage and rosemary in the tubs, which are then closed with a marble slab. The lardo is best eaten in thin slices, accompanied by slices of grilled bread. Traditionally the quarrymen would also add slices of tomato to their lunch of bread and lardo.

Pecorino toscano

MADE FROM FULL-FAT PASTEURIZED SHEEP'S MILK, curdled with calf rennet, Pecorino Toscano has been produced following a very specific production technique since it obtained DOP recognition. It can be found fresh, with a soft consistency, or aged. The rind is hard and brownish-yellow in color, the paste white or straw-yellow and the flavor distinctive, becoming sharper as the cheese ages. When fresh it is excellent eaten on its own, while the aged version is suitable for grating.

Crostini di fegatini di pollo
Chicken-Liver Crostini

Serves 4

14 oz (400 g) chicken livers
1/4 cup (60 ml) vinegar
7 Tbsps (3 ½ oz or 100 g) butter
at room temperature
1/2 onion, minced - 4 sage leaves
salt and pepper
1/2 cup (120 ml) beef broth
4-5 Tbsps salted capers, rinsed
4 anchovy fillets in oil, drained
1/2 baguette, sliced
2 Tbsps extra-virgin olive oil

Preparation time **15 minutes**
Cooking time **15 minutes**
Level **easy**
Wine **Rosso delle Colline Lucchesi**

Marinate the chicken livers in a mixture of vinegar and water for 10 minutes. Melt a pat of butter in a frying pan and sauté the onion and sage leaves.

Add the drained chicken livers and brown briefly. Season with salt and pepper, add the broth and continue cooking for 10-15 minutes.

Puree the liver mixture in a food processor with the capers, anchovies and remaining butter. Toast the baguette slices and top them with the chicken-liver spread. Drizzle with olive oil and serve.

Note *This traditional recipe can also be prepared without capers and anchovies, which gives a more pronounced chicken-liver flavor.*

Cecina
Chickpea Flatbread

Serves 6-8

6 cups (1 ½ l) water
3 ¼ cups (10 ½ oz or 300 g) chickpea flour
7 Tbsps extra-virgin olive oil
1 tsp salt
freshly ground pepper

Preparation time **5 minutes**
Cooking time **30 minutes**
Level **easy**
Wine **Bianco Vergine della Valdichiana**

Pour the water into a bowl and sprinkle in the chickpea flour little by little, whisking constantly to avoid lumps. Add 6 tablespoons of olive oil and the salt and mix to obtain a smooth batter. Let rest for 30 minutes.

Oil a baking sheet and pour on the batter. Bake until a crust forms on the surface.

Serve hot, topped with a sprinkling of freshly ground pepper.

Note *Cecina is a kind of very thin and wide flatbread, with a bright yellow color. The inside should be soft and the outside crunchy. It can be eaten plain, with salt and pepper, or sliced with salted focaccia, always with a glass of red wine on the side.*

Panzanella
Tomato and Bread Salad

Serves 6

14 oz (400 g) stale Tuscan-style bread, sliced
2 ripe tomatoes, sliced
2 red onions, sliced
1 celery stalk, sliced
1 bunch of basil
extra-virgin olive oil for dressing
salt and pepper
red wine vinegar for dressing

Preparation time **15 minutes**
Level **easy**

Soak the bread slices in cold water for
a few minutes until soft, then drain and
squeeze out excess water by hand. The
bread should form small, dry crumbs.

Place them in a salad bowl and add the
tomatoes, onions, celery and basil leaves
and dress with olive oil, salt and pepper
to taste. Keep chilled until ready to serve.
Just before serving sprinkle over
a little vinegar.

Note *The name* panzanella *comes from the
peasant tradition of eating leftover bread (*pane*)
with vegetables from the garden while sitting on
the banks of ditches, known as* zanelle.

Cecina

Panzanella

ribollita
bean and kale soup

Serves 6

4 cups (2 ¼ lb or 1 kg) dried cannellini beans
7 Tbsps extra-virgin olive oil - 1 leek, minced
3 onions, 2 minced and 1 sliced
4 garlic cloves, 2 minced and 2 smashed
2 carrots, 1 diced and 1 sliced
2 ripe tomatoes, peeled, deseeded and chopped
1 ham bone - 6 cups (1 ½ l) vegetable broth
1 piece of Parmesan rind - 1 celery stalk
10 ½ oz (300 g) curly kale leaves, roughly chopped
1 potato, peeled and diced
1 rosemary sprig
1 thyme sprig - salt and pepper
6 slices of stale Tuscan-style bread
1/4 cup (1 oz or 25 g) grated
Parmesan cheese

Preparation time **30 minutes**
Cooking time **1 hour 30 minutes**
Level **medium**
Wine **Chianti Classico**

Soak the beans overnight and drain. Heat 2 tablespoons
of olive oil in a heavy-bottomed saucepan. Sauté the 2 minced
onions and the 2 minced garlic cloves until soft, then add
the diced carrot, beans, tomatoes, celery, leek and ham bone.
Cover with the broth and cook over low heat for 1 hour. When
the beans are tender remove 4-5 spoonfuls and set aside.
Remove the ham bone and puree the mixture.

Return the puree to the heat and add the Parmesan rind,
reserved beans, cavolo nero, sliced carrot and potato. Sauté the
rosemary, thyme and 2 smashed garlic cloves in 5 tablespoons
olive oil. When the garlic is golden, strain the oil into the soup,
reserving the garlic cloves. Adjust salt and pepper and bring to
a boil. Cook until the cabbage is tender. Preheat the broiler and
toast the bread. Rub with the reserved garlic cloves.

Place the bread in the bottom of a terracotta bowl. Pour over
the soup and sprinkle with sliced onion and the Parmesan.
Broil for a few minutes and serve.

Traditional recipe

Minestra di farro
Farro Soup

Serves 6

1 cup (7 oz or 200 g) dried cranberry beans
3 Tbsps extra-virgin olive oil, plus extra for drizzling
1 white onion, minced
1 Tbsp ready-made tomato sauce
1 ½ cups (10 ½ oz or 300 g) farro
(also known as spelt or emmer)
2 cups (500 ml) vegetable broth
salt and pepper

Preparation time **15 minutes**
Cooking time **1 hour**
Level **easy**
Wine **Morellino di Scansano**

Soak the beans overnight, then drain them and boil until tender.

Heat the olive oil in a saucepan and sauté the onion until soft. Add the tomato sauce, farro, cooked beans and vegetable broth. Cook for about 40 minutes, then adjust the salt and pepper. Serve hot, drizzled with extra-virgin olive oil.

Pici con le briciole
Pici with Breadcrumbs

Serves 4

7 oz (200 g) stale Tuscan-style bread
2/3 cup (150 ml) extra-virgin olive oil
2 garlic cloves, minced
1 ¼ lb (600 g) fresh pici pasta
5 Tbsps grated Pecorino cheese
salt
4 Tbsps minced parsley (optional)

Preparation time **10 minutes**
Cooking time **20 minutes**
Level **easy**
Wine **Bolgheri Bianco**

Grate the bread crust, and break up the crumb into small pieces. Heat the olive oil in a frying pan and sauté the garlic. Add the breadcrumbs and cook over low heat until golden. Season with salt to taste.

Bring a large pot of salted water to a boil and cook the pici until they float. Drain with a slotted spoon and transfer to the pan with the breadcrumbs. Toss to coat.

Serve hot, sprinkled with Pecorino, and parsley if desired.

Pappardelle all' aretina
Arezzo-Style Pappardelle

Serves 4

1 duck - 1/2 celery stalk, minced
3 tomatoes (about 10 ½ oz or 300 g in total)
1/2 stick (2 oz or 60 g) butter - salt
1/2 onion, minced - 1/2 carrot, minced
1 ½ oz (40 g) prosciutto, diced
grated nutmeg
2 cups (500 ml) beef broth
3 oz (80 g) beef liver
14 oz (400 g) pappardelle

Preparation time **40 minutes**
Cooking time **1 hour**
Level **medium**
Wine **Chianti Classico**

Carefully clean the duck. Chop the liver and reserve. Blanch the tomatoes, drain, peel and pass through a sieve. Melt the butter in a saucepan and brown the duck, turning frequently, until evenly colored. Remove from the heat and cut into pieces. Season with salt.

In the same pan, sauté the onion, carrot, celery, prosciutto and tomatoes with a grating of nutmeg and add the duck pieces. Continue cooking over low heat for 40 minutes, stirring often and adding broth when necessary. Meanwhile clean the beef liver and blanch it in boiling water, then drain and chop.

Remove the duck pieces from the sauce, debone, chop the meat and return to the pan.

Add the beef liver to the sauce and continue cooking for a few minutes. Bring a large pot of salted water to a boil and cook the pappardelle. Drain and add to the sauce. Serve hot.

Pici con le briciole

Pappardelle all'aretina

Acqua cotta
Tuscan Egg Soup

Serves 6

2 large ripe tomatoes
3 medium onions, thinly sliced
1/2 cup (120 ml) extra-virgin olive oil
1 bay leaf - 4-5 basil leaves
1 celery stalk, sliced
6 cups (1 ½ l) vegetable broth
6 slices of Tuscan-style bread
salt and pepper - 6 eggs
5 Tbsps grated mild Pecorino cheese

Preparation time **20 minutes**
Cooking time **35 minutes**
Level **medium**
Wine **Rosso di Montalcino**

Preheat the oven to 350°F (180°C or Gas Mark 4). Blanch the tomatoes in boiling water for a few seconds. Drain, peel, cut into quarters and deseed. Place the onions in a saucepan with the olive oil and bay leaf and sauté for 5-7 minutes over low heat.

Add the basil, tomatoes and celery. Cook for a few minutes then add the broth and simmer for 20 minutes. Toast the bread in the oven for 5 minutes. Remove and keep warm. Season the soup with salt and a little pepper, remove from the heat.

Break the eggs into the soup and poach, keeping them whole. Place a slice of bread in each of 6 terracotta bowls (or shallow soup bowls) and sprinkle with Pecorino. Fill with soup and place 1 egg in each bowl. Serve immediately.

Pappa col pomodoro
Tomato and Bread Soup

Serves 4

1 ¼ lb (600 g) tomatoes, chopped
1 carrot, chopped
1 onion, chopped
1 celery stalk, chopped
5 Tbsps extra-virgin olive oil
salt and pepper
1 lb (500 g) stale Tuscan-style bread
2 garlic cloves
10 basil leaves
6 cups (1 ½ l) water

Preparation time **25 minutes**
Cooking time **1 hour 30 minutes**
Level **easy**
Wine **Etna Rosso**

Place the tomatoes, carrot, onion and celery in a saucepan of water and bring to a boil. Cook until the vegetables are soft, drain and then pass through a sieve or food mill.

Return the puree to the pan with some olive oil, salt and pepper and continue cooking.

Cut the bread into slices or cubes and place in a separate saucepan with olive oil, garlic, basil, salt, pepper and the water. Bring to a boil and stir frequently, breaking up the bread.

Add the tomato sauce and continue to simmer for 1 hour, adding a little water if necessary. Serve the soup hot or cold, as desired.

Penne al favollo
Penne with Crab and Tomato

Serves 4

2 ¼ lb (1 kg) crabs
4 cups (1 l) water
2 ¼ lb (1 kg) peeled plum tomatoes
3 Tbsps extra-virgin olive oil
3 garlic cloves, minced
2 sage leaves, minced
1/2 red chili pepper, minced
salt
10 ½ oz (300 g) ridged penne
2 pats of butter
3 Tbsps minced parsley

Preparation time **35 minutes**
Cooking time **1 hour 20 minutes**
Level **medium**
Wine **Bianco Vergine Valdichiana**

Wash the crabs well and place in a saucepan with the water and tomatoes. Bring to a boil and cook, uncovered, for about 20 minutes.

Remove the crabs with a slotted spoon, crack them and remove the meat, leaving the claws intact. Heat the olive oil in a non-stick frying pan and sauté the garlic, sage and chili.

Transfer the mixture to the saucepan with the water and tomatoes and add the crab meat and claws. Season with salt and cook for about an hour, until the sauce is thickened. Bring a large pot of salted water to a boil and cook the penne until al dente. Drain and transfer to the sauce. Stir in the butter and serve, sprinkled with parsley.

Pappa col pomodoro

Penne al favollo

Fegatelli di maiale
Pork-Liver Bundles

Serves 6

14 oz (400 g) caul fat
3 garlic cloves, minced
1 pinch of fennel seeds
salt and pepper
1 ½ lb (650 g) pork liver, rinsed and cubed
1 bunch of wild fennel or fresh bay leaves
6 Tbsps extra-virgin olive oil
1/2 cup (120 ml) red wine

Preparation time **20 minutes**
Cooking time **20 minutes**
Level **easy**
Wine **Carmignano Rosso**

Rinse the caul fat well and soak it in warm water for 5-10 minutes. Mix together the minced garlic, fennel seeds, salt and pepper.

Dip the pork liver cubes in the garlic mixture, then wrap each one in a small piece of caul fat. Secure each bundle with a sprig of wild fennel, or with a toothpick and a bay leaf.

Heat the olive oil in a frying pan until very hot, then brown the pork-liver bundles. Pour over the red wine and cook for 6-8 minutes over low heat. Serve hot.

Triglie alle livornese
Livorno-Style Mackerel

Serves 4

12 mackerel
all-purpose flour for flouring
2 Tbsps extra-virgin olive oil
salt and pepper
3/4 cup (180 ml) white wine
1 onion, minced
1 garlic clove, peeled
1 bay leaf
4 peeled plum tomatoes, chopped
4 Tbsps minced parsley

Preparation time **20 minutes**
Cooking time **20 minutes**
Level **easy**
Wine **Bolgheri Bianco**

Wash the mackerel and clean them carefully, then pat dry and dust with flour.

Heat the olive oil in a large, non-stick frying pan and brown the mackerel on both sides. Salt the fish and add the wine. Cook for a few minutes, then add the onion, garlic, bay leaf and pepper.

When the wine has evaporated, add the tomatoes. Cook, covered, for a few minutes. Sprinkle over the parsley and serve hot.

Fagioli all'uccelletto
Cannellini Beans with Tomatoes

Serves 4

1 lb (450 g) dried cannellini beans
salt and pepper
4 Tbsps extra-virgin olive oil
2 garlic cloves, smashed
1 sage sprig
1 cup (7 oz or 200 g)
peeled plum tomatoes, pureed

Soaking time **12 hours**
Preparation time **10 minutes**
Cooking time **30 minutes**
Level **easy**

Soak the beans for about 12 hours. Drain
and boil in salted water over low heat until
they start to fall apart. Drain.

Heat the olive oil in a large frying pan
or an earthenware pot and sauté the garlic
and sage. When the garlic is golden, add
the tomatoes. Cook for 10 minutes, until
thickened.

Add the beans, stir carefully and adjust salt
and pepper. Continue cooking for another
15 minutes, then serve hot.

Triglie alla livornese

Fagioli all'uccelletto

Tagliata di chianina
Porterhouse Steak

Serves 4

7 oz (200 g) roasted red and yellow peppers in oil, drained and finely chopped
salt and pepper
6 Tbsps Tuscan extra-virgin olive oil
2/3 cup (3 ½ oz or 100 g) salted capers, rinsed and minced
5 ½ oz (150 g) pickled long green peppers, drained and coarsely chopped
1 Porterhouse steak (about 2 ¼ lb or 1 kg; 2 inches or 4-5 cm thick)
coarse salt

Preparation time **15 minutes**
Cooking time **10 minutes**
Level **easy**
Wine **Brunello di Montalcino**

Mix together the roasted peppers, salt, pepper and 2 tablespoons olive oil and place in a serving bowl. Mix together the capers with 2 tablespoons olive oil and place in a serving bowl. Place the green peppers in a serving bowl.

Heat a grill about 2 inches (5 cm) above charcoal, or a cast-iron grill pan on the stove. Make cuts in the steak's fat to stop it curling up, and cuts near the bone to help it cook evenly.

Cook the steak on the hot grill or grill pan (if using the grill pan sprinkle it with salt before putting on the steak) for 5 minutes on each side, sprinkling with coarse salt.

Cut the steak into thick slices and serve with a drizzle of olive oil, accompanied by the green peppers, roasted peppers and capers.

Arrosto all'uva rosata
Roast Pork with Grapes

Serves 4

2 rosemary sprigs
5 sage leaves
salt and pepper
1 center-cut pork loin
4 slices of pancetta
4 tbsps extra-virgin olive oil
2 shallots, coarsely chopped
3/4 cup (180 ml) rosé wine
1 bunch of red grapes
4 bay leaves

Preparation time **20 minutes**
Cooking time **50 minutes**
Level **easy**
Wine **Morellino di Scansano**

Preheat oven to 350°F (180°C). Mince together the rosemary and sage leaves. Salt and pepper the meat and rub with the herb mixture. Wrap in the pancetta and tie with kitchen string.

Heat the olive oil in a frying pan and add the shallots. Add the meat and brown evenly on all sides. Add the wine and remove from heat.

Transfer the meat and pan juices to a baking dish and add the grapes and bay leaves. Bake for 45 minutes.

Tegamata di Pitigliano
Pitigliano-Style Beef Stew

Serves 4

1/2 cup (120 ml) red wine
1 carrot, thinly sliced - 1 onion, thinly sliced
1 rosemary sprig - 3-4 cloves
1 ¾ lb (800 g) beef, cut into cubes
5 Tbsps extra-virgin olive oil
2 ½ cups (1 lb or 500 g) peeled plum tomatoes, pureed and sieved
salt and pepper
1 ¼ lb (600 g) new potatoes

Preparation time **30 minutes**
Cooking time **3 hours 20 minutes**
Level **medium**
Wine **Morellino di Scansano**

Mix together the red wine, carrot, onion, rosemary and cloves and pour over the beef. Marinate overnight. Drain the beef, reserving the marinade.

Heat the olive oil in a saucepan and brown the beef. As soon as it starts to color, add 1-2 ladlefuls of the marinade. Cook over high heat until the liquid starts to boil, then lower the heat and continue cooking, covered, until the liquid has thickened. Remove the lid and add the tomatoes. Cook until the sauce has a creamy consistency, then cover the meat with hot water and bring to a boil.

Adjust salt and pepper and continue cooking for 2 hours, adding water when necessary. Add the potatoes and cook for another 30 minutes, until they are tender. Serve hot.

Arrosto all'uva rosata

Tegamata di Pitigliano

Castagnaccio toscano
Tuscan Chestnut Cake

Serves 6

3/4 cup (4 oz or 120 g) raisins
2 ⅓ cups (14 oz or 400 g)
sweet chestnut flour
2 ½ cups (600 ml) water
1/2 cup (120 ml) extra-virgin olive oil
salt
1/2 cup (2 ½ oz or 70 g) pine nuts
1 rosemary sprig, leaves only

Preparation time **20 minutes**
Cooking time **30 minutes**
Level **easy**
Wine **Vernaccia di San Gimignano Passito**

Preheat the oven to 400°F (200°C or Gas Mark 6). Soak the raisins in warm water until soft, then drain and squeeze out excess water.

Mix together the chestnut flour, water, 1 tablespoon olive oil and a pinch of salt. Stir until the mix is smooth and free of lumps. Stir in the pine nuts and raisins.

Pour the mixture into an oiled baking dish, sprinkle with rosemary leaves and drizzle over the remaining olive oil. Bake for 25-30 minutes. Serve at room temperature.

Note *Castagnaccio is a typical poor man's dessert that uses no sugar, but gets its sweetness from the chestnut flour. The rosemary gives it an extra layer of flavor. Use a high-quality olive oil.*

Buccellato di Lucca
Lucca-Style Sweet Raisin Bread

Serves 4-6

2/3 cup (3 ½ oz or 100 g) raisins
2 ½ tsps active dry yeast
3 ⅔ cups (1 lb or 450 g) all-purpose flour
1/2 cup (3 ½ oz or 100 g) sugar,
plus extra for sprinkling
2 eggs
3 ½ Tbsps (2 oz or 50 g) butter, softened
4 Tbsps milk
3 Tbsps aniseeds
salt

Preparation time **25 minutes**
Cooking time **1 hour**
Level **easy**
Wine not recommended

Soak the raisins in warm water until soft, then drain and squeeze out the excess liquid. Dissolve the yeast in a little warm water.

Mix together the flour, sugar, eggs, butter, milk, raisins, aniseeds and a pinch of salt. Lastly add the yeast mixture, little by little, and continue to knead the dough. Form the dough into a ball and cover with a kitchen towel. Leave to rise for 30 minutes in a warm place.

Form the dough into a rectangular loaf, or into many little rings. Make cuts in the surface of the dough and leave to rise for another hour. Preheat the oven to 350°F (180°C or Gas Mark 4).

Sprinkle the surface of the dough with sugar and transfer to a baking sheet. Bake for about 1 hour. Let cool before serving.

Buccellato di Lucca

Schiaccia all'uva
Grape Schiaccia

Serves 4-6

1 lb (500 g) black or red grapes
2 blocks of brewers' yeast
1/2 cup (120 ml) warm water
4 cups (1 lb 2 oz or 500 g) all-purpose flour,
plus extra for flouring
1 ½ cups (10 1/2 oz or 300 g) sugar
1 Tbsp extra-virgin olive oil
1 pat of butter

Preparation time **30 minutes**
Cooking time **1 hour**
Level **medium**
Wine **Moscato Bianco Passito**

Remove the grapes from the stems, taking
care not to break the fruit. Dissolve the
yeast in the warm water. Mound the flour
on a work surface and make a well in the
center. Add half the grapes, the yeast
water, sugar and olive oil. Mix well and
then knead for 10 minutes. If the dough
becomes too sticky add a little flour.

Form the dough into a ball and cover it
with a kitchen towel. Let rise for 1 hour
in a cool dry place. Preheat the oven to
300°F (150°C or Gas Mark 2). Butter and
flour a baking sheet.

Place the dough on the baking sheet and
spread out the dough by hand, pressing
with fingertips, until it covers most of the
pan. Distribute the remaining grapes over
the dough. Sprinkle generously with sugar.
Bake for 1 hour.

Schiaccia all'uva

Spongata di Pontremoli
Pontremoli-Style Fruit Cake

Serves 4

2/3 cup (3 ½ oz or 100 g) raisins
1 tsp brandy
1/2 cup (7 oz or 200 g) liquid Lunigiana honey
1 ¾ cups (7 oz or 200 g) chopped mixed nuts (almonds, walnuts, pine nuts, hazelnuts)
3 ½ oz (100 g) dry cookies, finely chopped
1 pinch of ground cinnamon
1 pinch of grated nutmeg
2 ⅓ cups plus 1 Tbsp (10 ½ oz or 300 g) all-purpose flour
7 Tbsps (3 ½ oz or 100 g) butter, softened
1/2 cup (3 ½ oz or 100 g) sugar
salt

Preparation time **1 hour**
Cooking time **35 minutes**
Level **medium**
Wine **Vin Santo**

Soak the raisins in warm water until soft, then drain and squeeze out excess liquid. Heat the honey in a saucepan and add the brandy, nuts, cookies, raisins, cinnamon and nutmeg. Stir well and transfer to a bowl. Cover and let sit overnight.

Mix together the flour, softened butter, sugar and a pinch of salt into a dough. Cover and let rest in a cool, dry place for about 1 hour. Preheat the oven to 350°F (180°C or Gas Mark 4).

Roll the dough out into two thick sheets. Lay one on a buttered baking sheet, top with the nut mixture, and cover with the other sheet of dough. Press around the edges to seal.

Bake for about 30 minutes.

Biscotti di Prato
Prato-Style Biscotti

Serves 4

1 cup (4 ½ oz or 130 g) almonds
4 cups (1 lb 2 oz or 500 g) all-purpose flour
2 ½ cups (1 lb 3 oz or 500 g) sugar
4 eggs
1 tsp baking soda
1 pinch of salt

Preparation time **30 minutes**
Cooking time **20 minutes**
Level **medium**
Wine **Vin Santo**

Preheat the oven to 300°F (150°C or Gas Mark 2). Toast the almonds for 10 minutes. Chop three-quarters and keep the rest whole.

Pour the flour onto a work surface and make a well in the center. Add the eggs, sugar, baking soda and salt to the center of the well. Mix well until uniform. Mix all the almonds into the dough. Line a baking sheet with waxed paper.

Form 2 long thin loaves with the dough. Place them on the baking sheet and bake for 10 minutes. Remove from the oven and slice the hot loaves on the diagonal to form biscotti.

Place the biscotti on the baking sheet and return to the oven until lightly browned.

Biscotti di Prato

Marche

A gastronomic culture marked by fishermen and farmers,

between the Appennine mountains and the Adriatic, with the best products from the land and sea. *Olive oil* of the highest quality, excellent *beef, cheeses* and *truffles* as well as *flavorful ciauscolo* salame, fish *brodetto* and stuffed *olive all'ascolana* are all waiting for visitors to the region's ancient villages and rolling hills.

MARCHE
local *products*

Brodetto *all'*anconetana

A COMPLEX LABYRINTH OF FLAVORS AND FRAGRANCES, based on the freshest fish caught in the Adriatic sea. Authentic brodetto from Ancona is a very thick soup made using 13 different kinds of fish, including scorpionfish, cod, sole, mullet, gurnard, squid and mantis shrimp. The cleaned fish is cooked in an earthenware pot with garlic, olive oil, parsley, tomato puree and a few drops of vinegar to help keep the fish whole. Variations exist along the Marche coast: In Fano they make brodetto with tomato preserves, while in San Benedetto the recipe comes from the neighborhood known as *u labirintu*, the maze-like fishermen's quarter, and is flavored with spicy chili and the local white wine, Falerio dei Colli Ascolani. In Porto Recanati no tomato is used, and the recipe calls for more cuttlefish, dusted with flour and browned, and saffron.

Carciofo violetto *di Jesi*

THIS PURPLE ARTICHOKE IS CULTIVATED AROUND THE TOWN OF JESI AS WELL AS THE VILLAGES OF OSTRENSE, MONSANO, MONTE SAN VITO, MORRÒ D'ALBA, SAN MARCELLO AND SAN PAOLO DI JESI. The tender artichoke has no spines and is mainly grown by the food industry to be frozen, brined or preserved in oil, or to extract its essence for medicinal uses. In fact it has many virtues, being rich in nutritional value and low in calories, with high iron, sodium, potassium, calcium, phosphorous and vitamins.

Fave *di* Ostra *e* Cicerchie

TWO VERY SPECIAL LEGUMES: OSTRA FAVA BEANS AND CICERCHIE FROM SERRA DE' CONTI. Fava beans have been a staple since ancient times. During famines the beans were even dried, ground into flour and used to make bread. Favas also have another significance, as they were used for voting during elections: A white bean for yes, a black one for no. Today they are eaten together with lonza, cured pork loin, and fresh sheep's milk cheeses. Cicerchie are small wild chickpeas which can flourish in even the poorest soil. Once very common, they were at risk of extinction before a small band of enthusiasts from the village of Serra de' Conti came together to promote the cicerchia and ensure its survival. They are commonly cooked in soup.

Cavolfiore *di Fano*

ONE OF THE STAR PRODUCTS OF THE MARCHE REGION, this cauliflower (*cavolfiore*) is very resistant to the cold and harvested from the end of February to mid-May following planting the previous summer. The production area includes all of the province of Fano and along the coast as far as Senigallia. Fano is one of the most prized varieties of cauliflower, low in calories and rich in vitamins A, B and C as well as minerals (phosphorous, potassium and copper) and very versatile in the kitchen. Usually it is boiled or stewed, but can also be eaten raw.

Ciauscolo

ONE OF THE MARCHE'S MOST CHARACTERISTIC CURED MEATS, ciauscolo is made from pork (shoulder or loin, lard and belly), seasoned with salt, pepper, crushed garlic, white wine, orange peel, thyme and fennel seeds, ground together three times and enclosed in a casing. It is then left to dry and lightly smoked. Ciauscolo is ready after two to three months of aging, and has a soft consistency so it can be eaten spread on bread or sliced. Styles vary: Around Ascoli Piceno it is more lean, and around Macerata it has a softer consistency.

Caciotta *di* Urbino Dop

MADE FROM WHOLE SHEEP'S MILK WITH THE ADDITION OF COW'S MILK, THIS CHEESE WAS TRADITIONALLY prepared either in terracotta or majolica vessels from the local ceramic-making industry, or in wooden forms made from oak or beech. These are still used today by some local artisanal producers. This tasty cheese was said to be Michelangelo's favorite, and since 1996 it has been protected by a European Union DOP (Denomination of Protected Origin). A classic table cheese whose flavor can vary from lightly acidic to more salty, it is best eaten fresh, paired with fig jam, a selection of cured meats and slices of grilled polenta.

Tartufo *bianco di* Acqualagna

IN THE METAURO VALLEY, IN THE PROVINCE OF PESARO AND URBINO, lies Acqualanga, one of the most renowned sources for white truffles (*tartufi bianchi*). The fungi are irregular in appearance, varying in size, with a smooth surface, an interior ranging from brown to pale hazelnut in color and a very intense fragrance. Their ideal habitat is the calcareous, marly or clayey soil of woods, where they grow symbiotically with oaks, lindens, willows, poplars and hazelnut trees. They can be found from October to the end of December and can be stored in glass for several years, but their unique scent is best appreciated when fresh.

Olive tenere Ascolane

ASCOLANA TENERA IS AN EXQUISITE VARIETY OF OLIVE, TRADITIONALLY STUFFED WITH MEAT, COATED IN BREADCRUMBS AND FRIED. The olive trees flourish in the fertile, rich soil of the hills around Ascoli Piceno, and the variety grows in an area of no more than a few hundred acres. The olive's distinguishing characteristic is its delicacy, the tenderness from which it gets its name (tenero means "tender"). The olives are large, with a thin yellowish-green skin and juicy, crunchy flesh. The Roman writer Pliny the Elder thought they were the finest of all olives. Preserved in brine, the olives are served as delicious snacks, found in all of Ascoli's best cafés to nibble on with drinks. Alternatively they can be used as an accompaniment to grilled or roasted meats. There are as many recipes for the typical stuffed and fried olive all'ascolana as there are families in Ascoli, but they always have four indispensable ingredients: Ascolana Tenera olives, Parmesan cheese, ground beef and ground pork. This unusual olive variety suffered from a period of anonymity, but is currently enjoying a resurgent popularity and is now protected by a Slow Food Presidium.

Olive all'ascolana
Ascoli-Style Fried Olives

Serves 6-8

3 ½ oz (100 g) pancetta, minced
2 Tbsps extra-virgin olive oil
2 oz (50 g) ground pork
2 oz (50 g) ground beef
2 oz (50 g) ground chicken
2 oz (50 g) prosciutto, minced - 2 eggs
2 Tbsps ready-made tomato sauce
2 Tbsps grated Parmesan cheese
1/2 cup (2 oz or 60 g) breadcrumbs
2 Tbsps milk - salt - grated nutmeg
40 large green olives, pitted
6 Tbsps all-purpose flour
sunflower oil for frying

Preparation time **20 minutes**
Cooking time **40 minutes**
Level **easy**
Wine **Falerio dei Colli Ascolani**

Sauté the pancetta with the olive oil until
browned, then add the pork, beef, chicken,
prosciutto and tomato sauce. Stir well and
cook over medium heat until the meat is
cooked through. Remove from the heat and
puree in a food processor with 1 egg, Parmesan,
1 tablespoon of breadcrumbs, milk, salt and
a grating of nutmeg. Stuff the olives with
the meat mixture. Beat the remaining egg.
Dip the stuffed olives in flour, then egg, then
breadcrumbs.

Heat the sunflower oil until very hot, then fry
the olives until golden, in batches if necessary.
Drain, dry on paper towels and serve.

Cascioni ripieni di erbette
Pan-Fried Spinach Pies

Serves 4

4 cups (1 lb 2 oz or 500 g) all-purpose flour
7 Tbsps extra-virgin olive oil
7 Tbsps warm milk
salt
2 ½ tsps active dry yeast
1 pat of butter
1 lb (500 g) spinach, chopped
3 ½ oz (100 g) Caciotta cheese, chopped

Preparation time **40 minutes**
Cooking time **30 minutes**
Level **easy**
Wine **Verdicchio dei Castelli di Jesi Spumante**

Mound the flour on a work surface and mix
in 5 tablespoons of olive oil, the warm milk,
a pinch of salt and the yeast. Knead
vigorously to obtain a smooth, uniform
dough.

Let the dough rest for 30 minutes, covered
with a clean kitchen towel. Divide the dough
into small portions and roll out into flat,
tortilla-like circles.

Melt the butter in a frying pan and sauté
the chopped spinach until wilted. Place a
little sautéed spinach in the middle of each
dough circle and top with some pieces of
cheese. Fold over the dough to create half-
moons and press down firmly around the
edges to seal well.

Heat the remaining 2 tablespoons of olive
oil in a frying pan and sauté the half-moons
on both sides until golden-brown. Serve hot.

Crescia sfogliata di Urbino
Urbino-Style Flatbreads

Serves 4

2 ⅓ cups plus 1 Tbsp (10 ½ oz or 300 g)
all-purpose flour
1/2 cup (3 ½ oz or 100 g) lard
3 eggs
salt

Preparation time **25 minutes**
Cooking time **15 minutes**
Level **easy**
Wine **Bianchetto del Metauro**

Mound the flour on a wooden pastry board
and make a well in the center. Break in the
eggs, add a pinch of salt, and work into
a smooth, firm dough. Cover with a kitchen
towel and let rest for 30 minutes.

Roll out the rested dough with a rolling pin
into a thick sheet and cover with pieces of
lard. Roll up the dough so the lard is in the
middle, then cut into 12-inch (30 cm) lengths
and press the ends together to stop the lard
coming out. Let rest for 1 hour in a cool place.

Roll out the dough into round, tortilla-like
disks. Heat a non-stick frying pan and cook
the flatbreads one at a time, turning them on
both sides until golden and browned in spots.
Serve hot.

Note *These flatbreads can be filled with cured
meats and vegetables.*

Cascioni ripieni di erbette

Crescia sfogliata di Urbino

Brodetto all'anconetana
Ancona-Style Fish Soup

Serves 4-6

2 ¼ lb (1 kg) mixed fish (halibut, turbot, cod, mackerel)
2 Tbsps extra-virgin olive oil
1 onion, minced
1 garlic clove, peeled
1/2 cup (120 ml) white wine vinegar
3 tomatoes, blanched, peeled and chopped
salt
4-6 slices of bread

Preparation time **20 minutes**
Cooking time **30 minutes**
Level **easy**
Wine **Verdicchio dei Castelli di Jesi**

Clean and fillet the fish. Heat the olive oil in a saucepan and sauté the onion and whole, peeled garlic clove until soft. Add the vinegar and let evaporate slightly, then add the tomatoes and cook for a few more minutes.

Add the fish fillets and other seafood, starting with the pieces that will take the longest to cook. Adjust salt and continue cooking until all the fish is cooked through.

Toast the bread in a non-stick frying pan or under the broiler. Serve the soup hot with the toasted bread.

Ciavattoni al pesce
Mixed Seafood Pasta

Serves 4-6

1 lb (500 g) clams - 1 lb (500 g) mussels
1 lb (500 g) mantis shrimp
1 lb (500 g) jumbo shrimp
2 Tbsps extra-virgin olive oil
1 pat of butter - 1 onion, minced
3 garlic cloves, minced
1 bunch of parsley, minced - salt
3/4 cup (180 ml) white wine
10 Pachino or large cherry tomatoes, chopped
1 pinch of chili pepper flakes
10 ½ oz (300 g) ciavattoni, paccheri or large rigatoni

Preparation time **15 minutes**
Cooking time **25 minutes**
Level **medium**
Wine **Falerio dei Colli Ascolani**

Cook the clams and mussels in a covered frying pan until they open, then remove the shells. Strain and reserve the resulting cooking liquid.

Boil the mantis shrimp and jumbo shrimp until cooked through. Peel the shrimp and chop the meat. Heat the olive oil and butter in a saucepan and sauté the onion, garlic and half the parsley. Add a pinch of salt and the wine and let evaporate briefly, then add the tomatoes and chili. After a few minutes add the clams, mussels, strained cooking liquid and chopped shrimp. Continue cooking until the sauce is creamy. Bring a large pot of salted water to a boil and cook the pasta until al dente. Drain and toss in the pan with the sauce. Serve hot, sprinkled with minced parsley.

Passatelli di carne
Chicken Passatelli

Serves 4

7 oz (200 g) chicken breast
10 ½ oz (300 g) spinach
salt
1 oz (30 g) beef marrow
1 large pat of butter, softened
1 ½ cups (5 ½ oz or 150 g)
grated Parmesan cheese
2/3 cup (3 oz or 80 g) breadcrumbs
4 egg yolks
grated nutmeg
4 cups (1 l) beef broth (from a stock cube)

Preparation time **20 minutes**
Cooking time **20 minutes**
Level **easy**
Wine **Falerno dei Colli Ascolani**

Poach the chicken breast in boiling water until cooked through, then drain. Wash the spinach, leaving water on the leaves, then wilt in a frying pan with a little salt. Drain and squeeze out any excess liquid.

Grind the chicken in a meat grinder with the beef marrow, passing it through twice. Transfer to a bowl and stir in the softened butter, half the grated Parmesan, the breadcrumbs, egg yolks, a grating of nutmeg and a pinch of salt. Work with the hands to obtain a smooth, firm mixture. Pass the mixture through a passatelli maker or again through the meat grinder to obtain strings.

Bring the broth to a boil and cook the passatelli for a few minutes. Serve sprinkled with the remaining Parmesan.

Spaghetti mare e monti
"Sea and Mountains" Spaghetti

Serves 4

14 oz (400 g) squid
2 Tbsps extra-virgin olive oil
1 garlic clove, peeled
14 oz (400 g) mixed wild mushrooms
3/4 cup (180 ml) white wine
2 ⅔ cups (14 oz or 400 g)
cherry tomatoes, chopped
salt
14 oz (400 g) spaghetti
ground chili pepper (optional)

Preparation time **15 minutes**
Cooking time **30 minutes**
Level **easy**
Wine **Verdicchio dei Castelli di Jesi Superiore**

Wash the squid under cold running water, then cut into small pieces.

Heat the olive oil with the whole peeled garlic clove in a large frying pan and add the squid. Add the mushrooms, and then the wine. Let evaporate briefly, then add the tomatoes. Adjust the salt and continue cooking until the sauce has thickened and the squid are cooked through.

Bring a large pot of salted water to a boil and cook the spaghetti until al dente. Drain and toss in the pan with the sauce. Serve hot, sprinkled with a little chili if desired.

Maccheroncini di Campofilone
Campofilone-Style Noodles in Capon Broth

Serves 4

1 capon (about 1 ½ lb or 700 g)
1/2 onion
1 carrot
1/2 celery stalk
1 bunch of mixed herbs, chopped
salt
1 ⅔ cups (7 oz or 200 g) all-purpose flour
2 eggs
1 Tbsp breadcrumbs
3 Tbsps grated Parmesan cheese
8 spears of wild or pencil asparagus, sliced
1/4 cup (1 oz or 20 g) shaved Pecorino di Fossa or other aged Pecorino cheese
8 cherry tomatoes, blanched, peeled, seeded and chopped

Preparation time **20 minutes**
Cooking time **2 hours**
Level **medium**
Wine **Bianchello del Metauro**

Place the capon, onion, carrot, celery and herbs in a large pot and cover with water. Bring to a simmer and let cook for about an hour, then salt to taste. Meanwhile, mix the flour and eggs together to form a smooth and elastic dough. Roll the dough into a thin sheet, roll up the sheet and slice into very thin noodles.

Remove the capon from broth, take the leg meat off the bone and chop finely. Mix together the chopped capon meat, breadcrumbs and Parmesan cheese. Roll the mixture into small balls to form dumplings. Strain the capon broth and bring it to a boil. Boil the dumplings in the broth until cooked through, then drain with a slotted spoon, leaving the broth in the pot. Bring to a boil and add the asparagus.

Cook briefly, then add the noodles and cook for a minute or so. Serve the soup with the dumplings, sprinkled with chopped tomatoes and shavings of Pecorino.

Filetti intrecciati di sogliola
Braided Sole Fillets with Mint

Serves 4

4 sole fillets (about 7 oz or 200 g each)
1 Tbsp all-purpose flour
2 Tbsps extra-virgin olive oil
1 garlic clove
salt and pepper
zest of 1/2 organic lemon, cut into thin matchsticks
juice of 1 lemon
1/2 cup (120 ml) white wine
2 ⅔ cups (14 oz or 400 g) cherry tomatoes, quartered
10 mint leaves, 6 chopped and 4 whole

Preparation time **20 minutes**
Cooking time **20 minutes**
Level **easy**
Wine **Verdicchio dei Castelli di Jesi**

Remove the skin from the sole fillets and slice the fillets into long, thin strips. Braid the strips and fix them with a toothpick at either end. Cover with plastic wrap and refrigerate for 10 minutes.

Dust the sole braids with flour. Heat the olive oil and whole peeled garlic clove in a frying pan and brown the sole. Season with salt and pepper and add the lemon zest, lemon juice and white wine. Let reduce, then remove the sole from the frying pan and set aside. Add the tomatoes to the frying pan with the chopped mint, stir, adjust salt and pepper and cook for 2-3 minutes.

Arrange the sole on serving plates and top with the tomato sauce. Garnish each plate with a mint leaf and serve.

Coniglio in porchetta
Rabbit with Wild Fennel

Serves 4

1 large rabbit - 3/4 cup (180 ml) vinegar
1 bunch of wild fennel
3 garlic cloves, 2 whole and 1 smashed
3 ½ oz (100 g) bacon, finely chopped
3 ½ oz (100 g) ham, finely chopped
3 ½ oz (100 g) salami, finely chopped
salt and pepper - 3 ½ oz (100 g) pancetta, sliced
3 Tbsps extra-virgin olive oil
3/4 cup (180 ml) white wine

Preparation time **40 minutes**
Cooking time **1 hour 15 minutes**
Level **medium**
Wine **Rosso Piceno**

Preheat the oven to 325°F (170°C or Gas Mark 3). Wash the rabbit with water and vinegar. Remove the giblets, wash, chop and set aside.

Bring a pot of water to a boil and blanch the wild fennel and whole garlic cloves. Drain, reserving the water. Chop the fennel. Sauté the bacon, ham and salami. Add the rabbit giblets and fennel and cook for a few minutes. Lay the rabbit out on a cloth. Season with salt and pepper and line the inside with slices of pancetta. Stuff with the bacon mixture and smashed garlic clove and sprinkle with pepper. Roll up carefully, sew closed the opening and tie with kitchen string.

Heat the olive oil in a large frying pan and brown the rabbit, then transfer to a roasting pan. Sprinkle over half the wine and some of the fennel cooking liquid. Roast for 1 hour, basting often with the remaining wine, cooking liquid and the pan juices.

Remove from the oven, remove the string, cut the rabbit into pieces and serve with slices of the stuffing.

Polenta, costarelle e salsicce
Ribs and Sausages with Polenta

Serves 4-6

8 cups (4 l) water
salt
3 cups (1 lb or 500 g) polenta cornmeal
(not instant polenta)
3 ½ oz (100 g) lardo (cured lard), chopped
1 lb (500 g) sausages, chopped
1 lb (500 g) pork ribs
1/2 cup (120 ml) white wine
4 Tbsps grated Pecorino cheese (optional)

Preparation time **5 minutes**
Cooking time **1 hour**
Level **easy**
Wine **Rosso Piceno Superiore**

Bring the water to a boil and sprinkle in the
cornmeal while whisking constantly to avoid
lumps forming. Adjust salt and continue
simmering for about 50 minutes, stirring with
a wooden spoon to prevent sticking.

Meanwhile brown the lardo in a frying pan
and add the sausages and ribs. Season with
salt and continue cooking, adding wine and
water when necessary, until cooked through.
Transfer the cooked polenta to individual
serving plates, using a cookie cutter to form
it into circles. Top with the sausages and ribs.
Sprinkle with grated Pecorino before serving,
if desired.

Coniglio in porchetta

Polenta, costarelle e salsicce

pizza al formaggio di Jesi
Jesi-style cheese bread

3 ½ tsps active dry yeast

2 ⅓ cups plus 1 Tbsp (10 ½ oz or 300 g) all-purpose flour

2 Tbsps milk

4 eggs

salt and pepper

3 Tbsps extra-virgin olive oil

7 Tbsps grated Pecorino Romano cheese

7 Tbsps grated Parmesan cheese

1 pat of butter

4 ½ oz (125 g) fresh Pecorino cheese, cut into matchsticks

Preparation time **40 minutes**

Cooking time **30 minutes**

Level **easy**

Wine **Verdicchio dei Castelli di Jesi**

Dissolve the yeast in a little warm water. Mix together 6 ½ tablespoons flour with the milk and yeast mixture. Mix well until smooth, then leave to rise until doubled in volume (about 3 hours). Mix the rest of the flour into the risen dough and add 3 eggs, pinches of salt and pepper, the olive oil, grated Pecorino and grated Parmesan. Knead until smooth.

Butter a high-rimmed baking dish and press the dough into it. Poke holes in the dough with the fingers and fill with the cheese matchsticks. Cover with a kitchen towel and let rise for another 40 minutes. Preheat the oven to 320°F (160°C or Gas Mark 3).

Beat the remaining egg and brush over the surface of the dough. Bake for about 30 minutes, until golden. Remove from the oven, let cool and turn out of the baking dish before serving.

Traditional recipe

Mungana
Marble Cake

Serves 4-6

4 cups (1 lb 2 oz or 500 g) all-purpose flour
3 eggs
3/4 cup (5 ½ oz or 150 g) sugar
1/4 cup (60 ml) Mistrà or other aniseed liqueur
3/4 cup (180 ml) milk
10 ½ Tbsps (5 ½ oz or 150 g) butter, softened,
plus extra for buttering
4 tsps baking powder
grated zest of 1/2 organic lemon
1/3 cup (1 oz or 25 g) cocoa powder

Preparation time **20 minutes**
Cooking time **30 minutes**
Level **easy**
Wine **Vernaccia di Serrapetrona Dolce**

Preheat the oven to 350°F (180°C or Gas
Mark 4).

Mound the flour on a work surface and add
the eggs, sugar, Mistrà, milk, butter, baking
powder and lemon zest. Knead to obtain a
smooth, uniform dough. Take a third of the
dough and knead in the cocoa powder.

Butter a baking dish and spread in half the
white dough. Top with the brown dough, then
finish with a layer of the white dough. Bake
until the top is golden. Serve warm or at room
temperature, cut into slices.

Note Mungana *means "spotted cow," and the*
brown and white patterns of this cake recall
a cow's hide.

Bostrengo
Raisin and Fig Cornbread

Serves 6

1/2 cup (3 ½ oz or 100 g) Carnaroli rice
1 cup (125 ml) milk
2/3 cup (3 ½ oz or 100 g) raisins
7 oz (200 g) stale crusty bread
3 cups plus 3 Tbsps (14 oz or 400 g)
all-purpose flour
1 ⅔ cups (7 oz or 200 g) finely ground cornmeal
zest of 1 organic orange, thinly sliced
1 apple, cored and thinly sliced
1 cup (3 ½ oz or 100 g) chopped walnuts
1 ⅓ cups (7 oz or 100 g) dried figs, chopped
1/2 cup (3 ½ oz or 100 g) sugar
1 Tbsp extra-virgin olive oil
confectioners' sugar

Preparation time **30 minutes**
Cooking time **1 hour**
Level **medium**
Wine **Vernaccia di Serrapetrona Dolce**

Preheat the oven to 325°F (170°C or Gas
Mark 3). Place the rice in a saucepan, cover
with milk and cook until al dente.

Soak the raisins in warm water until soft, then
drain and squeeze out excess liquid. Soak the
bread in a little milk until soft. Place in a bowl
and mix with the flour, cornmeal, orange zest,
apple slices, raisins, walnuts and figs.

Add the sugar and cooked rice and mix well.
Transfer to an oiled cake tin and bake for about
1 hour. Remove from the oven and let cool.
Sprinkle with confectioners' sugar and serve
in slices or cut into cubes.

Bostrengo

Umbria

A *forgotten rural world,*
where sheep and horses graze

on gentle grassy slopes and the traditional
cooking has a timeless quality. The true
essence of art and cuisine, making the
most of natural foods and flavors: excellent
sheep's milk cheeses, red potatoes,
intensely flavored legumes like *lentils*
and *cicerchie*, as well as *truffles* and
cured *meats*. A region of simple
gastronomic pleasures.

UMBRIA
local products

Olio d'oliva extravergine DOP

UMBRIA IS THE ONLY ITALIAN REGION TO HAVE BEEN AWARDED DOP (DENOMINATION OF PROTECTED ORIGIN) branding for its entire production of extra-virgin olive oil (*olio d'oliva extravergine*). Olive trees are grown mainly along the Appennines. Umbrian oil has an unmistakable fruity aroma and is primarily made from Moraiolo, Leccino, Frantoio, San Felice, Pendolino and Agogia olives. Depending on the blend, the oil can range from green to yellow and from bitter to spicy.

Farro di Monteleone di Spoleto

THE FARRO (SOMETIMES CALLED EMMER OR SPELT) FROM MONTELEONE IS UNUSUAL because when milled, it produces a flour that is brown instead of white. Farro is an important element in the local diet, and is low in fat, rich in starch and easy to digest. Umbria is home to many farro dishes, and it is often used in place of rice.

Lenticchie di Castelluccio

LENTILS (LENTICCHIE) FROM CASTELLUCCIO AND COLFIORITO are some of the most flavorful and tenderest. Castelluccio lentils have a thin skin, which almost disappears during cooking. Umbrian farmers use a rotation system (alternating wheat, lentils and pasture) so they can make the most of the land without having to use chemical fertilizers. The lentils, rich in protein and iron, are commonly used in soups.

Sagrantino di Montefalco

THE BEST-KNOWN UMBRIAN WINES ARE Montefalco Rosso DOC, Montefalco Bianco DOC and Montefalco Sagrantino DOCG (Denomination of Controlled Protected Origin). Sagrantino is made from the grape variety of the same name, and can be dry or sweet, with a minimum aging period of 30 months. For the sweet passito, particularly tough Sagrantino grapes are left to dry for months without fermenting, retaining all of their sugars. To make Montefalco Rosso, a structured, ruby-red wine, the rules call for other red grapes to be blended with Sagrantino. Montefalco Bianco has a straw-yellow color with greenish hues and a flowery, fruity bouquet.

Prosciutto di Norcia IGP

UMBRIA HAS A LONG TRADITION OF PORK BUTCHERY, and in fact in Italy pork butchers are known as *norcini* because so many of them originally came from Norcia. One of the highest-quality products is prosciutto di Norcia, an IGP (Indication of Protected Origin). Shaped like a pear or triangle, this cured ham has a slightly spiced aroma from the pepper used during production. Its flavor is delicate and not over-salted. The prosciutto is made from a pork leg, which is trimmed and then seasoned with salt, pepper and garlic. After two months of resting, the meat is again seasoned with garlic and pepper, and then cured for no less than a year.

Tartufi

BLACK TRUFFLES (TARTUFI) ARE FOUND THROUGHOUT UMBRIA, AND THE ONES FROM NORCIA AND SPOLETO ARE PARTICULARLY PRIZED. The truffles mature from November to March and can range in size from a walnut to an apple. The skin is black and wrinkly, the interior purplish black with thin white veining. White truffles are collected around Orvieto from October to the end of December.

Strangozzi di Spoleto
Spoleto-Style Strangozzi

Serves 4

3 cups plus 3 Tbsps (14 oz or 400 g)
all-purpose flour
1 ¾ cups (400 ml) water
salt and pepper
2 Tbsps extra-virgin olive oil
2 garlic cloves, smashed
1 bunch of parsley, roughly chopped
2 dried red chili peppers
1 lb (500 g) tomatoes, roughly chopped

Preparation time **25 minutes**
Cooking time **35 minutes**
Level **easy**
Wine **Orvieto Classico**

Mix the flour, water and a little salt to form a smooth dough. Roll out into a thick sheet and let dry slightly, then cut into irregular strips.

Heat the olive oil in a frying pan with the garlic, parsley and chili. Add the tomatoes, season with salt and pepper and cook for about 30 minutes to obtain a thick sauce.

Bring a pot of salted water to the boil and cook the strangozzi until they rise to the surface of the water. Drain with a slotted spoon and toss carefully with the sauce, then serve hot.

Pappardelle alla norcina
Norcian Pappardelle

Serves 4

1 garlic clove, minced
2 Tbsps extra-virgin olive oil
2 sausages, casings removed
3/4 cup (180 ml) white wine
2 Tbsps heavy cream
1 bunch of parsley, minced
salt and pepper
1 lb (500 g) pappardelle

Preparation time **5 minutes**
Cooking time **20 minutes**
Level **easy**
Wine **Sagrantino di Montefalco**

In a large frying pan, sauté the garlic in the olive oil. As soon as the garlic is golden, crumble in the sausage meat and brown for a few minutes, stirring occasionally.

Add the wine and let it cook off over medium heat. Add the cream, parsley (reserving some for garnish) and pepper.

Bring a large pot of salted water to a boil and cook the pappardelle until al dente. Drain and toss in the pan with the sauce. Serve hot, sprinkled with the reserved parsley and freshly ground black pepper.

Pappardelle alla norcina

Friccò
Tomato-Braised Chicken

Serves 4-6

6 Tbsps extra-virgin olive oil
2 rosemary sprigs
3 sage leaves
2 garlic cloves
1 chicken (around 2 ½ lb or 1 ⅕ kg),
cut into pieces
salt and pepper
1 ½ cups (360 ml) white wine
1/2 cup (120 ml) white wine vinegar
3 ripe tomatoes, deseeded

Preparation time **20 minutes**
Cooking time **50 minutes**
Level **medium**
Wine **Colli Perugini Rosato**

Heat the olive oil, rosemary, sage and garlic
in a Dutch oven or earthenware casserole.

Add the chicken and brown, turning often.
Season to taste with salt and pepper. As soon
as the meat is evenly browned, add the white
wine and vinegar and adjust the salt and pepper.
Cover and continue cooking over low heat.

When the meat is tender and starts to pull
away from the bone, add the tomatoes and
continue cooking for another 10 minutes.
Serve hot.

Pizza di Pasqua al formaggio
Easter Cheese Bread

Serves 6

4 eggs
3 cups plus 3 Tbsps (14 oz or 400 g)
all-purpose flour
6 Tbsps extra-virgin olive oil
1 ½ cups (5 ½ oz or 150 g)
grated Parmesan cheese
1 ¼ cups (4 ½ oz or 125 g)
grated Pecorino cheese
2 tsps active dry yeast
3/4 cup (180 ml) milk
salt and pepper
4 ½ oz (125 g) Pecorino cheese,
cut into matchsticks

Preparation time **20 minutes**
Cooking time **50 minutes**
Level **easy**
Wine **Orvieto Classico**

Break the eggs into a bowl and stir in the flour,
olive oil, Parmesan and half the grated Pecorino
with a wooden spoon.

Dissolve the yeast in the milk and add to the
mixture. Season with salt and pepper to taste.
Knead to obtain a smooth and uniform dough.

Spread the dough into a high-edged, narrow
baking tin. It should come halfway up the sides.
Insert the Pecorino sticks vertically into the
dough. Cover with a clean kitchen towel and let
rise for 2 hours in a warm, dry place. Preheat the
oven to 375°F (190°C or Gas Mark 5).

When the dough has doubled in volume, bake
for about 50 minutes, until the surface is golden.

Pizza di Pasqua al formaggio

Scaloppine alla perugina
Perugian-Style Veal Scaloppini

Serves 4-6

2 salted anchovies
2 Tbsps vinegar
4 Tbsps extra-virgin olive oil
2 garlic cloves, minced
2 ½ oz (70 g) prosciutto, minced
juice and grated zest of 1/2 organic lemon
2 Tbsps capers
1 chicken liver, finely chopped
salt and pepper
8 veal scaloppini (about 1 lb or 500 g in total)
3 Tbsps all-purpose flour
8 sage leaves

Preparation time **20 minutes**
Cooking time **15 minutes**
Level **medium**
Wine **Torgiano Bianco**

Wash the anchovies well under cold
running water, remove any bones and soak
them a mixture of vinegar and water for
a few minutes. Drain and pat dry.

Heat 2 tablespoons of olive oil in a frying
pan and sauté the garlic, prosciutto and
anchovies. Add the lemon zest, capers and
chicken liver. Cook for 5 minutes, then
drizzle with lemon juice and adjust salt and
pepper. Transfer the sauce to a bowl.

In the same pan, heat the remaining oil.
Dust the veal scaloppini with flour and pan-
fry. As soon as they start to brown, add the
sauce and sage leaves. Serve hot.

Scaloppine alla perugina

scafata
spring vegetable stew

Serves 4

1 ⅔ cups (9 oz or 250 g) fresh
shelled fava beans
salt and pepper
4 Tbsps extra-virgin olive oil
2 spring onions, sliced
1 bunch of wild fennel or dill, chopped
3 ½ oz (100 g) pancetta, diced
9 oz (250 g) Swiss chard, chopped
8 cherry tomatoes, diced
1 bunch of mint, chopped

Preparation time **15 minutes**
Cooking time **40 minutes**
Level **easy**
Wine **Rubesco**

Blanch the favas in boiling salted water for a few minutes,
then drain and peel.

Heat the olive oil in a saucepan and sauté the spring onions
until golden. Add the fennel or dill and pancetta and sauté for
a few minutes. Add the favas and chard and cook, covered, for
10 minutes.

Add the tomatoes and continue cooking, adding a little water
when necessary, for another 10 minutes. Season with salt and
pepper and add the mint. Serve hot.

Zuccherini di Bettona
Bettona-Style Cookies

Serves 4

4 cups (1 lb 2 oz or 500 g) all-purpose flour
2 ½ oz (70 g) risen bread dough
2 tsps active dry yeast
1 cup (5 ½ oz or 150 g) raisins
3/4 cup (3 ½ oz or 100 g) pine nuts
1 cup (7 oz or 200 g) sugar
3 Tbsps extra-virgin olive oil
1 tsp aniseeds
1 pat of butter

Preparation time **30 minutes**
Cooking time **30 minutes**
Level **medium**
Wine **Sagrantino di Montefalco Passito**

Knead the flour into the risen bread dough, adding water as necessary. Leave to rise until the volume has doubled.

Dissolve the yeast in a little warm water, knead it into the dough and let rise for another 2 hours. Soak the raisins in warm water until soft, then drain and squeeze out excess liquid. Knead the raisins, pine nuts, sugar, olive oil and aniseeds into the dough. Knead well until thoroughly mixed.

Divide the dough into many small sticks about the length of a finger and form each one into a doughnut-like ring. Butter a baking sheet and lay the rings on it, keeping them far apart from each other. Bake for about 30 minutes, until golden, then remove from the oven and let cool before serving.

Panpepato
Umbrian Fruitcake

Serves 6-8

2/3 cup (3 ½ oz or 100 g) raisins
1 cup (3 ½ oz or 100 g) walnuts
3/4 cup (3 ½ oz or 100 g) hazelnuts
2/3 cup (3 ½ oz or 100 g) blanched almonds
5 oz (150 g) dark chocolate
2/3 cup (3 ½ oz or 100 g) chopped candied fruit
grated nutmeg
pepper
2 tsps ground cinnamon
3/4 cup plus 1 Tbsp (200 ml) honey
all-purpose flour

Preparation time **10 minutes**
Cooking time **20 minutes**
Level **medium**
Wine **Grechetto Passito**

Preheat the oven to 350°F (180°C or Gas Mark 4). Soak the raisins in warm water for a few minutes. Drain and squeeze out the excess water. Finely chop the walnuts, hazelnuts, almonds, chocolate and candied fruit and mix together. Add pinches of nutmeg and pepper, and then the cinnamon and raisins.

Heat the honey and a little water in a saucepan and bring to a boil. Pour the boiling honey over the nut mixture. Mix until the chocolate melts and then sift in enough flour to combine the dough. Form 6 rounds and place them on a baking sheet lined with parchment paper. Bake for 10 minutes. Remove from the oven and cool completely before serving. The cakes may be stored for up to 2 weeks in an airtight container.

Pere al Sagrantino
Sagrantino-Poached Pears

Serves 4

4 large, slightly underripe pears
1 ¾ cups (400 ml) water
1 ½ cups (360 ml) Sagrantino Passito wine
3/4 cup (5 ½ oz or 150 g) sugar,
plus extra for dipping
1/2 cinnamon stick,
plus extra for garnish (optional)
1 organic lemon, sliced

Preparation time **10 minutes**
Cooking time **20 minutes**
Level **easy**
Wine **Sagrantino di Montefalco Passito**

Place the pears in a saucepan with the water
and wine. Add the sugar and cinnamon
stick, cover and cook over low heat for
about 20 minutes, or until the pears are
tender. Let them cool. Dip the lemon
slices in sugar.

Make a cut into each pear, pour in a little
of the cooking liquid, and insert a lemon
slice. Serve the pears drizzled with the rest
of the cooking liquid and garnished with
cinnamon sticks if desired.

Panpepato

Pere al Sagrantino

Abruzzo

Shepherding and farming are the most traditional

activities in this region, and they have left their mark on a cuisine of strong, authentic flavors. While coastal cooking is delicate and seafood-based, the mountainous interior is home to refined products like *saffron* and *truffles*. An excellent region for artisanal pasta like the renowned *maccheroni alla chitarra*.

ABRUZZO
local products

Aglio rosso di Sulmona

THIS VARIETY OF RED GARLIC (*AGLIO ROSSO*) IS FOUND ONLY IN THE SULMONA VALLEY. Also known as solimo, it is one of the finest garlics in Italy. Easily recognized by the purplish-red skin covering each clove, it has a larger head and higher essential-oil content than white or pink garlics. Traditionally it is worked into braids with 54 heads each, which are then hung in shops. The Abruzzian variety is unique in generating a flowering scape, which is cut off before harvesting to make the bulb grow bigger. The scapes are eaten fresh, blanched in vinegar or preserved in oil.

Carota del Fucino

GROWN ON THE FUCINO PLATEAU, IN THE PROVINCE OF L'AQUILA, this was the first vegetable variety to earn an IGP (Indication of Protected Origin) recognition, in 2005. The carrot (*carota*) is bright orange in color, cylindrical with a rounded tip, smooth to the touch and has a unique crunchiness and sweet flavor. The carrots are packaged under their brand, with "Carota dell'Altopiano del Fucino" written in green and the IGP label in white and blue.

Pecorino di *Farindola*

THIS SHEEP'S MILK CHEESE IS UNIQUE IN BEING MADE WITH PORK RENNET, using milk from Pagliarola-Appenninica breed sheep. It is produced in very limited quantities on the eastern slopes of the Gran Sasso mountain, including in the town of Farindola. The cheese is aged for 3 to 12 months, during which time the forms are rubbed with a mixture of extra-virgin olive oil and vinegar, giving them a saffron-yellow color and mouthwatering aroma. All the forms are labeled by individual producers and include the name of the woman who has cared for the cheese during its aging.

Zafferano di Novelli

THE "GOLD OF NAVELLI," IS GROWN IN THE NAVELLI HIGHLANDS IN AND AROUND THE PROVINCE OF L'AQUILA. The use of saffron (*zafferano*) in the local cuisine is linked to its supposed miraculous properties. The locals have the habit of carrying around a pinch of saffron with them at all times: dissolved in hot wine, it can cure colds, while mixed with oil it can help heal scars. Though the first color associated with saffron is the golden yellow of a saffron-scented risotto, the spice itself actually has a purplish-red color. It is sold absolutely pure, either in a powder made from grinding the stigmas, or in threads, leaving the stigmas whole. The saffron comes from *Crocus sativa* flowers, harvested entirely manually. When the plant blooms, the still-closed flowers are carefully collected so as not to break the precious stigma. The flowers are opened and the stigmas separated from the petals, then placed in sieves and dried over oak charcoal.

Fregnacce
Pasta Parcels

Serves 4

2 ⅓ cups plus 1 Tbsp (10 ½ oz or 300 g) all-purpose flour
3 eggs - salt
3 Tbsps extra-virgin olive oil
1 onion, minced
3 sausages, casings removed
10 ½ oz (300 g) ground beef
1 lb (500 g) ripe tomatoes, chopped
1 cup (3 ½ oz or 100 g) grated Parmesan cheese
1 pat of butter

Preparation time **40 minutes**
Cooking time **30 minutes**
Level **medium**
Wine **Montepulciano Cereasuolo**

Preheat the oven to 350°F (180°C or Gas Mark 4). Mix together the flour and eggs to obtain a smooth dough. Roll out into a thin sheet and cut out squares using a rolling cutter.

Bring a large pot of salted water to a boil and cook the pasta squares. Drain and dry on a kitchen towel. Let cool. Meanwhile heat the olive oil in a large frying pan and sauté the onion until soft. Add the sausage meat and beef and brown. Add the tomatoes, season with salt to taste and continue cooking until the sauce has thickened.

Place a spoonful of the sauce in the center of each pasta square, sprinkle over a spoonful of Parmesan and fold up into rectangular parcels. Place them in a buttered baking dish and bake for a few minutes, then serve.

Brodetto alla vastese
Vasto-Style Fish Soup

Serves 4-6

2 ¼ lb (1 kg) mixed fish for soup (cod, skate, halibut, mackerel, squid or cuttlefish, shrimp)
7 Tbsps extra-virgin olive oil
2 garlic cloves, peeled
1/2 hot chili pepper, minced
1 ¾ lb (800 g) tomatoes, chopped
salt
1 bunch of parsley, minced

Preparation time **30 minutes**
Cooking time **30 minutes**
Level **easy**
Wine **Trebbiano d'Abruzzo**

Clean the fish under cold running water, shell the shrimp and fillet the fish. Heat the olive oil in a saucepan and sauté the garlic and chili.

Add the tomatoes and cook down until thickened. Start adding the fish in order of cooking time, leaving cod, mullet and shrimp for last. Cook, covered, for 15 minutes; adjust salt, sprinkle with parsley and serve.

Zuppa di lenticchie
Lentil Soup

Serves 6

2 ½ cups (1 lb or 500 g) lentils
2 Tbsps extra-virgin olive oil,
plus extra for drizzling
1 onion, minced
1 celery stalk, minced
1 carrot, minced
7 oz (200 g) smoked pancetta, diced
12 cups (3 l) water
1 vegetable stock cube
pepper
crusty bread (optional)

Preparation time **5 minutes**
Cooking time **40 minutes**
Level **easy**
Wine **Montepulciano d'Abruzzo**

Soak the lentils for about 12 hours,
then drain.

Heat the olive oil in a saucepan and
sauté the onion, celery and carrot. Add
the pancetta and continue cooking until
browned. Add the lentils, water and stock
cube. Continue cooking until the lentils are
tender and the broth is creamy. Sprinkle
with pepper, drizzle with olive oil and serve.

The soup can be accompanied by crusty
bread, either grilled or cubed and fried.

Brodetto alla vastese

Zuppa di lenticchie

spaghetti con ragù d'agnello
spaghetti with lamb ragù

Serves 4

1 ⅔ cups (7 oz or 200 g)
all-purpose flour

3/4 cup (3 ½ oz or 100 g)
durum-wheat flour

2 eggs

3 egg yolks

5 Tbsps extra-virgin olive oil

salt

2 garlic cloves, peeled

1 lb (500 g) lamb, cut into strips

1/2 cup (120 ml) white wine

1 rosemary sprig

salt and pepper

1 red bell pepper

1 yellow bell pepper

1 large pat of butter

3 Tbsps grated Parmesan cheese

1/2 bunch of parsley, minced

Preparation time **30 minutes**
Cooking time **50 minutes**
Level **medium**
Wine **Pentro di Isernia Rosso**

Mix together the two flours, eggs, egg yolks, 1 tablespoon of olive oil and salt to obtain a smooth, uniform dough. Roll it out with a rolling pin, then use a "chitarra" cutter to form spaghetti (alternatively cut using a pasta machine). Heat 2 tablespoons of olive oil in a saucepan and brown the whole peeled garlic cloves. Add the lamb, brown well, then add the white wine, rosemary, salt and pepper. Cover and cook for 35 minutes.

Meanwhile roast the bell peppers over an open flame or under the broiler. Close in a plastic bag to steam, then peel, deseed and dice. Heat 2 tablespoons of olive oil in a wide frying pan and sauté the diced peppers for 5 minutes. Add the lamb mixture.

Bring a large pot of salted water to a boil and cook the spaghetti. Drain and toss in the pan with the sauce. Stir in the butter and Parmesan and sprinkle with parsley. Serve immediately.

Frittata di alici
Anchovy Frittata

Serves 4-6

1 lb (500 g) fresh anchovies
5 eggs
6 Tbsps grated Pecorino cheese
3 Tbsps minced parsley
1 hot chili pepper, minced
2 Tbsps extra-virgin olive oil
salt

Preparation time **20 minutes**
Cooking time **20 minutes**
Level **easy**
Wine **Abruzzo Bianco**

Gut the anchovies, wash them carefully and
leave to drain in a colander.

Beat the eggs with the Pecorino, parsley, chili
and a pinch of salt. Add the anchovies and stir
well. Heat the olive oil in a large frying pan
and pour in the mixture. Cook for 10 minutes
on each side.

Pat dry with paper towels and serve warm
or at room temperature, cut into wedges.

Arrosticini
Lamb Kebabs

Serves 6

1 ½ lb (700 g) lamb
salt
bread, sliced (optional)
olive oil (optional)

Preparation time **15 minutes**
Cooking time **10 minutes**
Level **easy**
Wine **Montepulciano Cerasuolo**

Prepare the barbecue or grill. Cut the lamb into
small, 1/2-inch (1 cm) cubes, then thread the
cubes onto wooden skewers.

Cook the skewers on a grill over hot coals for
about 10 minutes, turning often so they cook
evenly, and taking care not to overcook and dry
out the meat.

Once cooked, salt them generously and serve
very hot, accompanied, if desired, by slices of
grilled bread brushed with olive oil.

Note *This is a simple but very tasty dish, a
symbol of Abruzzo and the convivial spirit of its
gastronomy. The kebabs are often cooked at village
festivals, and served with garlic bruschetta.*

Agnello cacio e uova
Lamb with Cheese and Egg

Serves 4

1 leg of lamb
2 Tbsps extra-virgin olive oil
1 garlic clove, smashed
1 rosemary sprig
3/4 cup (180 ml) white wine
4 eggs
8 Tbsps grated Pecorino cheese
juice of 1 lemon
1 slice of country-style bread, crusts removed
salt

Preparation time **20 minutes**
Cooking time **40 minutes**
Level **easy**
Wine **Montepulciano d'Abruzzo Riserva**

Debone the leg of lamb and cut into pieces.
Heat the olive oil in a frying pan with the garlic and rosemary, then brown the lamb pieces. Add the wine and let cook off, then remove the rosemary.
Meanwhile beat the eggs with the Pecorino, lemon juice and salt. Crumble in the bread and stir. Pour the mixture over the lamb and cook until the sauce is thickened. Serve hot.

Arrosticini

Agnello cacio e uova

Pollo all'abruzzese
Abruzzian-Style Chicken

Serves 4

4 Tbsps extra-virgin olive oil
1 onion, minced
1 chicken (about 3 ½ lb or 1 ½ kg),
cut into pieces
salt and pepper
1 lb (500 g) peeled plum tomatoes, chopped
1 red bell pepper
1 yellow bell pepper

Preparation time **30 minutes**
Cooking time **1 hour**
Level **easy**
Wine **Val di Sangro Rosso**

Heat 3 tablespoons of olive oil in a saucepan
and sauté the onion. Brown the chicken for
a few minutes, season with salt and pepper
and add the tomatoes. Continue cooking for
about 40 minutes.

Meanwhile roast the peppers on a grill or
under a broiler. Close in plastic bag to steam,
then peel, deseed and cut into strips.

Heat 1 tablespoon of olive oil in another
frying pan and add the peppers. Cook, covered,
over medium heat for about 10 minutes. Just
before the chicken is done, add the peppers.
Continue cooking for another 10 minutes, then
serve hot.

Cozze allo zafferano
Saffron Mussels

Serves 6

2 ½ lb (1 ⅕ kg) mussels
1 bunch of parsley, minced
1 bay leaf
1 onion, minced
3/4 cup (180 ml) white wine
4 Tbsps extra-virgin olive oil
1 pinch of saffron

Preparation time **40 minutes**
Cooking time **20 minutes**
Level **easy**
Wine **Trebbiano d'Abruzzo Riserva**

Carefully clean the mussels, debearding them
and rinsing under cold running water. Place
in a large saucepan and add the parsley, bay leaf,
onion and wine. Cover and cook over high heat
until the mussels open. Discard any which stay
closed.

Drain the mussels, reserving the cooking
liquid, and transfer to serving plates. Keep
warm. Strain the cooking liquid, bring it to
a boil and let it reduce slightly. Whisk in the
olive oil and saffron and let sit for a few minutes
for the flavors to blend. Pour the sauce over
the mussels and serve.

Scapece alla vastese
Vasto-Style Pickled Fish

Serves 4-6

2 ¼ lb (1 kg) fish (halibut, cod, sole)
all-purpose flour for flouring
extra-virgin olive oil for frying
salt
2 cups (500 ml) vinegar
1/2 tsp saffron
2 rosemary sprigs

Preparation time **20 minutes**
Cooking time **10 minutes**
Level **easy**
Wine not recommended

Carefully clean the fish and cut into pieces.
Dust with flour.

Heat the olive oil until very hot and fry
the fish pieces until cooked through and
golden. Drain on paper towels to absorb
excess oil and sprinkle with salt.

Heat the vinegar in a saucepan. When just
starting to boil, remove from the heat and
stir in the saffron. Make layers of the fish
in a baking dish or earthenware casserole.
Pour over the vinegar so as to completely
cover the fish. Let marinate for 24 hours.

Drain the fish, garnish with rosemary and
serve at room temperature.

With a good, strong vinegar, the fish can
keep for 20-30 days.

Cozze allo zafferano

Scapece alla vastese

Pepatelli
Peppered Almond Cookies

Serves 6

1 ½ cups (1 lb or 500 g) honey
grated zest of 1 organic orange
2 cups (10 ½ oz or 300 g)
blanched almonds, finely chopped
2 pinches of ground white pepper
whole wheat flour
1 large pat of butter

Preparation time **30 minutes**
Cooking time **20 minutes**
Level **easy**
Wine **Moscato Bianco di Pescara**

Preheat the oven to 400°F (200°C or Gas
Mark 6). Heat the honey in a saucepan until
liquid, then stir in the orange zest and almonds.
Mix well, then add the white pepper. Stirring
constantly, sprinkle in enough flour to obtain
a dense dough.

Remove from the heat and turn the dough out
onto a clean work surface. Level it out and let
cool. Cut the dough into 2-inch (5 cm) wide
rectangles and arrange on a buttered baking
sheet. Bake for 15-20 minutes.

Note *Whole-wheat flour is obtained by grinding
the whole grain of the wheat, using the bran, germ
and endosperm. White, refined flours are made
from only the endosperm. Whole-wheat flour is
more nutritious than white flour, with more fiber,
protein and minerals.*

Bocconotti
Mini Chocolate-Almond Pies

Serves 6-8

4 ¾ cups (1 lb 5 oz or 600 g) all-purpose flour
2/3 cup (4 oz or 120 g) sugar
7 Tbsps (3 ½ oz or 100 g) butter, softened
2 eggs - 4 egg yolks
grated zest of 1 organic lemon
1 Tbsp milk
1/2 tsp baking powder
1 cup (5 ½ oz or 150 g) blanched almonds,
toasted and finely chopped
10 ½ oz (300 g) dark chocolate, finely chopped
5 Tbsps grape jam
1 Tbsp Centerbe or other herb liqueur
1 pinch of ground cinnamon
confectioners' sugar (optional)

Preparation time **30 minutes**
Cooking time **20 minutes**
Level **easy**
Wine **Torre de' Passeri**

Preheat the oven to 400°F (200°C or Gas
Mark 6). Mix together the flour, sugar, softened
butter, eggs, egg yolks, lemon zest, milk and
baking powder. Roll the dough out into a thin
sheet and use it to line fluted cupcake molds.
Reserve enough dough to make lids.

Mix together the almonds, chocolate,
jam, liqueur and cinnamon until thoroughly
combined. Fill the molds with the mixture and
cover with a thin layer of the remaining dough.
Bake for 15-20 minutes. Remove from the oven,
let cool and unmold. Serve sprinkled with
confectioners' sugar, if desired.

Parrozzo
Chocolate-Glazed Dome Cake

Serves 4

1 ⅓ cups (7 oz or 200 g) blanched almonds, finely chopped
8 bitter almonds, finely chopped
1 cup (5 ½ oz or 150 g) finely ground semolina
grated zest of 1 organic lemon
6 eggs, separated
salt
1 cup (7 oz or 200 g) sugar
5 ½ oz (150 g) dark chocolate
1 large pat of butter

Preparation time **40 minutes**
Cooking time **45 minutes**
Level **medium**
Wine **Moscato Bianco di Pescara**

Preheat the oven to 400°F (200°C or Gas Mark 6). Mix together the almonds, semolina and lemon zest to obtain a floury mixture.

Beat the egg whites to stiff peaks with a pinch of salt. Fold the egg whites into the almond mixture, add the egg yolks one at a time and then the sugar, stirring well to avoid lumps.

Line a dome mold with aluminum foil. Pour in the batter and bake for 45 minutes. Remove from the oven, unmold onto a plate, cover and let sit for 24 hours.

Melt the chocolate over a double boiler with the butter. Spread on the base of the cake. Once hardened, turn over and spread over the top part. Let harden, then serve.

Bocconotti

Parrozzo

Molise

Medieval villages, unspoilt nature and a past rich in history.

From grassy pastures to imposing mountains to the clear waters of its short coastline, Molise is firmly rooted in its agricultural traditions. The *fruits and vegetables* grown here are of the highest quality, as are the excellent, artisanally produced *ventricina, caciocavallo* cheese and *citrus oils*. There is a world of cuisine to discover in this beautiful and little-known landscape.

MOLISE
local products

Pasta secca

Triticum durum, hard wheat, grows well in Molisan soil, and this special grain, rich in protein, vitamins and minerals, is the ideal ingredient for producing the best *pasta secca* (dried pasta). Thanks to its fields of golden grain, Molise is considered the cradle of southern Italy's traditional pasta-making art, a tradition rooted in the distant past. Probably the first pasta here was wrapped up by housewives in large handkerchiefs for the herders to take with them during the transhumance, the seasonal migration of the flocks from the mountains to the plains for the winter and back again for the summer.

Caciocavallo *molisano*

The characteristic pear shape, the classic straw-yellow color and above all the unique flavor of this cheese have made it famous. Made from cow's milk with the addition of natural starter whey, Molisan Caciocavallo has obtained DOP (Denomination of Protected Origin) recognition. Tied and hung up, the forms age for around three months before being sold. The best known version comes from Agnone, but traditionally all Molisan cheesemakers make Caciocavallo.

Olio *extravergine* d'oliva

OLIVE OIL IS PRODUCED THROUGHOUT THE REGION, BUT PARTICULARLY IN THE PROVINCE OF CAMPOBASSO. At least 80% of Molise's extra-virgin olive oil (*olio extravergine d'oliva*) is pressed from Aurina, Gentile di Larino, Nera di Collotorto and Leccino cultivars, and Paesana Bianca, Sperone di Gallo Olivastro and Rosciola are also used. The color can range from yellow to green, and the fruity flavor is marked by hints of bitterness and spiciness. Molisan olive oil is best drizzled over local soups or fish pastas.

I fichi a scorza *nera*

THESE BLACK-SKINNED FIGS (*FICHI A SCORZA NERA*) ARE GROWN AROUND THE WHOLE REGION. The fruit are picked when they are completely ripe and unbruised. They are then laid out far apart from each on racks and set out in the sun to be dried. Open-air drying can take from one to two months, and they are then further dried in the oven. The figs might then be stuffed with toasted almonds, walnuts or chocolate. When the figs are ready they are usually strung onto a piece of cotton to form a chain, threaded onto wooden skewers forming a triangle or placed in glass jars, and then preserved in a dry place. They can be used in desserts and decoctions.

Ventricina

PRODUCED AROUND CAMPOBASSO, this was originally a cured meat for the poor, because it was made with lean cuts of meat. Today it has become more appreciated because better cuts are used. The hand-cut pieces of pork are seasoned with fennel and chili before being packed in casings or a bladder depending on whether a long or round shape is desired. Slow aging brings out the complex flavors.

Spaghetti con le noci
Spaghetti with Walnuts

Serves 4

10 ½ oz (300 g) pre-soaked salt cod,
cut into large pieces
2 Tbsps extra-virgin olive oil
2 garlic cloves, peeled
2/3 cup (3 oz or 80 g) chopped walnuts
14 oz (400 g) spaghetti
salt
4 Tbsps grated Pecorino cheese (optional)

Preparation time **15 minutes**
Cooking time **40 minutes**
Level **easy**
Wine **Trebbiano del Molise**

Boil the salt cod in, lightly salted water for about 20 minutes. Drain with a slotted spoon, reserving the cooking liquid. Break the fish up into smaller pieces.

Heat the olive oil in a frying pan and sauté the whole peeled garlic cloves until golden. Remove from the pan and add the walnuts. Toast briefly, then add the salt cod. Season with salt to taste and continue cooking, adding some of the reserved cooking water when necessary.

Bring a large pot of salted water to a boil and cook the spaghetti until al dente. Drain and toss in the pan with the salt cod and walnuts, stirring well to blend all the ingredients. Serve hot, sprinkled with grated Pecorino if desired.

Pasta lievitata
Leavened Pasta with Ragù

Serves 4-6

4 cups (1 lb 2 oz or 500 g) all-purpose flour
3 ½ tsps active dry yeast
2 eggs
salt
1 onion, minced
1 garlic clove, minced
2 Tbsps extra-virgin olive oil
2 oz (60 g) beef or veal tendons, chopped
10 ½ oz (300 g) ground beef or veal
3/4 cup (180 ml) red wine
3/4 cup (7 oz or 200 g) ready-made tomato sauce
4 Tbsps grated Parmesan cheese

Preparation time **30 minutes**
Cooking time **2 hours 20 minutes**
Level **easy**
Wine **Molise Rosso**

Energetically knead together the flour, yeast, eggs and salt to form a dough, then shape into a loaf. Cover and leave to rise until doubled in volume.

Meanwhile sauté the onion and garlic in the olive oil until soft. Add the tendons and ground meat. Brown, then add the red wine, tomato sauce and a pinch of salt and cook for 2 hours.

Take small portions of the risen dough and form them by hand into small sticks. Lay them out to dry slightly.

When the ragù is ready bring a large pot of salted water to a boil and cook the pasta. Drain, toss with the sauce and sprinkle with grated Parmesan before serving.

Pizza e minestra
Cornmeal Bread with Soup

Serves 6-8

2 pig's feet
2 pig's ears
1 celery stalk, chopped
1 onion, chopped
1 tomato, chopped
1 chili pepper
2 ¼ lb (1 kg) mixed seasonal vegetables, chopped
3 cups (1 lb or 500 g) finely ground cornmeal
salt

Preparation time **30 minutes**
Cooking time **3 hours**
Level **easy**
Wine **Tifernum Rosato**

Boil the pig's feet and ears for 30 minutes. Lightly salt the water and add the celery, onion and tomato and cook for another 1 hour 30 minutes, then add the chili and seasonal vegetables and cook for another 15 minutes.

Meanwhile, preheat the oven to 350°F (180°C or Gas Mark 4). Mix the cornmeal with salt and enough water to form a smooth dough. Roll out to about 1-inch (2 cm) thick and bake until browned. Remove from the oven and break into pieces.

When the soup is done, cut up the meat. Serve the soup over the pieces of cornmeal bread.

Pasta lievitata

Pizza e minestra

Capra alla molisana
Molisan-Style Goat

Serves 6

2 ¼ lb (1 kg) goat meat, cubed
4 cups (1 l) red wine
4 sage leaves
2 bay leaves
2 rosemary sprigs
4 Tbsps extra-virgin olive oil
1 onion, minced
1 lb (500 g) ripe tomatoes, deseeded and chopped
salt and pepper

Preparation time **20 minutes**
Cooking time **50 minutes**
Level **easy**
Wine **Montepulciano del Molise**

Place the goat in a bowl and add the wine, sage, bay leaves and rosemary. Refrigerate for 12 hours, turning the meat every so often.

Drain the meat and pat dry with paper towels. Heat the olive oil and sauté the onion. Add the goat, brown for a few minutes, then add the tomatoes. Season with salt and pepper and continue cooking for 45 minutes over low heat. Serve hot.

Polpette cacio e uova
Meatless Meatballs

Serves 6

2 Tbsps extra-virgin olive oil
1 onion, sliced
2 yellow bell peppers, deseeded and chopped
2 ripe tomatoes, chopped
6 eggs, beaten
10 ½ oz (300 g) stale bread with crusts removed
1 ½ cups (5 ½ oz or 150 g) grated Pecorino cheese
1 bunch of parsley, minced
salt

Preparation time **30 minutes**
Cooking time **15 minutes**
Level **easy**
Wine **Molise Rosato**

Heat the olive oil in a saucepan and sauté the onion and peppers. Add the tomatoes and salt and cook for a few minutes.

Mix together the eggs, bread, Pecorino, parsley and a pinch of salt to form a stiff mixture.

Form into walnut-sized balls, carefully add to the sauce and cook for a few minutes. Serve hot.

Affunniatelle
Stewed Peppers with Egg

Serves 4

6 Tbsps extra-virgin olive oil
1 onion, sliced
5 mixed bell peppers, deseeded and sliced
8 ripe tomatoes, blanched, peeled and chopped
1/2 bunch of parsley, minced
1 pinch of chili pepper flakes
5 basil leaves
salt
8 eggs, beaten

Preparation time **15 minutes**
Cooking time **20 minutes**
Level **easy**
Wine **Pentro di Isernia Rosato**

Heat the olive oil in a saucepan, add the onion and sauté gently over medium heat until soft. Add the peppers and sauté for a few minutes. Add the tomatoes, parsley, chili and basil, adjust salt and cook for 10 minutes.

When the sauce has thickened, stir in the eggs. Cook briefly, until just set, then serve immediately.

Polpette cacio e uova

Affunniatelle

Fiatone
Savory Cheese Tart

Serves 6

1 ⅔ cups (7 oz or 200 g) all-purpose flour
8 eggs
1 Tbsp sugar
salt
1 Tbsp extra-virgin olive oil
14 oz (400 g) aged goat's cheese, grated
10 ½ oz (300 g) fresh cheese, chopped
5 ½ oz (150 g) salami, chopped
3 Tbsps minced parsley

Preparation time **30 minutes**
Cooking time **1 hour**
Level **medium**
Wine **Biferno Rosato**

Preheat the oven to 350°F (180°C or Gas Mark 4). Mound the flour on a work surface, make a well in the middle and break in 2 eggs.

Add the sugar, olive oil and a pinch of salt and mix together, kneading to obtain a smooth dough. Cover with a kitchen towel and let rest. Meanwhile mix together the grated goat's cheese, fresh cheese, salami, parsley and 6 eggs. Stir well until thoroughly combined.

Roll the dough out into 2 sheets. Use one to line a baking dish lined with parchment paper, then pour in the filling and spread out with a spatula.

Cut the remaining sheet of dough into slices and lay them across the top to form a lattice. Pinch around the edges to seal well. Bake for 1 hour. Serve warm or at room temperature.

Capunata
Taralli Salad

Serves 4

4 taralli or large rusks
4 Tbsps white wine vinegar
2 eggs
4 tomatoes, sliced
2 celery stalks, sliced
1 bell pepper, sliced
1 cucumber, sliced
2 garlic cloves, minced
1/2 cup (2 oz or 50 g) green and black olives
3 ½ oz (100 g) anchovies in oil, drained and chopped
1 pinch of dried oregano
6 Tbsps extra-virgin olive oil
salt

Preparation time **20 minutes**
Cooking time **5 minutes**
Level **easy**
Wine **Trebbiano del Molise Riserva**

Sprinkle the taralli or rusks with vinegar, then leave to dry on a clean kitchen towel. Hard-boil the eggs, drain, cool, shell and cut into wedges.

Arrange the taralli on serving plates and top with tomato, celery, pepper and cucumber.

Add the eggs, garlic, olives and anchovies. Sprinkle over a little salt and oregano and drizzle with olive oil.

Let sit for 30 minutes in a cool place or the refrigerator before serving to allow the flavors the blend.

Insalata di maiale
Pork Salad

Serves 4

2 pig's ears
2 pig's feet
salt and pepper
4 Tbsps vinegar
1 celery stalk, sliced
1 garlic clove, minced
6 Tbsps extra-virgin olive oil
2 Tbsps lemon juice

Preparation time **20 minutes**
Cooking time **2 hours**
Level **easy**
Wine **Molise Rosato**

Chop the meat into large pieces with a sharp knife, then boil in lightly salted water with the vinegar for about 2 hours. Drain with a slotted spoon, chop into smaller pieces and arrange on a serving plate.

Let cool and then toss with the celery, garlic, extra-virgin olive oil, lemon juice, salt and pepper.

Note *Pork is much used in the local cuisine, particularly inland, where a series of cured pork products such as ventricina, sopressata and saggicciotto are made.*

Capunata

Insalata di maiale

Caggiunitti
fried sweet ravioli

Serves 6-8

3 ⅔ cups (1 lb or 450 g) all-purpose flour
2 eggs
milk
salt
5 ½ Tbsps (3 oz or 80 g) butter, softened
3/4 cup (5 ½ oz or 150 g) sugar
1 ¾ cups (9 oz or 250 g) chestnuts
3 ½ oz (100 g) dark chocolate, chopped
1/3 cup (2 oz or 50 g) blanched almonds, finely chopped
1/3 cup (2 oz or 50 g) candied fruit, chopped
grated zest of 1 organic lemon
1 ½ Tbsps baking soda
extra-virgin olive oil for frying
lard for frying
confectioners' sugar

Preparation time **40 minutes**
Cooking time **20 minutes**
Level **easy**
Wine **Moscato Bianco del Molise**

In a large mixing bowl, mix together the flour, eggs, softened butter, sugar and enough milk to form a soft dough. Let rest for 1 hour. Boil the chestnuts in lightly salted water until soft. Drain, peel and mash into a puree. Mix together the chestnut puree, chocolate, almonds, candied fruit and lemon zest.

Dissolve the baking soda in a little warm milk, then mix into the rested dough. Roll the dough out into a sheet. Place spoonfuls of the chestnut mixture around the dough, then use a round cookie cutter to cut out circles around the filling.

Make ravioli by folding over into half-moons. Press down well around the edges to close. Heat equal parts olive oil and lard in a frying pan and fry the ravioli until golden, in batches if necessary. Serve hot, sprinkled with confectioners' sugar.

Traditional recipe

Lazio

The capital of the country but also many villages, provincial towns

and ancient ports; modest but excellent
trattorias and Michelin-starred restaurants;
international tourists and skilled farmers.
A region with a thousand faces, a journey
through history that always finishes at the
dinner table, with succulent *pastas* and
simple fruits of the earth like *puntarelle*
and *Roman artichokes*. A varied cuisine,
packed with flavor.

LAZIO
local products

Pecorino romano

PRODUCED FOR MILLENNIA – IT WAS A STAPLE
FOOD FOR THE ROMAN LEGIONS – Pecorino
Romano is made from fresh, full-fat sheep's milk
from Lazio, Sardinia and the Tuscan province of
Grosseto. A DOP (Denomination of Protected
Origin) since 1996, the authentic cheese is
easily recognizable from the dotted writing
on the rind, with a stylized sheep's head. The
cooked-curd cheese has a hard texture, compact
and with a few small holes. The flavor is very
aromatic and slightly sharp, and finds its ideal
pairing with fresh fava beans. The more aged
version has a stronger flavor and can be grated.

Ricotta romana Dop

RICOTTA ROMANA IS MADE FROM THE WHEY LEFT
OVER AFTER PECORINO ROMANO PRODUCTION.
Its name means "re-cooked" and refers to the
process of reheating the whey again after
it has already been cooked for cheesemaking.
Ricotta Romana has a grainier texture and
more intense flavor than other ricottas. It is
produced throughout the region and can
be used in savory and sweet dishes.

Carciofo *romanesco* Igp

THESE LARGE, ROUNDED ARTICHOKES (*CARCIOFI*)
HAVE A PARTICULARLY TENDER TEXTURE. They can
be cooked in many different ways because almost
all of the artichoke can be eaten, and they are
perfect for stuffing. They are prominently
featured in traditional local cuisine, for example
in *carciofi alla romana* (stewed with mint)
and *alla giudea* (fried).

Olio *extravergine* d'oliva

THREE DOP EXTRA-VIRGIN OLIVE OILS ARE PRODUCED
LOCALLY, in the north of the region, near Viterbo
and Rieti, in Canino, Sabina and Tuscia. Olives
have been grown around Viterbo since the time
of the Etruscans, and this is where Canino DOP oil
comes from, of the highest quality, with a bright
green tinge, recognizable by its sweet, fruity aroma,
marked flavor and slightly spicy aftertaste.
Around Tuscia the oil of the same name is made,
delicate with a pleasantly spicy flavor.
The third DOP oil, Sabina, is from the province
of Rieti, made by pressing a variety of olives
including Moraiolo, Olivago, Carboncella and
Frantoio culitivars. Thanks to centuries of
experience in making oil, the pressing of the
olives results in an excellent oil with a bright
yellowish-green color and harmoniously balanced
flavors. Not all olives become oil: The south
of Lazio also produces table varieties like
the giant San Gregoria, Gaeta and Itri.

Mozzarelline in carrozza
Fried Mozzarella Sandwiches

Serves 4

10 slices of sandwich bread, crusts removed
10-12 small mozzarella balls
(bocconcini), halved
7-8 anchovy fillets in oil, drained and chopped
2 eggs, beaten
1 ¼ cups (5 ½ oz or 150 g) breadcrumbs
sunflower oil for frying
salt

Preparation time **15 minutes**
Cooking time **10 minutes**
Level **easy**
Wine **Prosecco di Conegliano
e Valdobbiadene Brut**

Cut the bread slices into squares a little
larger than the mozzarella balls. Place half a
mozzarella ball on each bread square and top
with a small amount of anchovy.

Brush the edges of the bread with beaten
egg and cover with a second bread square,
pressing down on the edges to seal. Continue
making the miniature sandwiches until the
ingredients have been used up.

Dip each one in beaten egg and then in
breadcrumbs, pressing on the breadcrumbs
with the hands. Heat sunflower oil in a frying
pan. Fry the sandwiches in the very hot
oil until golden and drain on paper towels.
Lightly salt and serve immediately.

Fiori di zucca fritti
Fried Squash Blossoms

Serves 4

8 squash blossoms
1/2 cup (2 ½ oz or 70 g) all-purpose flour
salt
1 ½ tsps active dry yeast
3 ½ oz (100 g) mozzarella, diced
16 anchovies in oil, drained and halved
sunflower oil for frying

Preparation time **30 minutes**
Cooking time **20 minutes**
Level **easy**
Wine **Colli Albani Spumante**

Remove the pistils from the squash blossom.
Wash the flowers under cold running water,
then gently pat dry.

Mix the flour with a pinch of salt and the yeast
and stir in enough water to obtain a smooth,
liquid batter.

Place a cube of mozzarella and a half anchovy
inside each flower. Heat the sunflower oil until
very hot. Working in batches, dip the flowers in
the batter and then fry until golden. Drain with
a slotted spoon and dry on paper towels.

Serve hot.

Fiori di zucca fritti

Canata
Bread and Tomato Salad

Serves 4

4 tomatoes, halved
1/2 loaf of stale crusty bread, sliced
3 baby artichokes in oil,
drained and quartered
4 Tbsps extra-virgin olive oil
1 Tbsp red wine vinegar
salt and pepper
6-8 basil leaves, torn into pieces

Preparation time **15 minutes**
Level **easy**
Wine **Aprilia Trebbiano**

Rub the tomato halves on the bread slices.
Break the bread into irregular pieces
of different sizes and place in a salad bowl.
Chop the tomatoes and add to the bowl
along with the artichokes, extra-virgin
olive oil, vinegar, salt and pepper. Add
the basil, and stir again before serving.

Note *The word* canata *means a mix
of different ingredients.*

Canata

Supplì
Fried Rice Balls

Serves 6-8

2 ½ cups (1 lb or 500 g) Carnaroli rice
4 cups (1 l) vegetable broth
1 ½ sticks (6 ½ oz or 180 g) butter
1 cup (3 ½ oz or 100 g) grated
Parmesan cheese
1 onion, minced
3 ½ oz (100 g) prosciutto, finely chopped
2/3 cup (2 oz or 50 g) sliced mushrooms
2 oz (50 g) chicken giblets, chopped
2 oz (50 g) veal, chopped
2 oz (50 g) lamb sweetbreads, chopped
salt and pepper
3/4 cup (180 ml) white wine
5 Tbsps all-purpose flour
1 egg, beaten
4 Tbsps breadcrumbs
sunflower oil for frying

Preparation time **50 minutes**
Cooking time **1 hour**
Level **medium**
Wine **Cerveteri Rosato**

Cook the rice in the broth for about 20 minutes, then drain and stir in 7 Tbsps (3 ½ oz or 100 g) of butter and the Parmesan. Transfer to a work surface and let cool.

Melt the remaining butter in a large frying pan and sauté the onion until soft. Add the prosciutto, mushrooms, giblets, veal, giblets and sweetbreads. Season with salt and pepper and add the wine. Continue cooking until the wine has reduced, adding a little flour if necessary to thicken the sauce. Using two tablespoons, form the rice into balls. Make a cavity in the middle and fill with a spoonful of the meat ragù, then reform into a ball with the filling in the center.

Place the flour in a bowl, the beaten egg in another and the breadcrumbs in another. Heat the sunflower oil in a large frying pan. Dip each rice ball first in the flour, then the egg and finally the breadcrumbs then fry, working in batches if necessary. Drain as soon as they are golden-brown, dry on paper towels and serve hot.

Note *The traditional version of these rice balls is called* al telefono, *with a cube of mozzarella inside. When the fried rice balls are bitten into, the melted cheeses stretches out like telephone wires.*

Gnocchi alla romana
Roman Semolina Dumplings

Serves 4

4 cups (1 l) milk
7 Tbsps (3 ½ oz or 100 g) butter
salt
1 ½ cups (9 oz or 250 g) finely ground semolina
1 ¼ cups (4 ½ oz or 125 g) grated Parmesan cheese

Preparation time **20 minutes**
Cooking time **1 hour**
Level **easy**
Wine **Velletri Bianco**

Preheat the oven to 400°F (200°C or Gas Mark 6). Heat the milk, half the butter and a pinch of salt in a saucepan. Bring to a boil and whisk in the semolina flour. Cook for 30 minutes, stirring constantly. Remove from the heat and add 1 cup (3 ½ oz or 100 g) Parmesan cheese.

Pour the semolina into a damp baking dish and spread to form a thin, even layer. Let cool. Using a round cookie cutter cut the semolina into small circles. Reserve the scraps. Melt the remaining butter in a small saucepan. Butter a baking dish and place the leftover semolina scraps on the bottom.

Pour half of the melted butter over the semolina and sprinkle with Parmesan cheese. Cover with semolina circles and top with remaining butter and Parmesan cheese. Bake until golden-brown and serve immediately.

Bucatini all'amatriciana
Amatrice-Style Bucatini

Serves 4

7 oz (200 g) pancetta, diced
3/4 cup (180 ml) white wine
2 small tomatoes, blanched, peeled and diced
1 pinch of ground chili pepper
salt
14 oz (400 g) bucatini or thick spaghetti
4 Tbsps grated aged Pecorino cheese

Preparation time **10 minutes**
Cooking time **30 minutes**
Level **easy**
Wine **Velletri Rosso**

Brown the pancetta in a large frying pan for a few minutes. Add the wine and let reduce. Add the tomatoes and cook for a few minutes, stirring every so often. Season with chili pepper.

Bring a large pot of salted water to a boil and cook the pasta until al dente. Drain and toss in the frying pan with the sauce. Serve hot, sprinkled with Pecorino.

Bucatini all'amatriciana

Pasta e fagioli
Pasta and Beans

Serves 4-6

3 Tbsps extra-virgin olive oil,
plus extra for drizzling
1 onion, minced
2 garlic cloves, minced
1 celery stalk, minced
1 piece of prosciutto fat, minced
2 peeled plum tomatoes, finely chopped
2 cups (500 ml) vegetable broth
2 cups (1 lb or 500 g) fresh cranberry beans
salt and pepper
1 ham bone
7 oz (200 g) cannolicchi, penne or fusilli

Preparation time **20 minutes**
Cooking time **1 hour**
Level **medium**
Wine **Cesanese di Olevano Romano**

Heat the olive oil in a saucepan. Sauté the
onion, garlic, celery, tomatoes and prosciutto
fat. Add the vegetable broth and let simmer.
In a separate saucepan, boil the beans in
salted water with the ham bone.

When the meat starts to come away from
the bone, drain it and transfer to the other
pan. When the beans are tender, drain and
add to the other pan also.

Add the pasta and cook for another
10 minutes. Serve hot, drizzled with olive
oil and sprinkled with pepper.

Spaghetti alla carbonara
Spaghetti Carbonara

Serves 4-6

2 Tbsps extra-virgin olive oil
1 onion, minced
4 oz (120 g) pancetta, diced
3 eggs
salt and pepper
14 oz (400 g) spaghetti
3 Tbsps grated Pecorino Romano cheese
3 Tbsps grated Parmesan cheese

Preparation time **5 minutes**
Cooking time **20 minutes**
Level **easy**
Wine **Bianco Capena Superiore**

Heat the olive oil and sauté the onion and
pancetta until browned. Beat the eggs in a bowl
with a pinch of salt.

Bring a large pot of salted water to a boil and
cook the spaghetti until al dente, then drain and
toss in the pan with the pancetta. Remove from
the heat and stir in the eggs, 1 tablespoon
of Pecorino, 1 tablespoon of Parmesan and pepper.
Stir well. Sprinkle over the remaining cheeses
and serve hot.

Strozzapreti al pomodoro
Strozzapreti in Tomato Sauce

Serves 6-8

4 Tbsps extra-virgin olive oil
14 Tbsps (7 oz or 200 g) butter
1 lb (500 g) pancetta, diced
1 lb (500 g) smoked pancetta, diced
4 dried chili peppers - salt
1 ¼ cups (10 ½ oz or 300 g)
tomato passata (pureed tomatoes)
2 cups (500 ml) hot water
8 cups (2 lb 3 oz or 1 kg) all-purpose flour
1 egg
grated nutmeg

Preparation time **20 minutes**
Cooking time **3 hours**
Level **medium**
Wine **Cerveteri Rosso**

Heat the olive oil and butter together in a frying pan. Add the two types of pancetta and sauté for about 15 minutes. Crumble in the chili peppers and season with salt. Add the tomato passata and hot water. Bring to a boil and cook for about 2 hours over low heat.

Meanwhile mix together the flour, egg, nutmeg and salt with enough warm water to make a soft dough. Knead on a wooden board, then let cover and let rest for 10-15 minutes. Roll out the dough into a thick sheet. Dust with flour, then roll up and cut into strips. Unroll the strips and break them into pieces about 2 inches (5 cm) long. When the sauce is almost ready, bring a large pot of salted water to a boil and cook the pasta for 10-15 minutes. Drain and toss in the sauce. Sprinkle with Parmesan and serve.

Timballo alla ciociara
Ciociara-Style Timbale

Serves 4-6

3 cups plus 3 Tbsps (14 oz or 400 g)
all-purpose flour
salt - 4 eggs
2 Tbsps extra-virgin olive oil
1/2 onion, sliced
14 oz (400 g) ground meat (pork and beef)
1/2 cup (120 ml) red wine
3 tomatoes, peeled and pureed
6 basil leaves - salt and pepper
1 pat of butter - 2 eggs, hard-boiled
1 large mozzarella ball, thinly sliced
1 cup (3 ½ oz or 100 g) grated Parmesan cheese

Preparation time **40 minutes**
Cooking time **1 hour 30 minutes**
Level **easy**
Wine **Cesanese del Piglio**

Mix the flour with a pinch of salt and the 4 eggs to form a dough. Shape into a ball, cover and let rest for 30 minutes. Roll the dough out with a rolling pin and cut into large squares using a rolling cutter. Heat the olive oil and sauté the onion. Add the meat and brown. Add the wine, and once reduced add the tomatoes, basil, salt and pepper and cook for 1 hour. Bring a large pot of salted water to a boil and cook the pasta squares. Drain and lay on a damp kitchen towel. Hard-boil 2 eggs, then shell and slice them.

Butter a baking dish and start making layers of sauce, pasta squares, slices of mozzarella, hard-boiled egg and Parmesan. Continue until the ingredients are finished. The last layer should be sauce and Parmesan. Bake for about 15 minutes.

Saltimbocca alla romana
Roman-Style Veal with Sage

Serves 4

8 thinly sliced veal steaks
8 slices of prosciutto (about 5 ½ oz or 150 g)
8 sage leaves
3 Tbsps (1 ½ oz or 40 g) butter
salt
1/2 cup (120 ml) white wine

Preparation time **20 minutes**
Cooking time **10 minutes**
Level **easy**
Wine **Cesanese di Olevano Romano**

Pound out the veal slices until very thin.
Lay a slice of prosciutto and a sage leaf
on each one and roll up the veal, fixing
with a toothpick to secure.

   Melt the butter in a frying pan and sauté
the veal rolls until evenly browned. Season
with salt, add the wine and let reduce,
cooking over medium heat for around
5 minutes, and turning halfway through.
Serve hot with the cooking liquid.

Abbacchio alla cacciatora
Braised Spring Lamb

Serves 6

2 Tbsps extra-virgin olive oil
2 garlic cloves
3 ½ lb (1 ½ kg) deboned leg of spring lamb,
cut into large pieces
salt and pepper
1 rosemary sprig
2 sage leaves
1/2 cup (120 ml) vinegar
1/2 Tbsp all-purpose flour

Preparation time **20 minutes**
Cooking time **45 minutes**
Level **easy**
Wine **Aprilia Sangiovese**

Heat the olive oil in a large frying pan with
the garlic. Brown the lamb pieces for about
15 minutes over high heat. Season with salt
and pepper, add the rosemary and sage and
lower the heat.

   Add the vinegar and continue cooking for
a few more minutes. Stir in the flour to thicken
the sauce. Cook, covered, adding water if
necessary, until the lamb is cooked through
and the sauce thickened (about 15 minutes).
Serve hot.

Coda alla vaccinara
Roman-Style Oxtail

Serves 6

1 oxtail (around 3 ½ lb or 1 ½ kg)
2 ½ Tbsps lard
2 oz (50 g) lardo (cured lard), minced
1 carrot, minced - 1 onion, minced
2 garlic cloves, minced
4 Tbsps minced parsley
salt and pepper
1/2 cup (120 ml) white wine
4 Tbsps ready-made tomato sauce
2 cups (500 ml) water
5 cups (1 ¼ l) vegetable broth

Preparation time **20 minutes**
Cooking time **2 hours 20 minutes**
Level **easy**
Wine **Cesanese del Piglio**

If necessary, trim the oxtail (removing any bristles and washing well), then cut into pieces. Melt the lard in a saucepan and add the lardo, carrot, onion, garlic and parsley. Sauté briefly then add the oxtail and brown evenly over high heat, stirring often. Season with salt and pepper, add the wine and let evaporate.

Mix the tomato sauce with the water nd pour over the oxtail. Cook for 3-6 hours over a very low heat, adding a little vegetable broth when necessary. Serve hot.

Note Pancetta, *cured pig cheek, is sometimes added to this dish. The sauce can also be used as a pasta sauce with rigatoni.*

Coda alla vaccinara

castagnole alla romana
lemon fritters

Serves 4

7 Tbsps (3 ½ oz or 100 g) butter
3 cups plus 3 Tbsps (14 oz or 400 g)
all-purpose flour
1/4 cup (2 oz or 50 g) sugar
4 eggs
1/4 cup (60 ml) rum
grated zest of 1 organic lemon
sunflower oil for frying
confectioners' sugar
salt

Preparation time **30 minutes**
Cooking time **20 minutes**
Level **easy**
Wine **Aleatico di Gradoli**

Clarify the butter in a double boiler and then transfer to a bowl. Sift the flour into the butter and then add the sugar, eggs, rum, lemon zest and a pinch of salt. Mix well.

Roll the dough into chestnut-sized balls. Heat the sunflower oil. Fry the cookies until they puff up. Drain on paper towels and sprinkle with confectioners' sugar.

Pastiera con grano e ricotta
Ricotta and Wheat Tart

Serves 6

7 Tbsps (3 ½ oz or 100 g) butter
1/2 cup (3 ½ oz or 100 g) sugar
1 egg
2 egg yolks
2 ¼ cups (9 oz or 250 g) all-purpose flour
1/2 cup (120 ml) milk
3/4 cup (5 1/2 oz or 150 g) cooked wheat
2 Tbsps orange-flower water
2 Tbsps sugar
4 oz (120 g) ricotta

Preparation time **30 minutes**
Cooking time **35 minutes**
Level **medium**
Wine **Albana Passito**

Preheat the oven to 350°F (180°C or Gas Mark 4). Beat together the butter, sugar, egg and 1 egg yolk. Add the flour and mix to form a smooth and elastic dough. Let rest for 20 minutes.

Roll out the dough and use it to line 6 miniature tart tins. Heat the milk and add the cooked wheat and orange-flower water. Let simmer for 5 minutes. Remove from heat and let cool.

In a mixing bowl beat the remaining egg yolk with the sugar and then add the ricotta. Add the cooked wheat mixture. Pour the filling into the tart tins and bake for 25 minutes. Let cool completely before serving.

Maritozzi
Sweet Rolls

Serves 6

2/3 cup (3 ½ oz or 100 g) raisins
1 lb (500 g) risen bread dough
4 Tbsps extra-virgin olive oil
1/3 cup (2 oz or 50 g) chopped candied citron
1/3 cup (2 oz or 50 g) pine nuts
4 Tbsps sugar
salt
whipped cream

Preparation time **40 minutes**
Cooking time **10 minutes**
Level **easy**
Wine **Cesanese di Affile Spumante Dolce**

Soak the raisins in warm water for 10 minutes. Drain and carefully squeeze out the excess water. Place the prepared bread dough on a work surface and knead in the olive oil, raisins, candied citron, pine nuts, 2 tablespoons of sugar and a pinch of salt. Knead vigorously to obtain a smooth dough. Divide the dough into 20-24 equal pieces. Form oval-shaped rolls with the dough pieces. Let the rolls rise in a warm place for 2 hours. Preheat the oven to 485°F (250°C or Gas Mark 10). Oil a baking sheet and place the rolls on the sheet. Bake for 7 minutes.

Meanwhile, dissolve the remaining 2 tablespoons sugar in a little water. Remove the rolls from the oven, brush them with the syrup and bake for 2 more minutes. Serve the maritozzi filled with whipped cream.

Pangiallo
Chocolate-Nut Cookies

Serves 6

2 cups (10 ½ oz or 300 g) raisins
1 ⅓ cups (7 oz or 200 g) blanched almonds
2 cups (7 oz or 200 g) walnuts
1 ½ cups (7 oz or 200 g) blanched hazelnuts
3/4 cup (3 ½ oz or 100 g) pine nuts
2/3 cup (7 oz or 200 g) honey
2 cups (5 ½ oz or 150 g) cocoa powder
3/4 cup plus 1 Tbsp (3 ½ oz or 100 g)
all-purpose flour
2 oz (50 g) dark chocolate, grated

Preparation time **40 minutes**
Cooking time **30 minutes**
Level **easy**
Wine **Colli Albani Spumante Dolce**

Preheat the oven to 400°F (200°C or Gas Mark 6). Soak the raisins in warm water for 10 minutes, then drain and squeeze out excess liquid. Place the raisins, almonds, walnuts, hazelnuts and pine nuts in a food processor and roughly chop.

Melt the honey over a double boiler or in a saucepan over very low heat. Transfer the raisins and nuts to a bowl and add the cocoa powder, flour, grated chocolate and melted honey. Stir with a wooden spoon until thoroughly combined.

Form the mixture into small balls and arrange on a baking sheet. Bake for about 30 minutes.

Maritozzi

Pangiallo

Campania

Though known for its pizza and pasta, this sun-kissed,

volcanic land offers much more. Everything grown or produced here, whether tomatoes, lemons or mozzarella, has more concentrated flavor than elsewhere. Lose yourself along the tortuously winding roads of the Amalfi Coast or under the rocky cliffs of Capri, following ancient paths to seek out Roman mosaics and sampling dishes that are packed with flavor. Campania is always an experience.

CAMPANIA
local products

Mozzarella di **bufala** campana DOP *e* fiordilatte

TWO FRESH STRETCHED-CURD CHEESES
WITH SIMILAR APPEARANCE but made from
milk from different animals. Mozzarella
di Bufala is made from the milk of water
buffalos raised in Campania, while
Fiordilatte uses milk from cows of a local
breed. Fiordilatte has a very particular
flavor and is delicious eaten on its own.
However in Naples it is most used to
top Margherita pizza, and in cooking
in general. Mozzarella di Bufala is best
uncooked, as in the classic Caprese salad,
and is probably Campania's best-known
cheese, though the DOP (Denomination
of Protected Origin) production zone
includes part of the neighboring regions
of Lazio and Puglia. The name comes
from the technique of pinching off
pieces of the curd by hand (*mozzare*
means "to lop off"), using the thumb
and index finger. Mozzarella comes in
many shapes and sizes, such as bocconcini
(little balls), larger balls and even braided.

Pomodori *San* Marzano *dell'Agro* Sarnese

THESE TOMATOES (*POMODORI*) ARE TRADITIONALLY GROWN IN THE AGRO SARNESE-NOCERINO ZONE in the province of Salerno, though today they can also be found in the provinces of Naples and Avellino. Authentic San Marzano tomatoes are cultivated like grapevines and are harvested progressively between July and September. The fruit has an elongated shape, bright red color, sweet and tart flavor and firm flesh. With fewer seeds and fibers than other varieties, the tomato is excellent eaten raw in salads, though it is most often canned and used in sauces. San Marzano tomato sauces are known for sticking very well to the pasta, without passing on acidity, but they are most often found in Naples on authentic Neapolitan pizza.

Castagna *di* Montella

CAMPANIA IS THE MOST IMPORTANT CHESTNUT (*CASTAGNA*) PRODUCER in the Appennines. The Montella variety, harvested around the town of the same name in the province of Avellino, was the first to obtain the protective IGP (Indication of Protected Origin) mark. Also grown in the province of Avellino is the Serino chestnut, in the Verdone and Montemarano varieties. The Alto Casertano is known for the production of the Tempestina di Roccamorfina chestnut, while in Cilento the Marrone di Roccadaspide is particularly prized.

Mela Annurca campana Igp

A TYPICALLY CAMPANIAN FRUIT, HIGHLY RECOGNIZABLE BY ITS CHARACTERISTICS (streaked red skin, pale and firm flesh, juiciness, lightly acidic and sweet flavor), the Annurca Campana apple (*mela*) is grown according to traditional methods. The fruit quickly becomes too heavy for the trees, so it is harvested prematurely, when still green. They then turn red not on the tree, but spread out in a melaio, an apple field, where they are turned regularly.

Frutta secca: noci *e* nocciole

SORRENTO WALNUTS (NOCI) ARE REPUTED TO BE THE BEST IN ITALY and have a thin shell, a rounded oval shape and pleasant flavor and are not too oily. Used to make Nocino liqueur, they are grown in the province of Naples, around Vesuvius, where they flourish in the volcanic soil. Other Campanian walnut varieties are Malizia and San Martino. Another of the region's stars is the Giffoni hazelnut (*nocciola*), native to the Irno and Picentini valleys in the province of Salerno. Around Avellino another hazelnut variety, Mortarella, is cultivated. The hazelnuts are used in many desserts and sweets, including the celebrated Benevento torrone, a kind of nougat.

Fico bianco del Cilento *Dop*

THE CILENTO WHITE FIG (*FICO BIANCO*) IS ONE OF THE MOST PRIZED FIG VARIETIES out of the 700 that grow around the Mediterranean basin. It has a pale yellow skin, soft flesh, honeyed flavor and strong fragrance. The fruit is eaten fresh on its own, or paired with cured meats and cheeses. It is also well-adapted to drying or preserving in syrup. The dried figs can be filled with hazelnuts, walnuts or almonds or covered in chocolate. Alternatively they can be stuffed with wild fennel seeds and citrus zest, two other typical local products.

Limone *di* Sorrento *Igp* e Limoncello

THE LIMONE DI SORRENTO IGP (SORRENTO LEMON PROTECTED GEOGRAPHICAL INDICATION) covers a specific area in the Sorrentino peninsula where the lemons can be grown. The fruit is large (never less than 3 oz/85 g), with an oval shape and bright straw-yellow, very juicy pulp. The rind is also bright yellow and very fragrant. In fact the rind is used to flavor many dishes, from appetizers to desserts. The juice and pulp are much used for marinating local fish and preparing babàs and sorbets. The rind is the essential ingredient for a noted product of the Amalfi Coast: Limoncello. This liqueur is made from infusing the skins of very fresh lemons in pure alcohol.

Mozzarella in carrozza
Fried Mozzarella Sandwiches

Serves 4

8 slices of crusty bread, crusts removed
1 large mozzarella ball, thinly sliced
all-purpose flour for dusting
2 eggs
salt
extra-virgin olive oil for frying

Preparation time **15 minutes**
Cooking time **10 minutes**
Level **easy**
Wine **Ischia Bianco**

Make 4 sandwiches with the bread and mozzarella slices. Dust the edges with flour and then sprinkle with cold water, pressing closed to seal the edges.

Beat the eggs with a pinch of salt and soak the sandwiches in the egg for a few minutes so that the bread absorbs all of the egg.

Heat olive oil in a large saucepan and fry the sandwiches, turning so they cook evenly on both sides. Work in batches if necessary. Drain with a slotted spoon as soon as they are golden and dry on paper towels before serving hot.

Caponata di pomodori
Tomato Salad

Serves 4

2 whole-wheat freselle or large rusks
2 Tbsps extra-virgin olive oil
4 ripe tomatoes, thinly sliced
1 garlic clove, minced
1 pinch of dried oregano
4 basil leaves, chopped
salt

Preparation time **15 minutes**
Level **easy**
Wine **Falerno del Massimo Bianco**

Quickly dip the freselle or rusks in cold water to soften them slightly, without letting them disintegrate. Drain and cut into large pieces.

Place in a large salad bowl and toss with the olive oil, tomatoes, garlic, a pinch of oregano and the basil. Season with salt to taste and stir well. Let sit for a few minutes before serving.

Note *Freselle are a kind of crisp, hard bread, similar to a rusk, typical to Campania. They are available as toasts or rounds, and come in regular and whole-wheat versions.*

Insalata Caprese
Tomato and Mozzarella Salad

Serves 4

1 lb (500 g) buffalo mozzarella
1 lb (500 g) fresh tomatoes
4 Tbsps extra-virgin olive oil
salt
1 Tbsp dried oregano
10 basil leaves

Preparation time **10 minutes**
Level **easy**
Wine **Capri Bianco**

Slice the mozzarella and tomatoes into fairly thick slices.

Arrange the slices on a serving plate, either covering the tomatoes with mozzarella or alternating the slices.

Dress with olive oil, a pinch of salt and oregano. Serve immediately, decorating the plate with basil leaves.

Note *For a richer version, add 1 thinly sliced Tropea onion or other sweet red onion, a few capers and anchovies, and serve with toasted bread.*

Caponata di pomodori

Insalata Caprese

Migliaccio praianese
Praiano-Style Pasta Frittata

Serves 4

salt and pepper
10 ½ oz (300 g) mixed pasta
(matagliati, spaghetti, ziti, mafalde)
1 cup (5 ½ oz or 150 g)
coarse durum-wheat semolina
3 eggs, beaten
2 Tbsps lard
2 oz (50 g) Caciotta cheese, grated
7 oz (200 g) mozzarella, diced
9 oz (250 g) cured smoked sausages,
casings removed and meat chopped

Preparation time **15 minutes**
Cooking time **30 minutes**
Level **easy**
Wine **Capri Rosso**

Bring a large pot of salted water to a boil
and start adding the pasta shapes, starting
with the largest ones. After about 5 minutes
add the semolina and stir with a wooden
spoon.

When the pasta and semolina are cooked,
remove from the heat and stir in the eggs,
1 tablespoon of lard, the Caciotta, mozzarella
and sausage. Adjust salt and pepper and stir
well until thoroughly combined.

Melt the remaining tablespoon of lard
in another pan and pour in the mixture.
Smooth off the surface with a spatula. Cook
over medium heat, flipping so it cooks
evenly, until golden on both sides.

Gnocchi alla caprese
Capri-Style Gnocchi

Serves 6-8

3 Tbsps extra-virgin olive oil, plus extra for oiling
1/2 onion, minced
5 ½ oz (150 g) ground beef
2 ¼ lb (1 kg) peeled, canned tomatoes
3-4 basil leaves
salt
2 ½ lb (1 1/5 kg) potato gnocchi
9 oz (250 g) mozzarella, chopped
4 Tbsps grated Parmesan cheese

Preparation time **20 minutes**
Cooking time **50 minutes**
Level **easy**
Wine **Capri Rosso**

Preheat the oven to 350°F (180°C or Gas
Mark 4). Heat the olive oil in a large frying
pan and add the onion. Sauté briefly and
add the beef. Brown the meat and then add
tomatoes and the basil leaves. Reduce the heat
and simmer for 30 minutes.

Bring a large pot of salted water to the boil
and cook the gnocchi until they rise to the
surface. Using a slotted spoon drain half of the
gnocchi directly into a well-oiled baking dish.
Top with half of the chopped mozzarella and
then add the remaining gnocchi.

Add the remaining cheese and cover with
the beef sauce. Sprinkle with Parmesan cheese
and bake for 5-10 minutes until the top is
golden-brown. Remove from the oven and serve
immediately.

Gnocchi alla caprese

Scialatielli alla pescatora
Fisherman's Scialatielli

Serves 4

7 oz (200 g) mussels
4 Tbsps extra-virgin olive oil
1 garlic clove, minced
1/2 bunch of parsley, minced
3 ½ oz (100 g) small shrimp
7 oz (200 g) clams
3 ½ oz (100 g) squid, sliced into rings
3/4 cup (180 ml) white wine
3 Tbsps ready-made tomato sauce
salt and pepper
12 ½ oz (350 g) scialatelli,
fettuccine or tagliatelle

Preparation time **15 minutes**
Cooking time **30 minutes**
Level **easy**
Wine **Greco di Tufo**

Scialatielli alla pescatora

Cook the mussels in a covered pan
until they open. Heat the olive oil in
a large frying pan and sauté the garlic
until golden. Add the parsley (reserving
a little for garnish), then add the shrimp,
clams, squid and cooked mussels.

Pour over the wine and as soon as it
has evaporated add the tomato sauce and
continue cooking for about 15 minutes
over medium heat.

Bring a large pot of salted water to a boil
and cook the scialatelli or other pasta.
Drain and toss in the frying pan with the
seafood. Stir well and serve hot, sprinkled
with pepper and the remaining parsley.

cianfotta a minestra
summer vegetable soup

Serves 4

2 eggplants, cubed
salt and pepper
3 Tbsps extra-virgin olive oil
1 celery stalk, finely chopped
1 carrot, thinly sliced
1 lb (500 g) San Marzano or plum tomatoes, thinly sliced
2 red or green bell peppers, chopped
6 potatoes, cubed
2 large onion, thickly sliced

Preparation time **15 minutes**
Cooking time **50 minutes**
Level **easy**
Wine **Vesuvio Lacryma Christi**

Place the eggplant in a colander and sprinkle with salt.
Leave for 10 minutes to purge, then drain and squeeze out
excess liquid. Rinse under cold running water.
   Heat 2 tablespoons of olive oil in a large saucepan
and sauté the celery, carrot and tomatoes, then add
the eggplant, peppers, potatoes and onions. Adjust salt
and pepper, cover with water, drizzle with the remaining
oil and continue cooking until all the vegetables are tender
and the soup has thickened. Serve hot.

Tubetti cacio e uova
Tubetti with Cheese and Egg

Serves 4

2 eggs
salt and pepper
1 bunch of parsley, minced
14 oz (400 g) tubetti, ditalini or pennette pasta
7 Tbsps (3 ½ oz or 100 g) butter
3 Tbsps grated Parmesan cheese
1 ½ cups (5 ½ oz or 150 g)
grated Pecorino cheese

Preparation time **5 minutes**
Cooking time **15 minutes**
Level **easy**
Wine **Falerno del Massico Bianco**

Beat the eggs with a fork and season
with salt and pepper. Stir in the parsley.
   Bring a large pot of salted water to a boil
and cook the pasta until al dente. Drain
with a slotted spoon.
   Melt the butter in a frying pan and add
the pasta. Stir in the egg mixture, add
the Parmesan and Pecorino and stir well
with a wooden spoon until the eggs set.
Serve hot.

Vermicelli di Scammaro
Scammaro-Style Vermicelli

Serves 4

1 Tbsp raisins
6 Tbsps extra-virgin olive oil
1 garlic clove
2 salted anchovies, rinsed, deboned and chopped
1 Tbsp capers, minced
3/4 cup (3 ½ oz or 100 g) black Gaeta olives,
pitted and thinly sliced
1 Tbsp pine nuts
3 Tbsps breadcrumbs, plus extra for sprinkling
salt
14 oz (400 g) vermicelli
3 Tbsps minced parsley

Preparation time **10 minutes**
Cooking time **15 minutes**
Level **easy**
Wine **Vesuvio Bianco**

Soak the raisins in warm water, drain and
squeeze out excess liquid.
   Heat the olive oil in a wide frying pan and
sauté the whole garlic clove until golden.
Add the anchovies and smash them with a
wooden spoon. Add the capers, olives, raisins
and pine nuts. Cook for a few minutes then
remove the garlic and stir in the breadcrumbs.
   Boil the pasta in salted water until al dente,
then drain and toss in the frying pan with the
sauce, stirring well to distribute it evenly.
   Top with a sprinkling of parsley and another
spoonful of breadcrumbs. Serve hot.

Minestra sposata
Wedding Soup

Serves 6

1 celery stalk, chopped
1 onion, chopped - 1 carrot, chopped
1 cup (5 ½ oz or 150 g) cherry tomatoes
1 ham bone - 1 lb (500 g) pork cheek
14 oz (400 g) pork ribs
7 oz (200 g) pork leg
1/2 Savoy cabbage, chopped
1/2 spring cabbage, chopped
1 lb (500 g) escarole, chopped
1 lb (500 g) chicory, chopped
10 ½ oz (300 g) borage, chopped
9 oz (250 g) new potatoes, chopped
6 Tbsps grated Parmesan cheese
1 pinch of chili pepper flakes

Preparation time **20 minutes**
Cooking time **1 hour 40 minutes**
Level **medium**
Wine **Taburno Rosso**

Place the celery, onion, carrot, tomatoes, ham bone and all the pork (cheek, ribs and leg) in a large saucepan and cover with water. Boil for about 1 hour 30 minutes, skimming off foam as necessary.

In a separate pan boil the Savoy cabbage, spring cabbage, escarole, chicory, borage and potatoes until tender, then drain and add to the other pan. Once the soup is cooked, remove the meat and cut into small pieces, removing any bones. Return to the pan. Serve the soup hot, sprinkled with Parmesan and chili flakes.

Vermicelli di Scammaro

Minestra sposata

Zucchine alla scapece
Zucchini with Mint

Serves 4-6

6 zucchini, thinly sliced lengthwise
salt
3 Tbsps extra-virgin olive oil
1 garlic clove
3 Tbsps vinegar
4 mint leaves, torn into pieces

Preparation time **15 minutes**
Cooking time **15 minutes**
Level **easy**

Place the zucchini slices in a bowl and
sprinkle with a pinch of salt. Let rest for
2 hours.

Heat the olive oil in a frying pan and sauté
the whole garlic clove until golden. Add
the zucchini and brown for a few minutes.
Sprinkle with salt, then remove from the
pan and pat dry with paper towels.

Arrange in a bowl in layers and add the
vinegar and mint leaves. Serve warm.

Pizza regina classica
Classic Margherita Pizza

Serves 1 pizza

1 ¾ tsps active dry yeast
3/4 cup plus 1 Tbsp (200 ml) warm water
salt
1 tsp sugar
3 Tbsps extra-virgin olive oil,
plus extra for oiling and drizzling
3 cups plus 3 Tbsps (14 oz or 400 g)
all-purpose flour
4 tomatoes, blanched, peeled,
deseeded and chopped
7 oz (200g) mozzarella, diced
20 cherry tomatoes, quartered
4 fresh basil leaves

Preparation time **20 minutes**
Cooking time **20 minutes**
Level **easy**
Beer **Pilsner**

Preheat the oven to 400°F (200°C or Gas
Mark 6). Mix the yeast into the warm water,
then add the salt, sugar and olive oil. Stir with
a spoon and pour the mixture over the flour.
Mix to form a dough, knead and then leave
to rise, covered, for 2 hours. Roll out the dough
into a 1/4-inch (1/2 cm) thick sheet, or
4 circles, on a lightly floured work surface.

Transfer the dough to an oiled baking sheet.
Spread the tomatoes on the pizza and top with
the mozzarella. Season with salt, drizzle with
olive oil and bake for 20 minutes. Remove from
the oven and garnish with the cherry tomatoes
and basil leaves. Serve immediately.

Parmigiana di melanzane
Eggplant Parmesan

Serves 4

3 eggplants, sliced lengthwise - salt
5 Tbsps extra-virgin olive oil
2 garlic cloves, minced
3 cups (700 ml) crushed tomatoes
4 basil leaves, chopped
5 Tbsps grated Parmesan cheese
9 oz (250 g) mozzarella, sliced

Preparation time **15 minutes**
Cooking time **1 hour**
Level **easy**
Wine **Falanghina**

Place the eggplant slices in a colander, sprinkle with salt and let sit for 30 minutes, then drain and squeeze out excess liquid. Preheat the oven to 400°F (200°C or Gas Mark 6). Heat a little olive oil in a large frying pan until very hot and fry the eggplant slices, in batches if necessary.

In another frying pan heat a drizzle of oil and sauté the garlic until golden. Add the tomato and cook down until thickened. Remove from the heat, add the basil and salt to taste, then pass through a food mill or puree in a food processor.

Spread a layer of eggplant in an oiled baking dish. Top with 1 ladleful of tomato sauce, sprinkle with Parmesan and cover with mozzarella slices. Continue making layers until all the ingredients have been used up. Finish with a layer of tomato sauce, drizzle with oil and bake for around 45 minutes. Serve hot.

Pomodori gratinati
Stuffed Tomatoes

Serves 4

8 round tomatoes
1/2 cup (2 oz or 50 g) black Gaeta olives, pitted and finely chopped
1 bunch of parsley, minced
1 Tbsp capers, minced
1 pinch of dried oregano
4 Tbsps breadcrumbs
4 Tbsps extra-virgin olive oil
salt
4 salted anchovies, rinsed and deboned

Preparation time **20 minutes**
Cooking time **15 minutes**
Level **easy**
Wine **Falerno del Massico Bianco**

Preheat the oven to 350°F (180°C or Gas Mark 4). Cut a lid off the top of the tomatoes and scoop out the inner liquid and seeds.

Mix together the olives, parsley, capers, oregano, breadcrumbs and 3 tablespoons of olive oil. Season with salt to taste. Arrange the tomatoes in a baking dish and fill with the mixture.

Top with the anchovies and drizzle with the remaining olive oil. Bake until golden on top. Serve hot.

Coniglio all'ischitana
Ischia-Style Rabbit

Serves 4

1 rabbit (about 3 ½ lb or 1 ½ kg)
2 Tbsps extra-virgin olive oil
3/4 cup (180 ml) white wine
1 lb (500 g) ripe tomatoes, chopped
1 rosemary sprig, leaves only
salt and pepper
6 basil leaves, torn

Preparation time **20 minutes**
Cooking time **30 minutes**
Level **easy**
Wine **Vesuvio Rosato**

Cut the rabbit into pieces, wash and dry. Reserve the liver.

Heat the olive oil in a frying pan and brown the rabbit pieces. Add the white wine and let evaporate. Add the tomatoes, rosemary, salt and pepper. Cover, lower the heat and continue cooking until the rabbit is cooked through, adding a little water if necessary. 10 minutes before the end of cooking add the liver. Serve hot, garnished with basil.

Pomodori gratinati

Coniglio all'ischitana

Pastiera napoletana
Neapolitan Ricotta Cake

Serves 6

1/2 cup (3 oz or 80 g) wheat berries
2 cups (500 ml) milk - 2 egg yolks
1 ¾ cups (12 ½ oz or 350 g) sugar
grated zest of 1 organic lemon
14 oz (400 g) fresh ricotta, sieved
2/3 cup (3 ½ oz or 100 g) chopped candied
citron and orange peel
1/2 tsp ground cinnamon - 3 eggs
1 Tbsp orange-flower water
4 cups (1 lb 2 oz or 500 g) all-purpose flour
1 cup (7 oz or 200 g) lard, softened

Preparation time **1 hour**
Cooking time **1 hour**
Level **easy**
Wine **Vesuvio Lacryma Christi Liquoroso**

Place the wheat, milk, 6 tablespoons of sugar
and the lemon zest in a saucepan and bring to
a boil. Simmer until the wheat is tender. Mix
together the ricotta, 6 tablespoons of sugar,
2 egg yolks, candied citrus, cinnamon and orange-
flower water in a mixing bowl. Stir the cooked
wheat mixture into the ricotta mixture and cover
the bowl. Mound the flour on a work surface and
make a well in the middle. Break in the 3 eggs
and add the softened lard and 1 cup (7 oz or
200 g) of sugar. Mix energetically to form an
elastic dough. Cover and let rest for 30 minutes.
Preheat the oven to 350°F (180°C or Gas Mark
4). Roll out the dough. Butter and flour a round
baking dish and use half the dough to line it.
Pour in the ricotta filling. Cut the remaining
dough into strips and form a lattice pattern
over the top. Bake for 45 minutes.

Babà
Rum Cakes

Serves 4

2 ½ tsps active dry yeast
2 cups minus 1 Tbsp (8 ½ oz or 240 g)
reinforced white flour (like Manitoba)
4 eggs
9 Tbsps (4 ½ oz or 130 g)
butter at room temperature
1 cup (7 oz or 200 g) sugar
salt
1 ¼ cups (300 ml) water
2/3 cup (150 ml) rum

Preparation time **30 minutes**
Cooking time **15 minutes**
Level **difficult**

Dissolve the yeast in 3 tablespoons of warm
water. Mix together with 2/3 cup (3 oz or 80 g)
of the flour. Let rise for 30 minutes on a floured
plate. Transfer the risen dough to a bowl and
mix with the eggs, 5 ½ Tbsps (3 oz or 80 g)
of butter at room temperature, the remaining
flour, 3 tablespoons of sugar and a pinch of salt.

Once a soft dough has formed, work it by
raising it up with the fingers and beating it in
the bowl so that bubbles form in the dough.
Let rest for 40 minutes. Preheat the oven to
350°F (180°C or Gas Mark 4). Divide the dough
between 10 buttered round molds, each
2 ½-inches (6 cm) in diameter and 5 inches
(2 cm) high. Fill the molds halfway. Let rise
again, then bake. Meanwhile boil the water
with the remaining sugar for 2 minutes.

Drench the baked cakes with the syrup.
Just before serving, pour over the rum.

Babà

Zuppa inglese alla napoletana
Neapolitan-Style Trifle

Serves 6-8

1 ¼ lb (600 g) sponge cake
1/4 cup (60 ml) rum
10 ½ oz (300 g) ricotta
3/4 cup (5 ½ oz or 150 g) sugar
2 oz (60 g) extra-dark chocolate, finely chopped
1 tsp vanilla extract
3 egg whites
2 ½ Tbsps confectioners' sugar
colored sprinkles

Preparation time **40 minutes**
Level **easy**

Cut the sponge cake horizontally into layers. Brush each layer with the rum. The cake should be moist and very soft.

Stir the ricotta, sugar, chocolate and vanilla extract together. Mix well to form a smooth cream. Place a little sponge cake at the bottom of 6 small glass bowls. Top with a layer of the ricotta cream. Continue making alternating layers until all of the ingredients have been used up.

Beat the egg whites until they form stiff peaks. Carefully fold in the confectioner's sugar. Spread a layer of the meringue over the trifles, top with the colored sprinkles and refrigerate overnight.

Sciù al cioccolato
Chocolate Cream Puffs

Serves 6

12 ½ oz (350 g) dark chocolate
1 cup (250 ml) whipping cream
1 ½ Tbsps water - 3 Tbsps milk
1 pat of butter, plus extra for buttering
6 ½ Tbsps all-purpose flour,
plus extra for flouring
2 eggs

Preparation time **50 minutes**
Cooking time **20 minutes**
Level **medium**

Preheat the oven to 425°F (220°C or Gas Mark 7). Melt 9 oz (250 g) chocolate in a double boiler. Whip the whipping cream to stiff peaks and then fold it into the chocolate. Set the chocolate cream aside.

Bring the water, milk and butter to a boil in a saucepan. Remove from the heat and sift in the flour, stirring constantly with a wooden spoon. Return the saucepan to the stove and cook the mixture for 2 minutes, stirring constantly. Let the mixture cool and then add the eggs, one at a time, stirring to incorporate completely. Butter and flour a baking sheet.

Transfer the batter to a pastry bag and form beignets or doughnut shapes. Bake for 6-7 minutes until the beignets are puffy and reduce the oven temperature to 375°F (190°C or Gas Mark 5).

Bake until cooked through. Fill the puffs with chocolate cream. Melt the remaining chocolate and drizzle over each cream puff.

Struffoli
Honeyed Fritters

Serves 6

3/4 cup plus 2 Tbsps (6 oz or 170 g) sugar
3 cups plus 3 Tbsps (14 oz or 400 g)
all-purpose flour, plus extra for dusting
3 eggs
2 egg yolks
3 Tbsps (1 ½ oz or 40 g) butter, softened
grated zest of 1 organic lemon
salt
sunflower oil for frying
4 Tbsps water
1 cup (12 ½ oz or 300 g) honey
4 Tbsps chopped candied fruit

Preparation time **45 minutes**
Cooking time **30 minutes**
Level **medium**
Wine **Vesuvio Lacryma Christi Liquoroso**

Reserve 2 tablespoons of sugar and mix
the remainder with the flour, eggs, egg yolks,
butter, lemon zest and a pinch of salt. Let
rest for 2 hours.

Form the dough into sticks about 1/5-inch
(1/2 cm) thick, cut them into cubes and dust
with flour. Heat the sunflower oil until very
hot and fry the dough until golden. Drain
and dry on paper towels. Bring the honey,
reserved 2 tablespoons of sugar and water to
a boil. When the syrup starts to turn golden,
lower the heat and add the fritters and
half the candied fruit. Stir well, then
immediately turn out into a bowl.

Garnish with the remaining candied fruit.

Sciù al cioccolato

Struffoli

Basilicata

A *small but varied region,* with hidden natural

beauties and fascinating historical sites like the Sassi di Matera rock houses. From the mountains to the crystal-clear sea, medieval churches and Doric columns, it's a gastronomic journey that features strongly flavored *cheeses* and *cured meats* like *cacioricotta* and *soppressata*, *salsiccia lucana* and *capocollo*.

BASILICATA
local products

Il Peperone di *Senise*

THE INDICATION OF PROTECTED ORIGIN (IGP) PEPERONE DI SENISE (SENISE PEPPER) COVERS THREE KINDS OF PEPPERS: pointed, truncated and hooked. The peppers are thin, with a low water content, so they dry quickly and naturally in the sun. They are harvested at the start of August and can be eaten fresh or dried. When dried, they are hung in dark, airy, dry environments on cloths or nets, and then threaded into chains. These are known as serte and are left out to dry further in the sun. Some peppers are dried again in the oven before being ground into a powder.

Il Pecorino *Canestrato*

A SPECIALTY OF MOLITERNO, PRODUCED FROM SHEEP'S MILK WITH THE OCCASIONAL ADDITION OF GOAT'S MILK. After being heated with kid or lamb rennet, the curd is placed in wicker baskets, heated again, dry-salted and left to mature. It is aged for around eight months, during which time the forms are turned often and treated with oil and vinegar. The marks of the baskets are evident on the rind. The cheese is white and oily, with an intense, sharp flavor.

Aglianico *del Vulture*

THE AGLIANICO GRAPE HAS FLOURISHED ON THE VOLCANIC SLOPES OF MT. VULTURE, and finds its best expression in the DOC (Denomination of Controlled Origin) Aglianico del Vulture, known as the "Barolo of the South" in tribute to its quality and nobility. The ruby red or bright garnet color depends on the aging (from 36 to 60 months), with a winy perfume that improves over time and a dry, almost velvety texture. Aglianico del Vulture pairs best with ragùs, game birds, poultry, roast suckling pig and semi-hard cheeses. The aged versions pair with game meats, lamb and hard cheeses. The wine is generally the perfect accompaniment to traditional local dishes.

Fagioli *di Sarconi*

THESE IGP-DESIGNATED BEANS (*FAGIOLI*) GROW IN THE SANDY SOIL of the province of Potenza, at 2,000 feet (600 m) above sea level. Legumes have been cultivated for centuries in the Alta Val d'Agri area, but Sarconi is the only place to grow these particular beans, a cross between local varieties of cannellini and borlotti (cranberry) beans. They are oval, whitish-yellow with dark streaks, particularly prized for their flavor and because they cook a *prima acqua*, "at first water," i.e. very quickly. Sarconi beans can be found on the tables of Basilicata whole or pureed, in soups, with pasta, with rice, in salads and on toasted bread. All these dishes can be sampled at the *Sagra del Fagiolo*, the Bean Festival, held in Sarconi in the second half of August.

Cavatelli e cime di rape
Cavatelli with Bitter Greens

Serves 4

3 cups plus 3 Tbsps (14 oz or 400 g)
hard-wheat flour
salt
2 ¼ lb (1 kg) bitter greens
(turnip tops or broccoli rabe)
2 Tbsps extra-virgin olive oil
1 garlic clove, chopped
1 chili pepper, minced
2 salted anchovies, chopped

Preparation time **30 minutes**
Cooking time **30 minutes**
Level **easy**
Wine **Ostuni Bianco**

Mound the flour on a work surface, then
add a pinch of salt and mix in enough
warm water to make a smooth, soft dough.

Form the dough into thin ropes then cut
them into small pieces. Take each piece
and press it with a finger, rolling it on a
wooden board, to obtain small gnocchi
with a cavity in the middle. Boil the greens
in salted water until tender.

Heat the olive oil in a frying pan and sauté
the garlic, chili and anchovies, then add the
drained greens.

Bring a large pot of salted water to a boil
and cook the cavatelli. Drain and toss
in the pan with the greens. Serve hot.

Ferretti con la mollica
Ferretti with Breadcrumbs

Serves 4

2 Tbsps extra-virgin olive oil
1 Tbsp finely chopped lardo (cured lard)
3 ½ oz (100 g) fresh breadcrumbs
1 garlic clove, minced
1 chili pepper, minced
3 Tbsps minced parsley
14 oz (400 g) ferretti, casarecce or penne
3/4 cup (2 ½ oz or 70 g) grated Pecorino cheese
salt

Preparation time **30 minutes**
Cooking time **20 minutes**
Level **easy**
Wine **Colli Albani Spumante**

Heat the olive oil and lardo and sauté the bread,
garlic and chili until golden, then stir in the
parsley.

Bring a large pot of salted water to a boil and
cook the pasta until al dente. Drain and transfer
to serving bowls. Sprinkle the bread mixture
over the pasta and top with Pecorino.

Stir well and serve.

Note *Ferretti is a typical Basilicata pasta, called
after the ferro (iron stick) the dough is wrapped
around to form the curled shapes. Traditionally
this recipe should be prepared with crumb from
a panella loaf, made from hard-wheat flour and
natural leavening, baked in a wood-burning oven
after rising for at least 6 hours.*

Strangolapreti alla potentina
Potenza-Style Strangolapreti

Serves 4-6

3/4 cup (3 oz or 80 g) grated Pecorino cheese
1 garlic clove, minced - grated nutmeg
1 bunch of parsley, minced
1 pinch of ground chili pepper
14 oz (400 g) pork (in 1 piece)
2 oz (50 g) pancetta, minced
2 Tbsps extra-virgin olive oil - salt and pepper
1/2 cup (120 ml) white wine
2 cups (14 oz or 400 g) peeled
plum tomatoes, pureed
4 cups (1 lb 2 oz or 500 g) all-purpose flour

Preparation time **20 minutes**
Cooking time **3 hours 20 minutes**
Level **easy**
Wine **Cesanese del Piglio**

Mix 1/2 cup (2 oz or 50 g) of the Pecorino with the parsley, garlic, nutmeg and chili. Pound out the pork and spread the mixture over one side. Top with the pancetta. Roll up the meat and tie with kitchen string.

Brown the pork in the olive oil. Add the wine, let reduce, then add the tomatoes, salt and pepper and cook for 2 hours, adding water if dry. Mix together the flour, a pinch of salt and enough hot water to form a dough. Roll into little ropes, cut into 1-inch (2 cm) lengths, then flatten and roll up into curls.

Cook the strangolapreti in boiling water until they float. Drain and toss with the tomato sauce from the pork. Top with the remaining Pecorino cheese. Serve the pork as a main course.

Ferretti con la mollica

Strangolapreti alla potentina

Acquasale
Spicy Bread and Egg Soup

Serves 4

2 Tbsps extra-virgin olive oil
1 onion, thinly sliced
1 hot red chili pepper, minced
salt
4 eggs
4 slices of crusty bread
3 ½ oz (100 g) aged ricotta salata, grated

Preparation time **10 minutes**
Cooking time **40 minutes**
Level **easy**
Wine **Castel del Monte Rosato**

Heat the olive oil in a large frying pan
and sauté the onion.

Add the chili pepper and cook for a few
minutes, then add warm water, season with
salt and break in the eggs, stirring well with
a wooden spoon.

Cut the bread into cubes and divide
between shallow bowls. Pour over a ladleful
of soup and top with grated ricotta salata.

Note *This soup is a classic peasant dish in
Basilicata, with bread, eggs, chili, parsley,
oil and salt as the basic ingredients, enriched
with others, such as tomatoes or ricotta,
when available.*

Involtini di spada alla scilla
Swordfish Involtini with Tomato

Serves 4-6

6 Tbsps extra-virgin olive oil
1 garlic clove, minced
5 peeled plum tomatoes, chopped
2 bunches of parsley, minced
6 Tbsps salted capers, rinsed
1/2 cup (2 ½ oz or 70 g) pitted green olives
1 hot red chili pepper, minced
salt and pepper
2 Tbsps breadcrumbs
2 Tbsps grated Parmesan cheese
1 ¾ lb (800 g) swordfish, thinly sliced
2 Tbsps white wine vinegar

Preparation time **40 minutes**
Cooking time **50 minutes**
Level **medium**
Wine **Ostuni Bianco**

Heat 4 tablespoons of olive oil and sauté the
garlic. Add the tomatoes, half the parsley, the
capers, olives, chili and a pinch of salt. Simmer
until thickened.

Mix together the breadcrumbs, Parmesan,
remaining parsley, salt, pepper, 2 tablespoons
of olive oil and enough water to make a smooth
mixture.

Spread a spoonful of the breadcrumb mixture
on each swordfish slice, then roll up and fix
with a toothpick. Drizzle with vinegar and
cook in the tomato sauce until cooked through.
Serve hot.

Involtini di spada alla scilla

Ruccul (o Rucculo di Basilicata)
Basilicata-Style Focaccia

Serves 4

4 cups (1 lb 2 oz or 500 g) all-purpose flour
3 ½ tsps active dry yeast
salt
1 Tbsp sugar
1 cup (250 ml) warm water
6 Tbsps extra-virgin olive oil
2 garlic cloves, thinly sliced
1 dried chili pepper, minced
1 Tbsp dried oregano

Preparation time **20 minutes**
Cooking time **20 minutes**
Level **easy**
Wine **Maratea Bianco**

Mound the flour on a work surface and sprinkle the yeast, salt and sugar on the top. Gradually mix in the warm water, stirring until the yeast has dissolved. Knead vigorously to obtain a smooth, uniform dough. Cover and let rest in a dry place for 20 minutes.

Divide the dough into four equal parts and roll them out on a floured work surface to form four thin disks. Oil one or two baking sheets and arrange the disks on them. Brush the disks with olive oil and let rest for another 20 minutes.

Preheat the oven to 450°F (230°C or Gas Mark 8). Sprinkle each disk with a little garlic, chili and oregano. Bake for 20 minutes and serve drizzled with olive oil.

Cotechinata
Pork Rind Involtini

Serves 4

1 Tbsp lard
3 garlic cloves, minced
1 bunch of parsley, minced
2 chili peppers, minced
14 oz (400 g) pork rind
7 oz (200 g) lardo (cured lard), sliced
2 Tbsps extra-virgin olive oil
2/3 cup (150 ml) pureed tomatoes
salt

Preparation time **25 minutes**
Cooking time **40 minutes**
Level **easy**
Wine **Aglianico del Vulture**

Heat the lard in a saucepan and sauté the garlic, parsley and chili until the garlic is soft and golden.

Cut the pork rind into squares of about 4 inches (10 cm) on each side. Boil them for 10 minutes. Drain, dry and spread with the garlic mixture.

Lay a slice of lardo on top of each one, then roll them up and fix with toothpicks. Heat the olive oil in a large frying pan and heat the tomatoes. Add the pork rind rolls, adjust salt and cook for 20 minutes. Serve hot.

Baccalà in fior di zucca
Stuffed Squash Blossoms

Serves 4

9 oz (250 g) pre-soaked salt cod
1 stale crusty bread roll, crumb only
4 eggs
salt
1 bunch of parsley, minced
6 Tbsps grated Pecorino cheese
3 Tbsps milk
3 Tbsps all-purpose flour
20 squash blossoms, stalks and pistils removed
sunflower oil for frying

Preparation time **30 minutes**
Cooking time **40 minutes**
Level **easy**
Wine **Torre Quarto Bianco**

Remove any bones from the salt cod and boil it in salted water for about 30 minutes. Drain, chop finely and place in a bowl.

Add the bread crumb, 2 eggs, parsley, 4 tablespoons of Pecorino and a pinch of salt. Mix well and form into 20 small balls. Beat the remaining 2 eggs in a bowl with the remaining Pecorino, a pinch of salt and the milk.

Place a ball of salt cod mixture in each squash blossom. Dip them first in the flour and then the egg mixture. Heat the sunflower oil until very hot and fry the blossoms in batches until golden. Drain with a slotted spoon, dry on paper towels and serve immediately.

Cotechinata

Baccalà in fior di zucca

torta di fichi e noci
fig and walnut tart

Serves 6-8

1 ¾ cups (400 ml) milk
1 ¾ cups (12 ½ oz or 350 g) sugar
grated zest of 1 organic orange
1/3 cup (80 ml) vin cotto
7 Tbsps extra-virgin olive oil
1 Tbsp aniseed liqueur, like Pastis
1/2 tsp ground cinnamon - 1/2 tsp vanilla extract
2 cups (10 oz or 280 g) dried figs, finely chopped
1/3 cup plus 1 Tbsp (2 oz or 50 g) chopped walnuts
3 ½ oz (100 g) dark chocolate, roughly chopped
4 ¾ cups (1 lb 5 oz or 600 g) all-purpose flour
3 eggs - 1 tsp baking powder

Preparation time **50 minutes**
Cooking time **1 hour**
Level **medium**
Wine **Moscato del Vulture**

Preheat the oven to 350°F (180°C or Gas Mark 4). Place the milk, 3/4 cup (5 ½ oz or 150 g) of sugar, orange zest, vin cotto, 1 tablespoon of olive oil, aniseed liqueur, cinnamon and vanilla into a large saucepan. Bring to a boil and cook until the mixture thickens. Remove from heat and add the figs and walnuts. Let cool completely. Add the chocolate and puree the mixture in a food processor. Let sit for 15 minutes.

Meanwhile, mix together the flour, eggs, baking powder, 6 tablespoons of olive oil and remaining 1 cup (7 oz or 200 g) of sugar to form a smooth dough. Roll out the dough into a thin sheet on a lightly floured work surface.

Lightly oil a tart pan and line it with the dough. Cut off any excess dough and set it aside. Pour in the filling and roll out the remaining pastry dough. Cut the dough into strips and use the strips to create a lattice over the top of the tart. Bake for 1 hour. Serve the tart warm or cold.

Traditional recipe

Copete
Almond Macaroons

Serves 6-8

2 egg whites
3 cups plus 2 ½ Tbsps (13 ½ oz or 380 g) confectioners' sugar
1 cup (4 oz or 120 g) blanched almonds, toasted and finely chopped
1 pinch of ground cinnamon
3-4 sheets wafer paper, cut into 30 rounds (3 inches/8 cm in diameter)

Preparation time **20 minutes**
Cooking time **15 minutes**
Level **easy**
Wine **Malvasia di Rapolla Dolce**

Preheat the oven to 400°F (200°C or Gas Mark 6). Beat the egg whites to stiff peaks and stir in 3 cups (12 ½ oz or 350 g) of confectioners' sugar, the almonds and cinnamon.

   Place spoonfuls of the mixture on top of the wafer-paper rounds and arrange them on a baking sheet. Sprinkle with the remaining confectioners' sugar and bake for about 15 minutes. Let cool, then remove the wafer-paper. The cookies will keep for a long time in an airtight container.

Taralli dolci con il miele
Honey Taralli

Serves 6-8

5 ½ tsps active dry yeast
16 cups (4 ½ lb or 2 kg) hard-wheat flour
10 eggs
3 Tbsps extra-virgin olive oil
1 cup (10 ⅓ oz or 300 g) honey
1 ⅔ cups (7 oz or 200 g) confectioners' sugar
1/2 cup (120 ml) water

Preparation time **30 minutes**
Cooking time **30 minutes**
Level **easy**
Wine **Moscato di Trani**

Dissolve the yeast in a little warm water. Mix with the flour and enough warm water to form a smooth dough. Cover and let rise for about 2 hours or until doubled in size. Mix in the eggs, olive oil and honey. Knead well then form into small ropes and close into doughnut shapes about 8 inches (20 cm) in diameter. Let rest in a warm place for 3 hours.

   Preheat the oven to 350°F (180°C or Gas Mark 4). There are two ways to cook the taralli. The first is to bake them on an oiled baking sheet until hard and golden for 30 minutes. Alternatively cook them in boiling water until almost done, then finish cooking them in the oven. Once cooked and cooled, prepare the glaze. Heat the confectioners' sugar in a saucepan with the water and bring to a boil. The glaze is ready when it forms threads when dripped from a spoon. Remove from the heat, transfer to a work surface and work with a spatula until white, then spread on the taralli.

Torta di ricotta
Lemon-Ricotta Cake

Serves 6

2 ⅓ cups plus 1 Tbsp (10 ½ oz or 300 g) all-purpose flour
3 egg yolks - 2 cups (14 oz or 400 g) sugar
14 Tbsps (7 oz or 200 g) butter, softened
grated zest of 2 organic lemons
1/4 cup (60 ml) Cognac - salt
1 lb (500 g) fresh ricotta - 3 eggs, separated
1/3 cup (2 oz or 50 g) chopped candied citron

Preparation time **20 minutes**
Cooking time **35 minutes**
Level **easy**
Wine **Moscato Dolce**

Sift the flour into a mound on a work surface. Make a well in the center and add the egg yolks, 3/4 cup (5 ½ oz or 150 g) of sugar, the softened butter, the grated zest of 1 lemon, Cognac and a pinch of salt. Mix to form a dough. Let rest for 1 hour.

Preheat the oven to 400°F (200°C or Gas Mark 6). Whisk together the ricotta, remaining 1 ¼ cups (9 oz or 250 g) of sugar and 3 egg yolks to form a soft cream. Beat the egg whites to stiff peaks and fold into the ricotta mixture with the citron and grated zest of 1 lemon.

Divide the dough into two pieces and roll them out. Use 1 piece to line a round cake pan. Pour in the ricotta filling and top with the remaining piece of dough. Poke holes in the top with a fork and bake for 35 minutes.

Torta di ricotta

Puglia

An enormous plateau, changing color with the seasons,

spread out between two seas. Ancient olive trees and whitewashed walls and an agricultural tradition par excellence: characterful *extra-virgin olive oil, flour* unique in hold and flavor, sensual *cheeses* like creamy *burrata* and bold ones like strong *Pecorinos. Fish* and *seafood, vegetables in oil,* peasant recipes that make the most of tasty delights like *lampascioni,* in a landscape dotted with ancient farmhouses and baroque churches.

PUGLIA
local products

Burrata

BURRATA IS ORIGINALLY FROM ANDRIA, IN THE PROVINCE OF BARI, but is now produced throughout the region, following its growing popularity in Italy and abroad. A full-fat cheese, it has an exterior shell of cooked, stretched curd, like a shiny, milky bag, filled with a mixture of the same curd, finely chopped, and fresh cream. Cow's milk is curdled at room temperature, using the natural starter whey from the previous day's cheesemaking. The curd is broken up with a curd knife made of beechwood or steel, reducing it to walnut-sized balls. After the whey settles, the mass is extracted by hand and left to mature for a few hours before being cut and pulled at a temperature of 185-195°F (85-90°C). The forming is always done by hand; the curd is modeled into spheres, filled with cream and the curd scraps (called *stracciatella*, little rags). The top is then tied off to close the sack.

Cartellate
e *Mostaccioli*

THESE UNUSUAL NAMES REFER TO
TWO TYPICAL SWEETS, closely linked
to Puglia's gastronomy. *Cartellate* are
a traditional Christmas and carnival
dessert. Little spirals of serrated
dough, they are flavored with honey,
wine and vin cotto (a syrupy liquid
made from figs). The leftover dough
scraps are used to make *porcedduzzi*
or *cicirieddi*, fried in sunflower oil and
mixed with whole almonds and honey.

Mostaccioli are known in both Puglia
and Basilicata, with small variations.
In Puglia they are made with flour, grated
orange zest, toasted almonds, cinnamon
and fig vin cotto. The dough is cut into
irregular shapes or diamonds, baked and
then glazed with sugar syrup or melted
chocolate. In Basilicata the mostaccioli
are more spiced, made using flour, almonds,
coffee, sugar, dark chocolate, cinnamon
and cloves.

Lampascioni

LAMPASCIONI ARE A TRUE DELICACY OF PUGLIAN CUISINE. The bulbs of *Muscari comosum*, a grape hyacinth which grows wild in uncultivated land, they resemble squat spring onions, with a pinkish-white flesh wrapped in a series of thin dark-brown papery layers. They can be eaten roasted, stewed or sautéed, but the best way to sample them is preserved in oil. Washed, trimmed of the external layers and boiled in a mixture of water and vinegar for a few minutes, the lampascioni are then lightly pressed for a day, arranged in glass jars and covered with extra-virgin olive oil, sometimes flavored with bay, mint, celery, spicy chili, parsley or garlic. The jars are then cooked in a double boiler and stored in a dark place.

Pitta

PITTA IS ONE OF THE MEDITERRANEAN'S MOST ANCIENT FLATBREADS. Its name comes from the same origins as pizza, but pitta has its flavorings inside instead of on the top. There are two versions: simple pitta with potatoes, and pitta with vegetables. The first has a dough made from flour and boiled potatoes, while the second is made from a pizza-like dough stuffed with minced onions, tomatoes, peppers, eggplant and other vegetables, and sometimes anchovies, sardines or fresh cheese.

Olio d'*oliva extravergine*

THERE ARE MANY DIFFERENT KINDS OF HIGH-QUALITY EXTRA-VIRGIN OLIVE OIL (*olio d'oliva extravergine*) made in Puglia, such as the DOP (Denomination of Protected Origin) Terra di Bari, from the province of Bari, which includes Castel del Monte, yellowish-green with a bitter, spicy flavor; Bitonto, the fruitiest; and Murgia dei Trulli and delle Grotte, with an almond fragrance. Collina di Brindisi is made from Ogliarola, Frantoio, Coratina and Leccino olives and has a lightly spicy, fruity aroma. It is a DOP for the Gargano and Alto and Basso

Tavoliere denominations. One of the oldest varieties, Terra d'Otranto, also a DOP, is excellent, made in the provinces of Lecce, Brindisi and Taranto. It has bright green hues and a fruity perfume, with a lightly bitter but pleasant and intense flavor.

Alici all'aceto
Marinated Anchovies

Serves 6

2 ¼ lb (1 kg) fresh anchovies
2 Tbsps all-purpose flour
salt
3/4 cup plus 1 Tbsp (200 ml) extra-virgin olive oil
2 onions, minced
1 garlic clove, minced
1 bunch of parsley, minced
1 bay leaf
2 cups (500 ml) vinegar

Preparation time **15 minutes**
Cooking time **25 minutes**
Level **easy**

Clean the anchovies, removing the heads, guts and bones. Dust them with flour. Heat 3/4 cup (180 ml) olive oil until very hot and fry the anchovies until golden. Drain and dry on paper towels. Sprinkle with salt and arrange in a container.

Heat the remaining tablespoon of olive oil in another frying pan and sauté the onion, garlic, parsley and bay leaf. As soon as the onion is golden add the vinegar. Simmer for about 10 minutes.

Pour the vinegar mixture over the anchovies and let sit for a few days. Drain from the marinade before serving.

Note *The anchovies can be served with slices of tomato and sautéed onions if desired.*

Focaccia pugliese
Puglian Focaccia

Serves 6-8

2 potatoes - salt
3 ½ tsps active dry yeast
4 cups (1 lb 2 oz or 500 g) all-purpose flour
4 Tbsps extra-virgin olive oil
1 Tbsp dried oregano
10 cherry tomatoes - 4 pitted green olives
3 Tbsps extra-virgin olive oil - coarse salt

Preparation time **30 minutes**
Cooking time **50 minutes**
Level **medium**
Wine **San Severo Bianco Spumante**

Boil the potatoes in salted water until tender, then drain, peel and mash with a potato ricer. Dissolve the yeast in a little warm water. Mound the flour on a work surface and make a well in the center.

Add the potatoes, yeast mixture, a pinch of salt and enough water to form a smooth dough. Mix to combine, adjusting flour and water if necessary, and when the dough comes together knead vigorously until smooth. Form the dough into a ball and make an X-shaped incision on the top. Cover and let rise for 2 hours, or until doubled in volume. Preheat the oven to 350°F (180°C or Gas Mark 4). Oil a baking sheet and spread the dough onto the sheet until it is about 2 ½-inches (6 cm) thick. Sprinkle over the oregano and place the cherry tomatoes and olives on top at regular intervals, pressing them into the dough. Drizzle the focaccia with olive oil and sprinkle over a few pinches of coarse salt. Bake for 30 minutes, until the top of the focaccia is golden-brown. Serve immediately.

Focaccia pugliese

Polpette di pane
Meatless Meatballs

Serves 4

1 loaf of stale crusty bread
(preferably baked in a wood-burning oven)
1 cup (250 ml) milk
4 Tbsps grated Pecorino cheese
1 garlic clove, minced
1 bunch of parsley, minced
1 egg
salt
4 Tbsps extra-virgin olive oil
1/2 onion, minced
5 Tbsps ready-made tomato sauce

Preparation time **30 minutes**
Cooking time **1 hour 10 minutes**
Level **easy**
Wine **Nardò Rosso**

Scoop out the soft crumb of the bread,
discarding the crusts. Chop into small pieces
and soak in the milk until soft. Drain, squeeze
out excess milk and transfer to a bowl. Add
the Pecorino, garlic, parsley, egg and a pinch
of salt. Stir well until thoroughly combined.

Form the mixture into small balls about
the size of a walnut. Heat 2 tablespoons of
olive oil in a frying pan and brown the bread
balls, turning frequently, until evenly browned.

Heat the remaining 2 tablespoons of olive oil
in another frying pan and sauté the onion until
soft. Add the tomato sauce and cook for a few
minutes, then add the bread balls and cook
for 1 hour. Serve hot.

Taralli pugliesi
Puglian Crackers

Serves 6-8

8 cups (2 lb 3 oz or 1 kg) all-purpose flour
1 ¼ cups (300 ml) dry white wine
1 cup (250 ml) extra-virgin olive oil,
plus extra for oiling
1 tsp salt

Preparation time **30 minutes**
Cooking time **45 minutes**
Level **easy**
Wine **Locorotondo Spumante**

Mound the flour on a work surface and
make a well in the center. Add the wine,
olive oil and salt and work vigorously to
obtain a smooth, uniform and elastic dough.
Cover with a clean kitchen towel and let rest
for 20 minutes. Preheat the oven to 400°F
(200°C or Gas Mark 6). Divide the dough
into portions and from each one form little
ropes about 1/2-inch (1 cm) in diameter
and 3-inches (8 cm) long. Form them into
rings by pressing the ends together.

Bring a large pot of salted water to a boil
and boil the taralli in batches. As soon as
they come to the surface, drain them with
a slotted spoon and dry on a clean kitchen
towel. Arrange the boiled taralli on a lightly
oiled baking sheet and bake for around
40 minutes, until golden.

Note *Taralli can also be flavored with onion,
fennel seeds or chili.*

Pepata di cozze
Mussels with Garlic and Pepper

Serves 4

2 ¼ lb (1 kg) mussels
3 Tbsps extra-virgin olive oil
3 garlic cloves, peeled
1 handful of cherry tomatoes, quartered
freshly ground black pepper

Preparation time **20 minutes**
Cooking time **10 minutes**
Level **easy**
Wine **San Severo Bianco**

Scrub the mussels under cold running water and debeard them. Heat the olive oil in a large frying pan and sauté the whole peeled garlic cloves until golden.

Add the tomatoes, cook for a few minutes, then add the mussels. Cook over high heat for 5 minutes, until the mussels have opened. Discard any which do not open. Sprinkle with black pepper. Serve hot.

Note *This is the Puglian version of a dish common around southern Italy. The tomato can be left out.*

Taralli pugliesi

Pepata di cozze

Orecchiette ai frutti di mare
Orecchiette with Seafood

Serves 4

14 oz (400 g) cuttlefish
1 ½ lb (700 g) mixed shellfish
(clams, mussels, cockles)
2 Tbsps extra-virgin olive oil
1 garlic clove, peeled and smashed
2 small tomatoes, chopped
14 oz (400 g) orecchiette
1 handful of arugula
salt

Preparation time **20 minutes**
Cooking time **30 minutes**
Level **medium**
Wine **Lizzano Bianco**

Clean the cuttlefish, washing them under cold running water, then cut them into pieces of about 1-inch (2 cm). Clean the shellfish and sauté in a frying pan over medium heat until they open. Strain the resulting liquid and remove the shells. Place the meat in a bowl and cover with the strained liquid.

Heat the olive oil in a large saucepan and brown the garlic, then add the tomatoes and cuttlefish. Continue cooking over high heat until the cuttlefish are cooked through, then add the shellfish and their liquid. Cook over high heat for about 5 minutes, then adjust the salt.

Bring a large pot of salted water to a boil and cook the orecchiette until al dente. Drain and toss in the pan with the sauce. Add the arugula and serve immediately.

Orecchiette alle cime di rapa
Orecchiette with Bitter Greens

Serves 4

2 ¼ lb (1 kg) bitter greens
(turnip tops or broccoli rabe)
10 ½ oz (300 g) orecchiette
4 Tbsps extra-virgin olive oil
2 garlic cloves, peeled and smashed
4 anchovy fillets in oil, drained
3 slices of stale crusty bread, crusts removed
1 chili pepper, sliced (optional)
salt

Preparation time **20 minutes**
Cooking time **30 minutes**
Level **easy**
Wine **Ostuni Bianco**

Wash the greens under cold running water and remove the hard stalks. Bring a large pot of salted water to a boil and add the greens and the orecchiette. While they cook, heat the olive oil in a frying pan and sauté the garlic until golden. Add the anchovies and stir until they dissolve.

Grate the bread and toast the crumbs under the broiler for a few minutes.

When the orecchiette are al dente, drain them with a slotted spoon directly into the pan with the garlic and anchovies. Mix together and add the toasted breadcrumbs. Serve immediately, sprinkled with chili if desired.

Tiella di riso, patate e cozze
Rice, Potato and Mussel Bake

Serves 4

2 ¼ lb (1 kg) mussels
5 Tbsps extra-virgin olive oil
1 garlic clove, minced
1 lb (500 g) potatoes, peeled and sliced
salt and pepper
1 bunch of parsley, minced
1 onion, minced
1 ½ cups (10 ½ oz or 300 g) Carnaroli rice

Preparation time **20 minutes**
Cooking time **1 hour**
Level **easy**
Wine **Castel del Monte Bianco**

Preheat the oven to 350°F (180°C or Gas Mark 4). Scrub the mussels under cold running water and debeard them. Heat 1 tablespoon of olive oil in large frying pan with the garlic. Add the mussels and cook over high heat until opened. Discard any that do not open.

Remove the shells and strain the cooking liquid. Line the bottom of an oiled baking dish with half the potato slices. Sprinkle with pepper, half the parsley and half the onions.

Cover with rice, add the mussels and top with the remaining potatoes, parsley and onion. Sprinkle with salt and pepper, drizzle with olive oil and pour over the strained mussel cooking liquid. Bake for about 45 minutes, adding water if the casserole becomes too dry.

Orecchiette con le cime di rapa

Tiella di riso, patate e cozze

cavatelli con i ceci
cavatelli with chickpeas

Serves 4

1 ½ cups (10 ½ oz or 300 g) dried chickpeas
1 bay leaf
1 garlic clove
2 Tbsps extra-virgin olive oil
1 onion, minced
1 dried red chili pepper
10 ½ oz (300 g) tomatoes, chopped
salt
3 cups plus 3 Tbsps (14 oz or 400 g) semolina flour

Preparation time **20 minutes**
Cooking time **60 minutes**
Level **easy**
Wine **Orta Nova Rosato**

Soak the chickpeas in cold water overnight. Drain and place in a saucepan with water, the bay leaf and garlic and simmer over medium heat for about 50 minutes, then drain.

Meanwhile heat the olive oil in a large frying pan and sauté the onion. Crumble in the chili and add the tomatoes. Cook over low heat for around 30 minutes, and adjust the salt.

Mix the semolina flour for the pasta with enough water and a pinch of salt to form a smooth dough. Roll the dough into small, hazelnut-sized balls, and form each one into a cavatello by rolling it on a work surface with a finger tip, forming a little cavity in the middle.

Boil the cavatelli in salted water. Drain and place in a bowl. Mix with the chickpeas and tomato sauce and serve immediately.

Traditional recipe

Polpette al sugo
Meatballs in Tomato Sauce

Serves 4

10 ½ oz (300 g) ground beef
3 Tbsps grated Pecorino cheese
3 Tbsps breadcrumbs
3 eggs
1 garlic clove, minced
1 bunch of parsley, minced
salt and pepper
3 Tbsps extra-virgin olive oil
1 onion, minced
1 lb (500 g) ripe tomatoes, pureed and strained
3 basil leaves

Preparation time **25 minutes**
Cooking time **30 minutes**
Level **easy**
Wine **Rosso Barletta**

In a bowl, mix together the ground beef, Pecorino, breadcrumbs, eggs, garlic and parsley. Add pinches of salt and pepper and stir well.

Form the mixture into balls about 2-inches (5 cm) in diameter. Heat the olive oil in a frying pan and sauté the onion until golden. Add the meatballs and brown, then add the tomatoes and basil. Adjust salt and pepper and cook, covered, for about 20 minutes.

Serve the meatballs hot or warm, depending on taste and the season.

Alici "arraganate"
Baked Anchovies

Serves 6

5 Tbsps salted capers
1 garlic clove
4-5 mint leaves
1 oregano sprig
2 ¼ lb (1 kg) fresh anchovies
1 ⅔ cups (7 oz or 200 g) breadcrumbs
3 Tbsps extra-virgin olive oil
1 Tbsp vinegar
salt

Preparation time **10 minutes**
Cooking time **20 minutes**
Level **easy**
Wine **Locorotondo Spumante**

Preheat the oven to 350°F (180°C or Gas Mark 4). Wash the capers under running water and dry. Mince them together with the garlic, mint leaves and oregano.

Remove the heads, guts and bones from the anchovies, wash under cold running water, pat dry and then layer them in a baking dish (preferably earthenware) interspersed with layers of breadcrumbs and the garlic-herb mixture. Drizzle with olive oil and sprinkle over the vinegar.

Bake for around 20 minutes, until the fish are cooked through. Serve hot or warm, adjusting salt if necessary.

Orata al forno con le olive
Roasted Bream with Olives

Serves 4

1 gilthead bream (about 1 ¾ lb or 800 g)
3 Tbsps extra-virgin olive oil
salt and pepper
2 Tbsps vinegar
3/4 cup (3 ½ oz or 100 g) black olives
5 cherry tomatoes, chopped

Preparation time **20 minutes**
Cooking time **25 minutes**
Level **medium**
Wine **Castel del Monte Bianco**

Preheat the oven to 350°F (180°C or Gas Mark 4). Carefully clean the bream, gutting and descaling the fish. Wash well under running water, then dry and cut in half horizontally.

Oil a baking dish with olive oil and place the fish in it. Season with salt and pepper inside and outside, and drizzle with olive oil and vinegar. Sprinkle over the olives and cherry tomatoes. Bake for about 25 minutes, then serve hot.

Note *Another typical Puglian recipe for bream involves roasting the fish with sliced potatoes, grated Pecorino cheese, and minced garlic and parsley.*

Alici "arraganate"

Orata al forno con le olive

Sgombri all'aceto
Marinated Mackerel

Serves 6

2 ¼ lb (1 kg) fresh mackerel
salt
vinegar
4 Tbsps extra-virgin olive oil
1 bunch of mint, minced
2 garlic cloves, minced

Preparation time **15 minutes**
Cooking time **10 minutes**
Level **easy**

Clean the mackerel and debone them, then wrap the fillets in a clean linen cloth and place them in a saucepan. Cover with water, add salt and bring to a boil. Boil for a few minutes, then remove the mackerel from the pan.

Let them drain and then place in a bowl, still wrapped in the cloth. Cover with vinegar and let marinate for about 1 hour.

Remove the mackerel from the cloth and arrange on a serving plate. Drizzle with olive oil and sprinkle over the mint and garlic.

Note *This recipe can also be used to preserve mackerel for several months, covered with olive oil in sterilized glass jars.*

Seppie ripiene
Stuffed Cuttlefish

Serves 4

3 ½ lb (1 ½ kg) cuttlefish
3 eggs
1 cup (3 ½ oz or 100 g) grated Pecorino cheese
1 ⅔ cup (7 oz or 200 g) breadcrumbs
1 bunch of parsley, minced
2 garlic cloves, minced
salt and pepper
1 tomato, diced
4 Tbsps extra-virgin olive oil
10 cherry tomatoes, quartered

Preparation time **15 minutes**
Cooking time **15 minutes**
Level **easy**
Wine **Ostuni Bianco**

Preheat the oven to 350°F (180°C or Gas Mark 4). Clean the cuttlefish, removing the eyes, ink sacs and hard parts, and wash well under running water. Beat the eggs in a large bowl and stir in the Pecorino, breadcrumbs, parsley and garlic. Mix well.

Use the mixture to fill the cuttlefish and lay them in an oiled baking dish. Sprinkle over pinches of salt and pepper and the diced tomato. Drizzle with the remaining olive oil.

Bake for about 15 minutes, then serve hot or cold according to taste, garnished with cherry tomatoes and parsley leaves.

Caponata pugliese
Puglian Caponata

Serves 4-6

3 Tbsps extra-virgin olive oil
1 large eggplant, diced
2 carrots, diced - 2 celery stalks, diced
1 large zucchini, diced
1 onion, minced
1 red bell pepper, diced
2 San Marzano or plum tomatoes, diced
1 Tbsp capers
1 red chili pepper, minced
1 Tbsp sugar - 1 Tbsp vinegar
salt - 5 mint leaves, torn
1 oregano sprig, leaves only

Preparation time **25 minutes**
Cooking time **50 minutes**
Level **easy**
Wine **Gioia del Colle Bianco**

Heat the olive oil in a frying pan until
very hot and sauté the eggplant, then add
the carrots, celery, zucchini and bell pepper.

Cook for a few minutes all together,
until the vegetables are browned and crisp,
stirring every so often and adding more
oil when necessary. Drain the vegetables
with a slotted spoon and set aside. Add the
onion to the same pan and sauté, then add
the tomatoes, capers and chili, then all the
sautéed vegetables. Add the sugar, vinegar,
a pinch of salt and the mint.

Let cook for a few minutes, then transfer
to a bowl. Sprinkle with oregano and cool
before serving.

Seppie ripiene

Caponata pugliese

Pastatelle
Mini Cherry Pies

Serves 6-8

1 ½ cups (1 lb or 500 g) cherry jam
1 cup (3 ½ oz or 100 g) finely chopped walnuts
grated zest of 1 organic orange
1 tsp ground cinnamon
2 ¼ lb (1 kg) shortcrust dough
all-purpose flour for flouring
1 Tbsp sugar

Preparation time **30 minutes**
Cooking time **30 minutes**
Level **easy**
Wine **Primitivo di Manduria Liquoroso**

Preheat the oven to 350°F (180°C or Gas Mark 4). Mix together the jam, walnuts, orange zest and cinnamon in a mixing bowl.

Divide the pastry dough into smaller portions. Roll the portions out with a rolling pin on a floured work surface. Using a cookie cutter, cut out disks about 3 inches (8 cm) in diameter.

Place a spoonful of the jam mixture in the center of each disk, then fold over into a half-moon. Press well around the edges to seal. Arrange them on a baking sheet lined with parchment paper and sprinkle with sugar. Bake for about 30 minutes. Serve warm.

Cartellate
Honey Fritters

Serves 6-8

3/4 cup plus 1 Tbsp (200 ml) white wine
1 tsp salt
2 cups (500 ml) warm water
8 cups (2 lb 3 oz or 1 kg) all-purpose flour
1 ¾ cups (400 ml) extra-virgin olive oil
1/2 cup plus 1 Tbsp (70 g or 2 ½ oz) confectioners' sugar
1 Tbsp ground cinnamon
sunflower oil for frying
honey

Preparation time **20 minutes**
Cooking time **30 minutes**
Level **medium**
Wine **Moscato di Trani**

Heat the white wine until almost boiling. Mix the salt into the warm water. Mound the flour on a work surface and make a hollow in the middle. Pour in the hot wine and olive oil.

Add the salted water and mix to form a smooth, uniform dough. Divide the dough into smaller balls and roll out with a rolling pin. Cut them into strips about 1 ½-inches (3-4 cm) wide, preferably with a fluted rolling cutter. Fold the strips in half and bring the edges together, then roll them up on themselves into a spiral. Lay them out to dry for about 6 hours. Mix together the confectioners' sugar and cinnamon. Heat the sunflower oil until very hot and fry the spirals until golden, in batches if necessary. Drain with a slotted spoon and dry on paper towels. Dip them in the honey. Dust with the confectioners' sugar and cinnamon.

Mostaccioli
Chocolate-Almond Cookies

Serves 6-8

2 ⅔ cups (14 oz or 400 g) blanched almonds
2 oz (50 g) dark chocolate
8 cups (2 lb 3 oz or 1 kg) all-purpose flour
1 ¼ cups (3 ½ oz or 100 g) cocoa powder
1/2 cup (3 ½ oz or 100 g) lard
or shortening, softened
4 cups (1 l) fig vin cotto
2 ½ cups (1 lb 2 oz or 500 g) sugar
2 tsps baking powder
1 pat of butter

Preparation time **25 minutes**
Cooking time **20 minutes**
Level **easy**
Wine **Gioia del Colle Aleatico**

Preheat the oven to 350°F (180°C or Gas Mark 4). Toast the almonds in the oven for 10 minutes. Let cool and chop coarsely. Melt the chocolate over a double boiler or in the microwave.

   Place the flour in a large mixing bowl and add the almonds, cocoa powder, melted chocolate, softened lard, vin cotto, sugar and baking powder. Mix to form a smooth dough.

   Form the dough into small irregular balls and place on a buttered baking sheet. Bake for 20 minutes.

Cartellate

Mostaccioli

Calabria

A land with a complicated history

and a cuisine rich in flavor and ingenuity, spicy with omnipresent *chili pepper*, based on *fish* and the skilful preparation of *preserves* and *cured meats*. Cooking based on the fruits of the earth and the sea, and a culinary tradition that knows how to turn even a simple vegetable like the *Tropea onion* into a delicacy.

CALABRIA
local products

Peperoncino rosso
di Calabria

IT'S SAID THAT CALABRIA IS THE ITALIAN REGION WITH THE SPICIEST FOOD, and in fact there are many varieties of chili peppers (*peperoncini*) used to flavor local dishes and products. The use of chili is a legacy from the days before refrigeration, when vegetables like eggplants, mushrooms, olives and tomatoes were preserved with the help of chili, guaranteeing a food source during the famines that would frequently hit the mountainous areas.

Cipolla di *Tropea*

AN UNUSUAL VEGETABLE WHICH IS SYMBOLIC OF A LONGSTANDING FARMING TRADITION, Tropea onions (*cipolle*) have purplish-red skin and white flesh, but their most distinctive characteristic is their intense sweetness, which makes them adaptable to many different dishes and excellent in salads.

Olio *calabrese*

MANY OF CALABRIA'S EXCELLENT OLIVE OILS are protected by a DOP (Denomination of Protected Origin). Varieties include Colli di Tropea, Savuto, Locride, Conca degli Ulivi, Calabria, Lametia, Alto Crotonese and Bruzio: oils with bright green hues, natural perfumes and marked flavors.

Ricotta di *Calabria*

CALABRIAN RICOTTA, MADE FROM SHEEP'S, GOAT'S OR COW'S MILK, is shaped into truncated cones. Soft and white, it has a delicate taste when fresh, but can then be baked or smoked to give it a more intense flavor. Fresh salted ricotta (ricotta salata) is cylindrical, with a pinkish exterior and white interior, lightly salted and slightly smoky. The production involves smoking over chestnut wood, which can make the ricotta hard enough to grate. Baked ricotta, with a brown rind and a firm, white paste, is cooked in the oven at 400°F (200°C).

Sardella

ALSO KNOWN AS MUSTICA, NOVELLAME OR ROSMARINA, sardella was considered "the caviar of the poor" in Calabria. A typical preparation from the Ionian coast, it is made of preserved new-born anchovies and sardines. As soon as the tiny fish are caught, they are washed and laid out to dry in the sun. They are sprinkled with ground chili pepper and salt and left to dry for about two days so that they expel any excess salt. The mixture is then left to mature in large glass tubs. The product spoils easily, and once bought it should be refrigerated and consumed within a few days of opening.

Insalata di stocco
Salt Cod Salad

Serves 4-6

2 ¼ lb (1 kg) Mammola salt cod, pre-soaked
6 Tbsps extra-virgin olive oil
3/4 cup (3 ½ oz or 100 g) black olives, pitted
1 garlic clove, minced
juice of 1/2 lemon
1 chili pepper, minced
1/2 bunch of parsley, minced

Preparation time **10 minutes**
Cooking time **5 minutes**
Level **easy**
Wine **Melissa Bianco**

Blanch the salt cod for a few minutes, then crumble into smaller pieces. Let cool slightly, then toss with the olive oil, olives, garlic, lemon juice, chili and parsley.

Serve at room temperature.

Note *Mammola salt cod is from the town of the same name in the province of Reggio Calabria. This dish can be served as an appetizer or a main course.*

Crostini rossi piccanti
Spicy Crostini

Serves 4

3 Tbsps extra-virgin olive oil
1 red chili pepper, minced
2 garlic cloves, peeled
1 cup (7 oz or 200 g) peeled plum tomatoes
1 pinch of dried oregano
salt and pepper
1/2 loaf of crusty bread

Preparation time **10 minutes**
Cooking time **10 minutes**
Level **easy**
Wine **Melissa Bianco**

Heat the olive oil in a frying pan with the chili and garlic. Add the tomatoes and chop them with a knife in the pan.

Add the oregano and adjust salt and pepper to taste. Cook until reduced and thickened.

Meanwhile cut the bread into thick slices and toast in a non-stick frying pan or under the broiler. Let the sauce cool then spread over the hot toast. Serve immediately.

Crostini rossi piccanti

Cannaruozzi 'ncipuddrati
Ditalini with Tomato-Onion Sauce

Serves 4-6

3 Tbsps extra-virgin olive oil
1 lb (500 g) Tropea onions or other sweet red onions, thinly sliced
1 ½ cups (10 ½ oz or 300 g) peeled plum tomatoes, chopped
salt
1 chili pepper, minced
1 lb (500 g) ditalini or other small, short pasta
5 Tbsps grated ricotta salata

Preparation time **20 minutes**
Cooking time **30 minutes**
Level **easy**
Wine **Pollino**

Heat 2 tablespoons of olive oil in a large saucepan and add the onions. Sauté gently, adding a little water to stop them turning brown. Continue cooking until very soft.

Heat 1 tablespoon of olive oil in a large frying pan and add the tomatoes and salt. Cook until the tomatoes break up and the sauce thickens. Transfer the tomato sauce to the onions, add the chili and stir well.

Bring a large pot of salted water to a boil and cook the pasta until al dente. Drain and toss with tomato and onion sauce. Serve immediately, sprinkled with ricotta salata.

Tagliatelle alla reggina
Reggio Calabrian-Style Tagliatelle

Serves 4

2 sweet bell peppers
2 Tbsps extra-virgin olive oil
2 garlic cloves, minced
1 onion, minced
1 large zucchini, diced
salt and pepper
2 Tbsps ready-made tomato sauce
14 oz (400 g) tagliatelle
3 basil leaves, torn into pieces
4 Tbsps grated Pecorino cheese

Preparation time **20 minutes**
Cooking time **30 minutes**
Level **easy**
Wine **Donna Camilla Rosato**

Roast the peppers over an open flame then close in a plastic bag to steam. Peel, deseed and cut into thin strips.

Heat the olive oil in a saucepan and sauté the garlic and onion until soft. Add the pepper strips and zucchini. Season with salt and pepper and add the tomato sauce. Cook over low heat to obtain a thick sauce.

Bring a large pot of salted water to a boil and cook the tagliatelle until al dente. Drain and toss in the pan with the sauce. Add the basil and sprinkle with grated Pecorino. Serve immediately.

Fusilli al gusto di cedro
Fusilli with Mushrooms and Lemon

Serves 4

3 Tbsps extra-virgin olive oil
1 lb (500 g) mushrooms, sliced
salt and pepper
4 Tbsps minced parsley
grated zest and juice of 1 organic
citron or lemon
10 ½ oz (300 g) fusilli

Preparation time **10 minutes**
Cooking time **20 minutes**
Level **easy**
Wine **Cirò Bianco**

Heat 2 tablespoons of olive oil in a frying
pan and sauté the mushrooms over high
heat until cooked through. Remove from
the heat, season with salt and pepper and
sprinkle with parsley. Add half the citron
or lemon juice.

Bring a large pot of salted water to a boil
and cook the fusilli until al dente. Drain
and toss in the pan with the mushrooms.

Stir in the remaining tablespoon of olive
oil, remaining citron or lemon juice, the zest
and pepper. Serve immediately.

Fusilli al gusto di cedro

Spaghetti al nero di seppia
Squid-Ink Spaghetti

Serves 4

2 cuttlefish (about 5 ½ oz or 150 g each)
3 Tbsps extra-virgin olive oil
2 garlic cloves, minced
1 red chili pepper, minced
1 bunch of parsley, minced
3 small tomatoes, sliced
14 oz (400 g) spaghetti
salt

Preparation time **15 minutes**
Cooking time **25 minutes**
Level **easy**
Wine **Melissa Bianco**

Clean the cuttlefish, detaching the ink sac and reserving it. Slice the cuttlefish into thin strips with a sharp knife, wash them and pat dry.

Heat the olive oil in a frying pan and sauté the garlic, chili and half the parsley. Add the cuttlefish, then a few minutes later add the tomatoes and salt. Cover and cook over moderate heat for 15 minutes adding the squid ink halfway through.

Bring a large pot of salted water to a boil and cook the spaghetti until al dente. Drain and toss in the pan with the sauce. Sprinkle with parsley and serve hot.

Polpette di ricotta in brodo
Ricotta Dumplings in Broth

Serves 4

14 oz (400 g) fresh sheep's milk ricotta
5 ½ oz (150 g) bread with crusts removed, finely chopped
2 eggs
4 Tbsps minced parsley
salt and pepper
all-purpose flour (optional)
6 cups (1 ½ l) beef broth

Preparation time **20 minutes**
Cooking time **20 minutes**
Level **easy**
Wine **Melissa Bianco**

Pass the ricotta through a food mill into a bowl, then add the bread, eggs, 2 tablespoons of parsley, salt and pepper.

Mix well until smooth and quite firm, adding flour if necessary. Form the mixture into balls about the size of a walnut. Bring the broth to a boil and add the balls.

Cook for a few minutes, then serve hot, sprinkled with parsley.

Note *A more substantial version of this recipe involves adding ground meat (ham, sausage or pork) or grated cheese to the dumpling mixture.*

Zuppa di cipolle rosse
Red-Onion Soup

Serves 4

2 ¼ lb (1 kg) Tropea onions
or other sweet red onions, thinly sliced
4 cups (1 l) beef broth
1 Tbsp all-purpose flour
6 extra-virgin olive oil
salt
4 thick slices of day-old crusty bread
4 Tbsps grated Parmesan cheese (optional)

Preparation time **15 minutes**
Cooking time **30 minutes**
Level **easy**
Wine **Scavigna Bianco**

Wash the sliced onions under cold running water, then dry. Bring the broth to a boil in a saucepan. Toast the flour in a frying pan for a couple of minutes.

Heat the olive oil in a large saucepan and add the onions. Sauté until golden, then add the toasted flour. Stir, continue cooking for a few minutes, then add the hot broth. Simmer until the soup becomes thick and smooth. Adjust salt and continue cooking for a few more minutes.

Toast the bread under the broiler or in a frying pan. Place 1 slice in each soup bowl, then top with soup. If desired, sprinkle with Parmesan before serving.

Note *This is a traditional recipe from Capo Vaticano, a seaside village in the province of Vibo Valentia.*

Polpette di ricotta in brodo

Zuppa di cipolle rosse

bucatini con lo stocco
bucatini with spicy salt cod

Serves 4

2 Tbsps extra-virgin olive oil
1 onion, minced
1 garlic clove, minced
2 ¼ lb (1 kg) Mammola salt cod, pre-soaked and chopped
salt
1 lb (500 g) peeled plum tomatoes, chopped
1 red chili pepper, minced
14 oz (400 g) bucatini
4 Tbsps minced parsley

Preparation time **25 minutes**
Cooking time **30 minutes**
Level **easy**
Wine **Mantonico di Calabria**

Heat the olive oil in a saucepan and sauté the onion and garlic until soft. Add the salt cod and season with salt to taste. Cook for a few minutes, then remove the salt cod and set aside.

Add the tomatoes and chili and cook until thickened, then return the salt cod to the pan and continue cooking.

Bring a large pot of lightly salted water to a boil and cook the bucatini until al dente. Drain and toss in the saucepan with the sauce. Sprinkle with parsley and serve hot.

Stoccafisso con patate
Salt Cod with Potatoes

Serves 4

2 Tbsps extra-virgin olive oil
2 onions, thinly sliced
3 peeled plum tomatoes, chopped
4 Tbsps minced parsley - salt
2 large potatoes, peeled and cut into wedges
1 lb (500 g) pre-soaked salt cod
3 Tbsps raisins
3 Tbsps black olives
4 basil leaves, torn into pieces
1 chili pepper, minced

Preparation time **20 minutes**
Cooking time **50 minutes**
Level **easy**
Wine **Bianco di Enotria**

Preheat the oven to 350°F (180°C or Gas Mark 4). Heat the olive oil in a frying pan and sauté the onions until soft. Add the tomatoes and parsley and cook over medium heat until the sauce is thick.

Bring a pot of lightly salted water to a boil and blanch the potato wedges for 5 minutes, then drain and let dry. Boil the salt cod in lightly salted water for 10 minutes, then drain with a slotted spoon, dry and cut into pieces.

Soak the raisins in warm water until soft, then drain and squeeze out excess liquid. Spread half the tomato sauce on the bottom of a baking dish and cover with the potatoes. Top with the salt cod, then spread over the remaining tomato sauce. Sprinkle with olives, basil, raisins and chili. Bake for 40 minutes and serve hot.

Tortiera di pesce spada
Roast Swordfish Fillets

Serves 4

1 ¾ lb (800 g) swordfish fillets
salt
1 pinch of ground chili pepper
2 garlic cloves, minced
6 Tbsps extra-virgin olive oil

Preparation time **10 minutes**
Cooking time **30 minutes**
Level **easy**
Wine **Cirò Bianco**

Preheat the oven to 375°F (190°C or Gas Mark 5). Remove the skin and any bones from the swordfish. Slice and lay the slices in a baking dish.

Sprinkle over salt, the chili and garlic and drizzle with the olive oil.

Bake until golden. Serve immediately.

Note *Variations on this recipe call for capers in brine or diced tomatoes. In the swordfish recipe all'uso di Bagnara, Bagnara-style, the fish is steamed and seasoned with capers, parsley and oregano.*

Tortiera di pesce spada

Pizza al salamino piccante
Pizza with Spicy Salami

Serves 4-6

1 ½ tsps active dry yeast
3/4 cup plus 1 Tbsp (200 ml) warm water
1 tsp sugar
6 Tbsps extra-virgin olive oil
4 cups (1 lb 2 oz or 500 g) all-purpose flour
2 cups (14 oz or 400 g) tomato passata
(pureed tomatoes)
9 oz (250 g) mozzarella, diced
5 ½ oz (150 g) spicy salami, sliced
1 pinch of dried oregano
salt

Preparation time **15 minutes**
Cooking time **30 minutes**
Level **easy**
Beer **Italian Lager**

Dissolve the yeast in the warm water.
Add the sugar, salt and 3 tablespoons of
extra-virgin olive oil. Stir energetically
and pour over the flour. Mix well to form
a dough, then cover and let rise for 2 hours,
then knead again and let rise for another hour.

Preheat the oven to 425°F (220°C or Gas
Mark 7). Oil a baking sheet and press the
dough out on it. Cover with the tomato
passata and bake for 10 minutes.

Remove from the oven and sprinkle over
the mozzarella and salami. Sprinkle over
the oregano and a pinch of salt and drizzle
with olive oil. Return to the oven for
another 20 minutes. Serve hot.

Tonno alla calabrese
Calabrian-Style Tuna

Serves 4

1 ¾ lb (800 g) tuna in 1 piece
2 anchovy fillets, sliced
1 garlic clove, chopped
3 Tbsps extra-virgin olive oil
1 pat of butter
1 onion, minced
2 celery stalks, minced
1 carrot, minced
1 ½ oz (40 g) pancetta, diced
2 ½ cups (9 oz or 250 g) Caesar's mushrooms
or other wild mushrooms, sliced
1/2 cup (120 ml) white wine
salt and pepper
2 Tbsps minced parsley (optional)

Preparation time **15 minutes**
Cooking time **40 minutes**
Level **easy**
Wine **Melissa Bianco**

Wash the tuna. Cut small slits into the surface
and fill with pieces of anchovy and garlic.

Heat the olive oil and butter in a frying pan
and sauté the onion, celery and carrot until soft.
Add the pancetta and mushrooms. Brown for
10 minutes, then add the tuna. Cook for
15 minutes, then add the wine and let reduce.

Add a little water, adjust salt and pepper and
cook for 30 minutes over low heat.

Serve the tuna in slices with the mushrooms,
sprinkled with parsley if desired.

Morzeddu
Tripe and Onion Soup

Serves 4

1 lb (500 g) pre-cooked veal tripe
salt
1 Tbsp lard
1 lb (500 g) pearl onions, sliced
4 slices of stale crusty bread
2 hot red chili peppers, halved
7 Tbsps grated Pecorino cheese

Preparation time **15 minutes**
Cooking time **1 hour 10 minutes**
Level **easy**
Wine **Melissa Rosso**

Boil the tripe in boiling salted water for
10 minutes, drain and cut into thin strips.

Melt the lard in a frying pan and add the
onions. Sauté until golden, then add the tripe
and salt. Cover with water and cook, covered,
for 1 hour, adding extra water if necessary.

Toast the bread in a non-stick frying pan
or under the broiler, then rub with the chili
pepper halves. Place a slice of bread in each
soup bowl. Thinly slice the chili.

Pour the tripe soup over the bread and top
with grated Pecorino cheese and sliced chili.
Serve hot.

Note *This filling soup is often served as
an appetizer.*

Tonno alla calabrese

Morzeddu

Ciambelline 'ngiloppate
Glazed Ring Cookies

Serves 8-10

20 egg yolks
grated zest of 1 organic lemon
1/4 cup (60 ml) Strega liqueur
2 tsps vanilla extract
3/4 cup plus 1 Tbsp (200 ml)
extra-virgin olive oil
4 egg whites
salt - all-purpose flour
2 ½ cups (1 lb 3 oz or 500 g) sugar
3/4 cup plus 1 Tbsp (200 ml) water

Preparation time **40 minutes**
Cooking time **25 minutes**
Level **medium**
Wine **Greco di Bianco**

Preheat the oven to 325°F (170°C or Gas Mark 3). Beat the egg yolks and beat in the lemon zest, liqueur, vanilla and olive oil, mixing well until creamy. Beat the egg whites with a pinch of salt to soft peaks, then fold into the yolk mixture.

Sprinkle in the flour, mixing constantly, adding enough to make a firm dough, and knead 15 minutes until smooth and elastic. Break off small pieces and form them into small doughnuts around a finger. Make a cut on the top surface and place on an oiled baking sheet. Bake for 25 minutes, taking care not to let them become too brown.

Meanwhile make the glaze by cooking the sugar and water together to 250°F (121°C). When the cookies are warm, dip them in the syrup and lay on a wire rack. Serve when the glaze is dry.

Bucconotti alla calabrese
Calabrian Jam Pies

Serves 8-10

8 cups (2 lb 3 oz or 1 kg) all-purpose flour
1 ¾ cups (12 ½ oz or 350 g) sugar
4 tsps baking powder
2 tsps vanilla extract
2 ½ sticks plus 1 Tbsp (10 ½ oz or 300 g) butter, softened
8 eggs
grated zest of 1 organic lemon
3/4 cup (9 oz or 250 g) grape (or other fruit) jam
confectioners' sugar

Preparation time **30 minutes**
Cooking time **40 minutes**
Level **easy**
Wine **Vernaccia di Serrapetrona Dolce**

In a large mixing bowl, mix together the flour, sugar, baking powder, vanilla, softened butter, eggs and lemon zest. Mix quickly to form a smooth, uniform dough.

Butter individual molds and place a piece of dough in each one, make a cavity in the middle and fill with jam. Cover the molds with another piece of dough and press into the shape of the mold. Unmold, place on a buttered baking sheet and bake until golden.

Serve cooled, sprinkled with confectioners' sugar.

Cannariculi tradizionali
Honeyed Fritters

Serves 6

3/4 cup (180 ml) white wine
3/4 cup (180 ml) extra-virgin olive oil
1/2 cup (120 ml) water
1 tsp ground cinnamon
1 tsp vanilla extract
1 tsp ground cloves
grated zest of 1 organic orange
all-purpose flour
lard for frying
sunflower oil for frying
2 Tbsps honey
colored sprinkles

Preparation time **40 minutes**
Cooking time **20 minutes**
Level **medium**
Wine **Mantonico di Calabria**

Place the wine, olive oil and water in
a saucepan and bring to a boil. Transfer to
a bowl and let cool. Stir in the cinnamon,
vanilla, cloves and grated orange zest.

Stir with a wooden spoon and sprinkle in
flour, stirring constantly, until it forms a thick
dough. Cover with a kitchen cloth and
let rest for 30 minutes.

Break off pieces of the dough and form into
finger-length ropes. Cut into pieces about
1-inch (2 cm) long. Heat equal amounts
of lard and sunflower oil until very hot and
fry the dough pieces. In a separate saucepan
heat the honey and add the fritters. Stir well.
Serve decorated with colored sprinkles.

Bucconotti alla calabrese

Cannariculi tradizionali

Crostata al limone
Lemon Cream Tart

Serves 6

Crust

4 ¾ cups plus 1 Tbsp (1 lb 5 oz or 600 g) all-purpose flour

2 ¼ cups (9 oz or 250 g) sugar

3 eggs

11 Tbsps (5 ½ oz or 150 g) butter, softened

1 tsp baking powder

1 tsp vanilla extract

Lemon Cream

3 organic lemons

1 Tbsp cornstarch

3/4 cup plus 1 Tbsp (3 ½ oz or 100 g) all-purpose flour

2 cups (500 ml) water

1 cup (7 oz or 200 g) sugar

1 tsp vanilla extract

2 eggs

4 Tbsps (2 oz or 50 g) butter

Preparation time **40 minutes**
Cooking time **40 minutes**
Level **medium**
Wine **Mantonico di Calabria**

Pour the flour onto a work surface and make a well in the center. Break the eggs into the center. Add the sugar, softened butter, baking powder and vanilla extract. Mix to form a smooth and compact dough. Cover with a damp towel and refrigerate for at least 30 minutes.

Preheat the oven to 350°F (180°C or Gas Mark 4). Zest the lemons and then juice them. In a mixing bowl stir together the cornstarch and flour for the cream and slowly pour in the water, stirring constantly with a wooden spoon. Add the sugar and vanilla extract. Beat the eggs separately and then add them to the batter along with the lemon juice and zest. Mix well and transfer the batter to a saucepan. Bring to a simmer over low heat and cook, stirring constantly, until the cream thickens. Remove from heat, stir in the butter and cover.

Remove the pastry from the refrigerator and knead briefly. Roll three-quarters of the dough into an even sheet and use it to line a buttered tart tin. Fill the tart with the lemon cream.

Use the remaining dough to make a lattice to decorate the top of the tart. Bake until the lattice is golden-brown and cool before serving.

Sicily

One large island surrounded by many small ones, scattered

in the Mediterranean's bluest water.
A cultural and historical heritage among the
richest in Italy, from the Greek amphitheaters
to the splendid baroque churches to the
most graceful expressions of Art Deco. In the
kitchen, Arabic and Spanish influences melt
into a rich variety of flavors. Many specialties,
*sweet and table wines, citrus, capers,
almonds, cured meats, cheeses, preserved
fish* and excellent *desserts*.

SICILY
local products

Capperi

THE FLOWERS AND FRUIT OF THE CAPER PLANT are eaten everywhere in Sicily, and those from Salina and Pantelleria are particularly prized. The caper plant is a low, branching shrub, whose white flowers have striking reddish-violet stamens. It is the buds of these flowers that are commonly consumed as capers (*capperi*), thanks to their aromatic qualities. The buds are usually preserved in salt or brined in vinegar, while the fruits are preserved in oil. Known as *cucunci*, the fruits are long, green berries with a pinkish flesh full of black seeds. They have a more delicate flavor than the buds and are used mainly in the cooking of the Aeolian islands, to flavor fish dishes or season preserved vegetables.

Pomodoro di Pachino

WITH AN INTENSELY VEGETAL PERFUME AND A DENSE, FLAVORFUL FLESH, this tomato is of the highest quality and has even earned IGP (Indication of Protected Origin) status. Pachino is the name of the town in the province of Syracuse where various kinds of tomatoes (*pomodori*) are grown: smooth, round, ribbed, red and green. But the best known is the spherical small cherry tomato. Omnipresent in local cooking, it can be found in salads, in simple and flavorful sauces, and on top of pizzas.

Agrumi e *Arancia rossa* di Sicilia

CITRUS (AGRUMI) CULTIVATION HAS A LONG TRADITION IN SICILY and is deeply rooted in the island's landscape and cuisine, to the point of becoming one of the most representative symbols of the region. Oranges and lemons have found their natural habitat here, thanks to the ideal terrain and climate. Sicily's blood orange (*arancia rossa*), which the EU has granted IGP (Indication of Protected Origin) recognition, includes the Tarocco, Moro and Sanguinello varieties, grown in the provinces of Ragusa, Syracuse, Enna and Catania. The rind is reddish-orange, the fragrance intense and the taste sweet, with a final acidic note. The oranges can be found between late autumn and spring.

Passito di *Pantelleria* e *Malvasia* delle Lipari

MOSCATO PASSITO DI PANTELLERIA DOC (DENOMINATION OF CONTROLLED ORIGIN) IS A WINE OF THE HIGHEST QUALITY, of great nobility and with an intense flavor. The full-bodied wine has an amber color and a delicate but persistent bouquet. On the palate it is pleasantly sweet and lightly aromatic. Produced from locally grown, raisined Zibibbo grapes, the wine is excellent sipped on its own or paired with typical Sicilian desserts like cream-filled pastries, cookies, cakes and fruit tarts. Another world-famous sweet Sicilian wine is Malvasia delle Lipari DOC, made from Malvasia grapes. Very aromatic, it has a full, sweet taste with floral, honeyed notes. Served chilled, at 46-50°F (8-10°C), it pairs well with cookies but is also worthy of consideration on its own at the end of a meal.

Nero d'Avola

STRUCTURED, POWERFUL, INTENSE AND HARMONIOUSLY BALANCED: This is Nero d'Avola, the prince of Sicilian wines, made exclusively from the black grapes of the same name. It is also known as Calabrese, suggesting origins off the island in the mainland region of Calabria. However the name probably arises out of a misunderstanding, from the mistranslation into Italian of the Sicilian dialect word *calaurisi*, a union of *calea* (grape) and *aulisi* (Avola, in the province of Syracuse). The area around Syracuse is the best known for cultivation of this grape, but it is also grown in the center of the island and along the northern coast. The Nero d'Avola produced in the west of Sicily has a different character than that from the east—the former heavier and with a violent impact on the palate, the latter more refined. The bouquet has floral notes of violets and fruity notes of cherry, blackberry, blackcurrant, raspberry and dried fruit, with chocolate hints. The wine is best paired with meat-based main courses and aged cheeses.

Sfinciuni
Tomato and Anchovy Breads

Serves 4-6

2 lb (900 g) prepared bread dough
1/2 cup (120 ml) extra-virgin olive oil
1 lb (500 g) tomatoes
1 onion, sliced
salt
12 salted anchovies
3 ½ oz (100 g) Ragusano
or Provolone cheese, grated
8 Tbsps breadcrumbs

Preparation time **15 minutes**
Cooking time **40 minutes**
Level **easy**
Wine **Inzolia**

Preheat the oven to 425°F (220°C or Gas
Mark 7). Knead the bread dough with
3 tablespoons of olive oil. Blanch the
tomatoes, peel, deseed and coarsely chop.

Heat 2 tablespoons of olive oil in a frying
pan and sauté the onion for 8 minutes over
low heat. Add the tomatoes, season with salt
and cook for 10 minutes. Rinse the anchovies
under running water to remove the salt.
Dry, debone and mince, then add to the
tomatoes together with the grated cheese.

Divide the bread dough into 4 parts. Roll
each part out to a thickness of 1-inch (3 cm)
and lay them out on baking sheets, oiled
with 1 tablespoon of olive oil.

Divide the tomato mixture between each
one, top with breadcrumbs and the remaining
oil and bake for 20 minutes or until
the dough is cooked through. Serve hot.

Arancini con carne e piselli
Rice Balls with Beef and Peas

Serves 4-6

2 Tbsps extra-virgin olive oil
1 celery stalk, minced
1 bunch of parsley, minced
1/2 onion, minced
14 oz (400 g) ground beef
salt and pepper
3 cups (14 oz or 400 g) peas
1 lb (500 g) San Marzano or plum tomatoes, peeled
2 ½ cups (1 lb or 500 g) Carnaroli rice
5 Tbsps grated Pecorino cheese
2 eggs, beaten
3 Tbsps breadcrumbs
sunflower oil for frying

Preparation time **30 minutes**
Cooking time **1 hour 20 minutes**
Level **medium**
Wine **Etna Rosso**

Heat the olive oil in a saucepan and sauté
the celery, parsley and onion. Add the beef
and season with salt and pepper. Brown for
10 minutes, then add the peas and tomatoes
and continue cooking over low heat, adding
water if necessary, for about 1 hour.

Boil the rice until al dente, then stir in the
Pecorino and let sit for 5 minutes. Form the
rice into orange-sized balls, make a cavity in
the middle and fill with the beef and pea sauce,
then reclose and dip in the beaten egg and then
roll in the breadcrumbs. Heat the sunflower oil
until very hot and fry the rice balls, in batches
if necessary. Remove from the oil when golden-
brown and dry on paper towels. Serve hot.

Pomodori secchi all'olio
Sun-Dried Tomatoes in Oil

Serves 4

8 tomatoes, halved
grated Pecorino cheese
oregano sprigs
basil leaves
extra-virgin olive oil
salt and pepper

Preparation time **30 minutes**
Level **easy**

Sprinkle the tomatoes with salt, then
lay on a wire rack with the cut side down
to drain for 3 hours. Arrange them on
a table or work surface and let dry for 3 days.

Divide the tomatoes between glass jars,
forming a layer of olive oil, then tomatoes,
oregano, Pecorino, basil, salt, pepper and
finishing with more oil.

Continue until the ingredients are used up,
then close the jars (not hermetically), cover
with paper and set aside for at least 10 days
before eating.

Note *Sun-dried tomatoes in oil are excellent
for preparing* cappoliato, *a spread made from
grinding up the drained tomatoes after they
have marinated for a month. It's delicious
on fresh crusty bread.*

Arancini con carne e piselli

Pomodori secchi all'olio

Pasta alla norma
Pasta with Eggplant

Serves 4-6

3 eggplants, diced
salt and pepper
2 ¼ lb (1 kg) ripe tomatoes
3 Tbsps extra-virgin olive oil
2 garlic cloves, minced
1 onion, minced
1 tsp sugar
6 basil leaves, chopped
1 lb (500 g) fresh pasta (rigatoni or spaghetti)
8 Tbsps grated aged ricotta salata

Preparation time **20 minutes**
Cooking time **40 minutes**
Level **easy**
Wine **Etna Bianco Superiore**

Sprinkle the eggplant with salt and leave
to drain in a colander for 30 minutes. Blanch,
peel and deseed the tomatoes, and chop
the flesh.

Heat 1 tablespoon of olive oil in a frying pan
and sauté the garlic and onion until golden.
Add the tomatoes and sugar and stir well.
Season with salt and pepper, add the basil and
cook for a few more minutes.

Heat the remaining olive oil in another
frying pan and fry the eggplant. Drain and dry
on paper towels.

Bring a large pot of salted water to a boil and
cook the pasta until al dente. Drain and toss
with the tomato sauce. Stir in the eggplant
and sprinkle with ricotta salata. Stir and serve
immediately.

Lasagne alla siciliana
Sicilian Lasagna

Serves 6

4 cups (1 lb 2 oz or 500 g) all-purpose flour
3 eggs
6 Tbsps extra-virgin olive oil
1 onion, minced - salt
1 bunch of parsley, minced
1 ½ lb (700 g) ripe tomatoes, pureed and sieved
4 basil leaves
1 pat of butter
10 ½ oz (300 g) fresh ricotta
5 Tbsps grated Pecorino cheese

Preparation time **45 minutes**
Cooking time **50 minutes**
Level **medium**
Wine **Bianco d'Alcamo**

Preheat the oven to 350°F (180°C or Gas
Mark 4). Mix together the flour, eggs,
1 tablespoon of olive oil and a pinch of salt
to form a smooth dough. Roll the dough out
thinly with a rolling pin and cut into rectangles
about 1 ½ by 2 ½-inches (4 by 6 cm).

Bring a large pot of salted water to a boil with
a tablespoon of olive oil and cook the pasta
sheets. Drain and lay on a clean kitchen towel
to dry. Heat the remaining 4 tablespoons of
olive oil in a frying pan and sauté the onion
and parsley. Add the tomatoes and basil and
cook for 20 minutes. Butter a baking dish and
start making layers of pasta sheets, tomato sauce,
pieces of ricotta and grated Pecorino. Continue
until the ingredients are used up, finishing with
a sprinkling of Pecorino. Bake for 20 minutes
and serve immediately.

Spaghetti alla siracusana
Syracusan-Style Spaghetti

Serves 4

2 salted anchovies - 1 lb (500 g) ripe tomatoes
2 ½ Tbsps capers - 5 Tbsps pitted black olives
2 eggplants, peeled and diced - 2 bell peppers
6 Tbsps extra-virgin olive oil
1 garlic clove, peeled and smashed
salt and pepper
1/2 bunch of basil, chopped
14 oz (400 g) spaghetti
4 Tbsps grated Pecorino cheese

Preparation time **20 minutes**
Cooking time **40 minutes**
Level **easy**
Wine **Carricante**

Rinse the anchovies and remove any bones. Finely mince them together with the olives and capers. Blanch and peel the tomatoes then pass them through a sieve. Place the eggplant in a bowl and sprinkle with salt. Let sit until it gives off water, then drain and rinse. Roast the peppers over an open flame, close in a plastic bag to steam, then peel, deseed and slice. Heat the olive oil and sauté the garlic until golden. Remove from the pan and add the eggplant. Cook for a few minutes, then add the tomatoes. Season with salt and pepper and add the roast peppers, olives, capers, anchovies and basil. Continue cooking until the sauce thickens.

Bring a large pot of salted water to a boil and cook the pasta until al dente. Drain and place in bowl, then dress with the sauce and sprinkle with Pecorino. Serve immediately.

Lasagne alla siciliana

Spaghetti alla siracusana

Pasta con acciughe e mollica
Pasta with Anchovies

Serves 4

4 salted anchovies
4 ripe tomatoes
4 Tbsps extra-virgin olive oil
2 garlic cloves, peeled
1 ¼ cups (5 ½ oz or 150 g) breadcrumbs
salt
14 oz (400 g) short pasta (penne, cavateddi)
1 bunch of parsley, minced

Preparation time **10 minutes**
Cooking time **25 minutes**
Level **easy**
Wine **Etna Bianco**

Rinse the anchovies under cold running water and remove any bones. Blanch the tomatoes in boiling water for a few minutes, then drain, peel and pass through a sieve.

Heat 2 tablespoons of olive oil in a saucepan and sauté the whole peeled garlic cloves until golden. Remove from the pan and add the anchovies. Stir with a wooden spoon until they dissolve, then add the tomatoes. Cook over medium heat for about 15 minutes.

Heat 2 tablespoons of olive oil in another frying pan and add the breadcrumbs. Toast, stirring constantly, until golden, then add to the pan with the tomatoes.

Bring a large pot of salted water to a boil and cook the pasta until al dente. Drain and transfer to a bowl.

Pour over the sauce and stir to combine. Serve immediately, sprinkled with parsley.

Pasta con le sarde
Pasta with Sardines

Serves 4

10 ½ oz (300 g) fresh sardines
all-purpose flour for flouring
sunflower oil for frying - 1 bunch of wild fennel
1/3 cup (2 oz or 50 g) raisins
salt and pepper - 14 oz (400 g) penne
3 Tbsps extra-virgin olive oil
1 onion, minced - 1 garlic clove, minced
4 salted anchovies, rinsed and chopped
1 Tbsp pine nuts, toasted - 1 pinch of saffron

Preparation time **30 minutes**
Cooking time **30 minutes**
Level **medium**
Wine **Bianco d'Alcamo**

Preheat the oven to 400°F (200°C or Gas Mark 6). Clean the sardines, removing the heads, guts and bones. Dust with flour. Heat the sunflower oil until very hot and fry the sardines until golden. Drain and dry on paper towels. Blanch the fennel in boiling water for about 10 minutes, then drain, reserving the water, and finely chop. Soak the raisins in warm water until soft, then drain and squeeze out excess water. Bring the fennel water back to a boil, adding more if necessary, add salt and use it to cook the penne. Drain when al dente.

Meanwhile heat 2 tablespoons of olive oil in a frying pan and sauté the onion until soft. Add the anchovies, garlic, fennel, raisins, pine nuts, saffron, salt and pepper and sauté until well mixed. Toss the pasta with three-quarters of the sauce. Oil a baking dish and make layers of the pasta alternating with layers of the fried sardines. Top with the remaining sauce.

Bake for about 10 minutes. Serve hot.

Pasta con le sarde

Impanata alla messinese
Messina-Style Swordfish

Serves 4

2 ¾ cups (12 ½ oz or 350 g) all-purpose flour
14 Tbsps (7 oz or 200 g) butter, softened
2 egg yolks - 1 tsp sugar - salt and pepper
1 ¼ lb (600 g) swordfish - 3 ½ Tbsps pine nuts
all-purpose flour for flouring - 1 large onion, minced
1/2 celery stalk, minced - 2 bay leaves
3/4 cup plus 1 Tbsp (200 ml) extra-virgin olive oil
14 oz (400 g) ripe tomatoes, blanched,
peeled and deseeded
1/3 cup (2 oz or 50 g) pitted black olives
2 ½ Tbsps salted capers, rinsed - 1 carrot, minced
3 Tbsps raisins, soaked in water and squeezed out

Preparation time **1 hour**
Cooking time **2 hours 10 minutes**
Level **medium**
Wine **Catarratto**

Mound the flour on a work surface and form
a well. Add the butter, egg yolks, sugar and
a pinch of salt. Mix well, cover and let rest.

Cut the swordfish into bite-sized pieces. Dust
with flour. Sauté the onion, carrot and celery in
the olive oil until soft. Add the swordfish and
brown briefly. Add the tomatoes, olives, capers,
pine nuts and raisins. Adjust salt and pepper and
cook, covered, for 1 hour 30 minutes.

Preheat the oven to 350°F (180°C or Gas
Mark 4). Roll out the dough into 3 sheets. Line a
buttered and floured baking dish with 1 sheet
of dough. Add half the swordfish mixture and
1 bay leaf and cover with a sheet of dough.

Top with the remaining swordfish and bay leaf,
cover with the last dough sheet and seal the
edges. Bake for 30 minutes and serve.

Sarde a beccafico
Stuffed Sardines

Serves 4-6

2 ¼ lb (1 kg) fresh sardines
2 Tbsps grated Pecorino cheese
1 Tbsp breadcrumbs
2 garlic cloves, minced
1 bunch of parsley, minced
salt and pepper
2 eggs
extra-virgin olive oil for frying
1 handful of cherry tomatoes, quartered
4-6 parsley sprigs

Preparation time **30 minutes**
Cooking time **20 minutes**
Level **easy**
Wine **Corvo di Casteldaccia Bianco**

Remove the heads from the sardines, open
them and remove the guts and bones. Wash
and dry with paper towels. Mix the Pecorino,
breadcrumbs, garlic, parsley, salt and pepper
in a bowl. Add 1 egg and mix well. Beat
the remaining egg.

Fill each sardine with a little of the filling
and brush along the edges with the beaten
egg, then roll up. Secure with a toothpick
if necessary.

Heat the olive oil in a frying pan, and when
hot add the stuffed sardines. Fry, turning
when they become golden on one side. Drain
from the oil, dry on paper towels and place on
a serving plate. Serve garnished with cherry
tomatoes and parsley sprigs.

Caponata di melanzane
Sweet-and-Sour Eggplant

Serves 4

5 medium eggplants, cubed
salt
3 Tbsps extra-virgin olive oil
3/4 cups (3 ½ oz or 100 g) green olives
1 Tbsp capers, rinsed
1 celery stalk, finely chopped
1 lb (500 g) ripe tomatoes, sliced
4 Tbsps sugar
4 Tbsps vinegar

Preparation time **10 minutes**
Cooking time **1 hour 10 minutes**
Level **easy**
Wine **Bianco d'Alcamo**

Salt the eggplant and leave to rest in
a colander for 30 minutes to give off water.
    Heat the olive oil in a large saucepan and
brown the eggplant cubes. Add the olives,
capers and celery and cook for 10 minutes.
Add the tomatoes and cook for 1 hour.
Add the sugar and vinegar, stir, remove from
the heat and let cool slightly before serving.
    The caponata can also be canned in
sterilized glass jars.

Sarde a beccafico

Caponata di melanzane

Sarde in foglie di vite
Sardines on Vine Leaves

Serves 4

8 large, very fresh sardines
salt and pepper - 1 Tbsp raisins
3 Tbsps extra-virgin olive oil
1 garlic clove, smashed
1 red chili pepper, minced
1 Tbsp pine nuts, minced
1/2 cup (120 ml) white wine
1/2 cup (2 oz or 50 g) breadcrumbs
3 Tbsps minced parsley
vine leaves in water, drained

Preparation time **20 minutes**
Cooking time **15 minutes**
Level **easy**
Wine **Grillo**

Preheat the oven to 400°F (200°C or Gas Mark 6). Remove the heads and guts from the sardines and wash well under cold running water. Pat dry and salt them inside. Soak the raisins in warm water until soft, then drain and squeeze out excess liquid.

Heat 2 tablespoons of olive oil in a frying pan and sauté the garlic and chili. When the garlic is golden, remove and discard. Add the raisins and half the pine nuts. Add the white wine, let evaporate, then add the breadcrumbs, parsley, salt and pepper. Continue cooking until the breadcrumbs are lightly toasted.

Stuff the sardines with the mixture. Lay the vine leaves out in a baking dish, arrange the sardines on top and roll up, securing with toothpicks. Sprinkle with the remaining pine nuts and drizzle with oil. Bake for 7 minutes.

Acciughe marinate
Lemon-Marinated Anchovies

Serves 6

1 lb (500 g) very fresh anchovies
2 garlic cloves
1 bunch of parsley
1/2 hot red chili pepper
1/2 tsp dried oregano
salt
juice of 2 lemons

Preparation time **20 minutes**
Level **easy**
Wine **Sicilia Inzolia**

Wash the anchovies well under cold running water and remove the head, guts and backbone, taking care not to break them. Dry and set aside.

Mash together the garlic, parsley and chili with a mortar and pestle, then add the oregano, a pinch of salt and the lemon juice.

Pour the marinade over the anchovies and let sit for at least 3 hours. Serve at room temperature.

Note *Variations on this recipe often include olive oil as well as lemon juice. Marinated anchovies are often served with toasted bread and butter.*

Acciughe marinate

Frittedda
Sicilian Spring Vegetable Stew

Serves 6

4 small artichokes
juice of 1 lemon
1 ¾ lb (800 g) peas in pods
3 ½ lb (1 ½ kg) fava beans in pods
6 Tbsps extra-virgin olive oil
1 onion, minced
salt and pepper
1/2 Tbsp sugar
2 Tbsps vinegar

Preparation time **15 minutes**
Cooking time **30 minutes**
Level **easy**
Wine **Bianco d'Alcamo**

Trim the artichoke stems and remove the tough outer leaves and the choke. Cut the artichokes into wedges or slices. Soak the artichokes in cold water and lemon juice.

Meanwhile, shell the peas and favas and peel the fava beans. Heat the olive oil in a large frying pan. Add the onion and sauté until soft. Add the drained artichokes and cook for a few minutes. Add the peas and favas. Season to taste with salt and pepper. Add a little water, lower the heat and cook until the artichokes are tender, adding more water if necessary.

When the artichokes are cooked, add the sugar and vinegar, mix well and remove from the heat. Cool and serve immediately or refrigerate overnight and serve the next day.

Scaloppine al Marsala
Veal Scaloppini with Marsala

Serves 4

1 lb (500 g) veal scaloppini
3 Tbsps all-purpose flour
3 ½ Tbsps (2 oz or 50 g) butter
1/2 cup (120 ml) dry Marsala wine
salt

Preparation time **10 minutes**
Cooking time **10 minutes**
Level **easy**
Wine **Nero d'Avola**

Pound the veal scaloppini with a meat tenderizer until very thin. Dip in flour, coating on both sides.

Melt the butter in a large frying pan and brown the meat. Adjust salt and continue cooking until cooked through.

Remove the meat from the pan and keep warm. Add the Marsala wine, stir and reduce until it forms a creamy sauce. Pour over the veal and serve hot.

Note *Marsala is a fortified white wine made in Sicily in the town of the same name in the province of Trapani, using Grillo, Inzolia and Catarratto grapes.*

Tonno alla siciliana
Sicilian-Style Tuna

Serves 6

2 ¼ lb (1 kg) fresh tuna in 1 piece
6 Tbsps extra-virgin olive oil
1 garlic clove, thinly sliced
6 mint leaves
salt
3/4 cup (180 ml) white wine
1 onion, minced
1 ¼ lb (600 g) ripe tomatoes,
peeled, deseeded and chopped
salt and pepper
3/4 cup (180 ml) hot water

Preparation time **30 minutes**
Cooking time **40 minutes**
Level **medium**
Wine **Catarratto**

Clean, wash and dry the tuna. Cut into slices. Heat 3 tablespoons of olive oil in a saucepan and sauté the garlic. Add the tuna and mint. Brown the tuna, then add salt and white wine.

Once the wine has evaporated, remove from the heat and keep warm. In another saucepan, heat 3 tablespoons of olive oil and sauté the onion until soft. Add the tomatoes, adjust salt and pepper and continue cooking for 10 minutes.

Transfer the tomato sauce to the pan with the tuna, add the hot water and cook, covered, for 20 minutes. Let cool before serving.

Zucchine alla palermitana
Palermo-Style Zucchini

Serves 4

2 Tbsps extra-virgin olive oil
1 garlic clove, minced
2 salted anchovies, rinsed and deboned
1 lb (500 g) zucchini, thinly sliced
1 Tbsp sugar
3 Tbsps vinegar
salt

Preparation time **15 minutes**
Cooking time **40 minutes**
Level **easy**
Wine **Inzolia**

Heat the olive oil in a large frying pan and sauté the garlic until golden. Add the anchovies and stir with a wooden spoon until they dissolve and form a smooth cream.

Add the zucchini, brown for a few minutes, then add the sugar and vinegar. Stir well, season with salt to taste and cook, covered, over low heat for 20 minutes. Add water when necessary.

Serve hot.

cassata alla siciliana
Sicilian cassata

Serves 4-6

14 oz (400 g) ricotta

3 ⅓ cups (14 oz or 400 g) confectioners' sugar

1 ⅓ cups (7 oz or 200 g) chopped candied fruit

3 ½ oz (100 g) dark chocolate, chopped

1 tsp vanilla extract

4 Tbsps rum

1 lb (500 g) round of sponge cake

2 oz (50 g) pistachio paste

juice of 1/2 lemon

whipped cream for garnish (optional)

Preparation time **40 minutes**

Level **medium**

Wine **Zibibbo**

Sieve the ricotta into a bowl. Add half of the confectioners' sugar, half the candied fruit and all the chocolate. Add the vanilla extract and the rum and mix well.

Cut the sponge cake into 2 rounds. Slice 1 round into strips and line the edges of a deep cake pan with the strips. Fill the pan with the ricotta mixture and place the remaining sponge cake round over the top of the filling. Refrigerate for 3-4 hours.

Prepare the glaze by mixing the remaining confectioners' sugar, pistachio paste, lemon juice and a little hot water to form a thick syrup. Unmold the cassata on a serving dish and cover with the glaze.

Decorate with the remaining candied fruit and whipped cream if desired.

Traditional recipe

Granita al caffè
Coffee Granita

Serves 4

1 cup (250 ml) water
6 ½ Tbsps sugar
1 cup (250 ml) coffee
1 vanilla bean or 2 tsps vanilla extract
1 pinch of ground cinnamon
1/2 cup (120 ml) whipping cream
2 Tbsps confectioners' sugar

Preparation time **30 minutes**
Cooking time **3 minutes**
Level **easy**

Place the water and sugar in a saucepan and bring to a boil. Boil for 1 minute, stirring constantly. Add the coffee, stir well and remove from the heat. Add the seeds from the vanilla bean or the vanilla extract and the ground cinnamon. Stir well and let cool.

Strain the mixture through a fine sieve and collect the liquid in a stainless-steel or plastic container. Freeze for at least 2 hours, stirring often with a spatula to keep soft.

Just before serving, whip the cream with the confectioners' sugar. Divide the granita between serving glasses or bowls and top with whipped cream. Serve immediately.

Cannoli siciliani
Sicilian Cannoli

Serves 4-6

2 ⅓ cups plus 1 Tbsp (10 ½ oz or 300 g) all-purpose flour
1 egg, separated - 14 oz (400 g) fresh ricotta
1 large pat of butter, softened - salt
2 tsps dry Marsala wine - 2 ½ Tbsps sugar
1 ½ cups (7 oz or 200 g) confectioners' sugar
2/3 cup (3 ½ oz or 100 g) chopped candied orange, citron and pumpkin
1/4 cup (1 oz or 30 g) pistachios, chopped
2 oz (50 g) dark chocolate, chopped, plus extra grated for garnish
sunflower oil for frying - lard for frying
vanilla sugar, ground cinnamon and candied orange rind for garnish

Preparation time **50 minutes**
Cooking time **30 minutes**
Level **medium**
Wine **Zibibbo**

Mix together the flour, egg yolk, sugar, butter, a pinch of salt and enough Marsala wine to make a soft dough. Cover and let rest for 2 hours.

Pass the ricotta through a sieve and stir in the confectioners' sugar, candied fruit, pistachios and chocolate. Roll out the dough and cut into squares 4 inches (10 cm) on each side. Brush with egg white and wrap around metal cannoli molds.

Heat the sunflower oil with a little lard until very hot and fry the cannoli on the molds until golden, in batches, then drain, dry on paper towels and let cool. Remove the cannoli from the molds and fill with the ricotta mixture. Serve sprinkled with vanilla sugar and cinnamon, garnished with orange rind and grated chocolate.

Biscotti di pasta di mandorle
Almond Cookies

Serves 6

3 ⅓ cups (11 ½ oz or 330 g)
almond flour
2 ⅓ cups (11 ½ oz or 330 g)
confectioners' sugar
2 egg whites
3 drops of almond extract
2 Tbsps honey
2 Tbsps sunflower oil
candied fruit pieces for garnish
almond slices for garnish

Preparation time **20 minutes**
Cooking time **10 minutes**
Level **easy**
Wine **Moscato Passito di Pantelleria**

Mix together the almond flour,
confectioners' sugar, egg whites, almond
extract and honey until smooth.

Use a pastry bag with a ridged tip to form
walnut-sized cookies on a baking sheet
ined with parchment paper and oiled.
Let rest for 2-3 hours.

Preheat the oven to 350°F (180°C or Gas
Mark 4). Bake the cookies for 5 minutes,
then top with pieces of candied fruit or
almond slices. Continue baking for another
5 minutes, until golden.

Serve warm or at room temperature.

Cannoli siciliani

Biscotti di pasta di mandorle

Sardinia

Crystal seas
and the scent of myrtle,

beautiful beaches and paths winding
through fantastically shaped pink granite
rocks. A unique island that inspires strong
emotions and whose cuisine is shaped
by the excellent products from sea and
mountain, from splendid *lobsters* to
delicious *Pecorino cheeses*, from salty
bottarga to rare *strawberry-tree honey*.

SARDINIA
local products

Mirto *di Sardegna*

ONE OF SARDINIA'S MOST CHARACTERISTIC LIQUEURS AND CERTAINLY THE BEST KNOWN OUTSIDE THE REGION. Mirto's perfume and flavor come from myrtle, which grows wild all over the island and gains aromatic qualities from the soil and microclimate. The evergreen bush produces bluish-purple berries, which are used to infuse the alcohol. Sugar or honey is added, and the end result is a fragrant liqueur with a purple color, *Mirto rosso*. The leaf buds are used to make a whitish or pale-green spirit, *Mirto bianco*. They are served cold, either as an aperitif before the meal, or as a digestif after.

Piccola pasticceria

THE PHRASE *PICCOLA PASTICCERIA* literally means small pastries and covers a wide range of little treats, flavored with sweet and bitter almonds, walnuts, soft cheeses like ricotta and fresh Pecorino, raisins, honey, lemons or oranges. Among the most common varieties are diamond-shaped *papassinas* with almonds, walnuts and raisins; *bianchittos* made from egg white, almonds and lemon zest; *mustazzolus*, little cakes of flour, sugar and yeast, typical of Oristano; and *gueffus* or *sospiri*, balls of almonds with orange-flower water.

Pane Carasau

THE MOST RENOWNED SARDINIAN BREAD comes from the north of the island, and is also known as *carta da musica* (music paper) because it resembles sheets of parchment. Pane carasau is made from very thin circles of unleavened dough and is very crisp. If seasoned with olive oil and salt it is called *pane guttiau*, and this is used to make *pane frattau*, a classic one-dish meal. It was once made exclusively with carasau, Pecorino cheese and broth, but these days it is usually enriched with tomato sauce or poached eggs.

Bottarga *di* muggine *e di* tonno

WHETHER MADE FROM MULLET OR TUNA, bottarga (cured fish roe) has become a gastronomic symbol of Sardinia. The eggs are extracted from the fish as soon as they are caught, then washed, salted and pressed until compact. The roes are then dried for at least 15 days. Mullet bottarga has a balanced flavor a strong marine scent, while tuna bottarga has a stronger taste. Bottarga is used in Sardinian cooking in all its variants (whole, grated or cut into thin shavings) and throughout the meal: over bread crostini for a starter, to flavor a simple pasta with olive oil or with clams and other local seafood.

Cassatedde fritte di Tuma
Fried Cheese Pies

Serves 4

4 cups (1 lb 2 oz or 500 g) all-purpose flour
salt and pepper
6 salted anchovies
3 tomatoes, peeled and chopped
4 Tbsps minced parsley
9 oz (250 g) Tuma (goat's milk cheese), chopped
sunflower oil for frying

Preparation time **20 minutes**
Cooking time **15 minutes**
Level **easy**
Wine **Torbato di Alghero**

Mound the flour on a work surface and make a well in the center. Add a pinch of salt and enough water to mix a smooth, elastic dough. Form a ball and let rest for 1 hour.

Meanwhile remove any bones from the anchovies and rinse the anchovies well under cold running water. Chop them and place in a bowl with the tomatoes, parsley, Tuma and pinches of salt and pepper and mix well.

Roll the dough out into a thin sheet and cut out disks with a cookie cutter. Place 1 tablespoon of filling in the middle of each one and fold over to form half-moons.

Heat the sunflower oil until very hot and fry the half-moons until golden, in batches if necessary, then drain and dry on paper towels. Serve hot or warm, according to taste.

Arselle e cozze a schiscionera
Sautéed Clams and Mussels

Serves 4

1 ¼ lb (600 g) clams
1 ¼ lb (600 g) mussels
2 Tbsps extra-virgin olive oil
2 garlic cloves, minced
1/2 bunch of parsley, minced
salt

Preparation time **20 minutes**
Cooking time **10 minutes**
Level **easy**
Wine **Vermentino di Gallura**

Wash the clams and mussels well and debeard the mussels. Place them a large frying pan and cook over high heat until they open and give off their liquid. Remove from the heat and set aside.

Meanwhile heat the olive oil in another frying pan and sauté the garlic and parsley.

Add the clams and mussels, still in their shells, together with their liquid. Cook for around 10 minutes, adding salt to taste.

Serve hot.

Note *According to tradition, this dish is served in a shallow soup bowl accompanied by toasted bread rubbed with a garlic clove.*

Aragosta alla sarda
Sardinian-Style Lobster

Serves 4

2 lobsters
salt and pepper
5 Tbsps extra-virgin olive oil
1 Tbsp vinegar
juice of 1 lemon
parsley sprigs for garnish (optional)

Preparation time **20 minutes**
Cooking time **20 minutes**
Level **easy**
Wine **Vermentino di Sardegna**

Tie the lobsters with kitchen string so the tail is folded in towards the head. Boil them in salted water for about 20 minutes. Drain and let cool.

Cut off the lobster tails and remove the meat, taking care not to break it. Slice the tails into 1/2-inch (1 cm) thick slices and arrange on a serving plate.

Remove all the meat remaining in the heads and the body cavity and puree it with any roe in a food processor with the olive oil, vinegar, lemon juice and pinches of salt and pepper until smooth, adding more olive oil if necessary.

Drizzle the lobster tail meat with the sauce. Garnish with parsley, if desired, and the lobster claws.

Arselle e cozze a schiscionera

Aragosta alla sarda

Ciciones
Dumplings with Pork

Serves 4

2 cups (14 oz or 400 g) semolina flour
salt
3 oz (80 g) lardo (cured lard), diced
1/2 onion, minced
10 ½ oz (300 g) ground pork
2 tomatoes, diced (optional)
1 pinch of saffron
4 Tbsps grated Pecorino cheese

Preparation time **10 minutes**
Cooking time **40 minutes**
Level **easy**
Wine **Carignano del Sulcis Rosato**

Mound the flour on a work surface, add
a pinch of salt and mix in enough warm
water to obtain a smooth, uniform and
compact dough. Form into ropes by hand,
then cut into pieces the size of a chickpea.
Lay out to dry on a clean kitchen towel.

Brown the lardo in a saucepan for a
few minutes. Add the onion, cook until
transparent, then add the ground pork.

Cook for 30 minutes over low heat, stirring
occasionally and adding water if necessary.
If desired, add chopped tomatoes. Season
with a pinch of saffron and salt to taste.

Bring a large pot of salted water to the boil
and cook the dumplings. Drain and add
to the sauce. Serve immediately, sprinkled
with grated Pecorino.

Spaghetti all'aragosta
Spaghetti with Lobster

Serves 4

2 Tbsps extra-virgin olive oil
1/2 onion, minced
1 carrot, minced
1 cup (7 oz or 200 g) peeled plum tomatoes,
chopped
1 live lobster (around 1 ½ lb or 700 g)
14 oz (400 g) spaghetti
salt

Preparation time **10 minutes**
Cooking time **30 minutes**
Level **easy**
Wine **Torbato di Alghero Spumante**

Heat the olive oil in a large saucepan and
sauté the onion and carrot until soft. Add
the tomatoes and cook over moderate heat
for 15 minutes.

Add the whole lobster, still alive, to the pan.
Cover, lower the heat and cook for about
10 minutes. Remove the lobster from the pan,
cut into pieces using poultry scissors, return
to the pan and cook for another 8 minutes.

Bring a large pot of salted water to a boil
and cook the spaghetti until al dente. Drain
and toss in the pan with the sauce. Serve hot.

Spaghetti all'aragosta

Malloreddus con salsiccia
Malloreddus Pasta with Sausage

Serves 4

1 ¼ lb (600 g) tomatoes
2 Tbsps extra-virgin olive oil
1 small onion, minced
1 garlic clove, minced
7 oz (200 g) sausage, casing removed
and meat crumbled
salt
1 bay leaf
2 basil leaves, torn into pieces
1 pinch of saffron
10 ½ oz (300 g) malloreddus,
gnocchetti or cavatelli
4 Tbsps grated Pecorino cheese (optional)

Preparation time **5 minutes**
Cooking time **25 minutes**
Level **easy**
Wine **Monica di Sardegna**

Blanch, drain, peel, deseed and chop the
tomatoes. Heat the olive oil in a large frying
pan and sauté the onion and garlic until
golden. Add the sausage meat and brown
for a few minutes.

Add the tomatoes, adjust the salt and add the
bay leaf, basil and saffron. Cook over medium
heat, stirring every so often and adding water
when necessary, until the meat is cooked
through and the sauce has thickened.

Bring a large pot of salted water to a boil and
cook the pasta until al dente, then drain and
transfer to the pan with the sauce. Toss to coat,
then serve, sprinkled with Pecorino if desired.

Fregola con le arselle
Fregola with Clams

Serves 4

1 ¾ cups (10 ½ oz or 300 g) coarse semolina
salt
2 ¼ lb (1 kg) clams
2 Tbsps extra-virgin olive oil
2 garlic cloves
1 sun-dried tomato, chopped
4 Tbsps tomato passata (pureed tomatoes)
4 cups (1 l) water
3 Tbsps minced parsley

Preparation time **20 minutes**
Cooking time **40 minutes**
Level **medium**
Wine **Nuragus di Cagliari**

Place the semolina in a bowl and sprinkle over
a little water, stirring by hand in circles until
the semolina forms small balls (fregola). Lay
them out on a clean kitchen towel to dry.

Meanwhile wash the clams and soak them
in cold water for about 2 hours, until they have
expelled all their sand. Drain the clams and
place in a saucepan. Cook over high heat until
the clams open, then remove the shells and
strain the cooking liquid.

Heat the olive oil in a frying pan and sauté the
garlic and sun-dried tomato. Add the tomato
passata and the water and bring to a boil. Add
the clams and their cooking liquid and the
parsley. Return to a boil and add the fregola.

Cook until it rises to the surface, then remove
from the heat and serve immediately.

Spaghetti alla bottarga
Spaghetti with Bottarga

Serves 4

1 ¼ lb (600 g) clams
salt
2 Tbsps extra-virgin olive oil
2 garlic cloves, minced
2 bunches parsley, minced
14 oz (400 g) spaghetti
6 Tbsps grated or shaved bottarga

Preparation time **5 minutes**
Cooking time **20 minutes**
Level **easy**
Wine **Vermentino di Sardegna**

Soak the clams in salted water for 1-2 hours so they expel any sand. Drain and wash well under cold running water.

Heat the olive oil in a large frying pan and sauté the garlic until golden-brown. Add the clams, cover, and cook over medium heat until they open. Discard any of the clams that stay closed and then season to taste with salt and sprinkle with parsley.

Bring a large pot of salted water to the boil and cook the spaghetti until al dente. Drain and add the pasta to the pan with the clams.

Toss the spaghetti to coat evenly with the clam sauce. Serve hot in shallow soup bowls, topped with bottarga.

Fregola con le arselle

Spaghetti alla bottarga

Tonno all'algherese
Alghero-Style Tuna

Serves 4

1 ¾ lb (800 g) fresh tuna
juice of 1/2 lemon
3 Tbsps extra-virgin olive oil
1/2 onion, minced
1 celery stalk, minced
3 bay leaves
1/2 cup (120 ml) white wine
1/4 cup (1 oz or 30 g) pitted black olives
salt

Preparation time **20 minutes**
Cooking time **30 minutes**
Level **easy**
Wine **Torbato di Alghero**

Place the tuna in a bowl, cover with water
and lemon juice and let soak for 2 hours.

Heat the olive oil in a frying pan and sauté
the onion, celery and bay leaves. Drain
the tuna and add to the frying pan.

Cook over low heat for 20 minutes,
turning carefully every so often. Add the
white wine, let evaporate, and add the
olives. Season with salt to taste, cover and
cook until the tuna is done.

Serve the tuna hot, sliced, with the olives
and pan juices.

Triglie alla Vernaccia
Mackerel with Vernaccia Wine

Serves 4

2 Tbsps extra-virgin olive oil
4 mackerels, cleaned
2 Tbsps parsley, minced
4 Tbsps breadcrumbs
3/4 cup (180 ml) Vernaccia wine
grated zest of 1 organic lemon
salt
lemon wedges for garnish

Preparation time **20 minutes**
Cooking time **15 minutes**
Level **easy**
Wine **Vernaccia di Oristano**

Heat the olive oil in a large frying pan
and brown the mackerel on both sides.
Mix together the parsley and breadcrumbs
and sprinkle over the fish.

Sprinkle over the Vernaccia wine and lemon
zest and adjust the salt. Cook over low heat
until the mackerel are cooked through.

Serve accompanied with their pan juices,
garnished with lemon wedges.

Note *Vernaccia di Oristano is a white wine with
a golden-yellow color, with a characteristic almond
and walnut bouquet, soft and warm on the palate
with an aftertaste of bitter almonds. It generally
pairs well with desserts.*

Pane frattau
Pane Carasau with Eggs

Serves 4

4 cups (1 l) vegetable broth
4 eggs
salt
8 sheets of pane carasau
1 ¾ cups (400 ml) ready-made tomato sauce
5 ½ oz (150 g) aged Pecorino cheese, grated

Preparation time **5 minutes**
Cooking time **20 minutes**
Level **easy**
Wine **Monica di Sardegna**

Divide the broth between 2 large saucepans
and bring to a boil. In one, immerse the sheets
of pane carasau for a few seconds, drain and
place on a serving plate, layered with a few
spoonfuls of tomato sauce, a pinch of salt
and some grated Pecorino between each sheet.
  In the other pan, poach the eggs one at
a time. Lay on top of the pane carasau and
sprinkle with Pecorino. Serve immediately.

Note *Another version of this recipe uses water
instead of vegetable broth.*

Triglie alla Vernaccia

Pane frattau

sebadas
sweet cheese fritters with honey

Serves 6–8

2 ¼ lb (1 kg) soft mild cheese
1/2 cup (120 ml) warm water
1 Tbsp vanilla extract
grated zest of 1 organic orange
8 cups (2 lb 3 oz or 1 kg) plus
6 ½ Tbsps all-purpose flour
1 cup (7 oz or 200 g) lard
sunflower oil for frying
strawberry-tree (arbutus) honey
or other bitter honey,
such as chestnut, for drizzling
salt

Preparation time **40 minutes**
Cooking time **30 minutes**
Level **medium**
Wine **Nasco di Cagliari Liquoroso Dolce**

Slice the cheese and place in a saucepan with the warm water, vanilla and orange zest. Cook over medium heat until the cheese melts. Remove from the heat and whisk in the 6 ½ tablespoons of flour.

Divide the cheese mixture into walnut-sized balls and place them on a damp cutting board. Press down on the balls to flatten and set aside.

Meanwhile, pour the remaining flour onto a work surface and work in the lard and salt. Slowly add enough warm water to form a smooth, elastic dough. Roll out the dough into a thick sheet. Using a cookie cutter, cut out several circles. Place 1 piece of the cheese filling on half of the dough circles.

Cover with the remaining circles of dough. Press down around the edges to seal. Heat the sunflower oil in a saucepan and fry the fritters until golden-brown, working in batches if necessary. Drizzle with honey and serve.

Traditional recipe

Gesminus
Orange-Flower Cookies

Serves 4-6

4 egg whites
2 ½ cups (10 ½ oz or 300 g)
confectioners' sugar
3 cups (10 ½ oz or 300 g) sliced
almonds, toasted
1/4 cup (60 ml) orange-flower water

Preparation time **30 minutes**
Cooking time **30 minutes**
Level **easy**
Wine **Malvasia di Bosa**

Preheat the oven to 350°F (180°C or
Gas Mark 4). Beat the egg whites and
confectioners' sugar together in a bowl
until soft and fluffy. Fold in the almonds
and orange-flower water.

Line a baking sheet with parchment paper
and place evenly spaced spoonfuls of the
mixture on it. Bake until golden.

Serve hot or at room temperature.

Note *The Sardinian name of these cookies,
gesminus, derives from gelsomino, "jasmine,"
because they used to be flavored with jasmine
essence, which these days has been replaced
by orange-flower water. If you can't find
orange-flower water, you can use the juice
of 1 lemon instead.*

Matassine dolci
Honey Twists

Serves 4

2 cups (9 oz or 250 g) all-purpose flour
2 eggs
1 egg yolk
4 Tbsps sugar
3 Tbsps lard
salt
sunflower oil for frying
2/3 cup (7 oz or 200 g) honey
sugar for sprinkling (optional)

Preparation time **30 minutes**
Cooking time **20 minutes**
Level **medium**
Wine **Malvasia di Bosa**

In a mixing bowl, mix together the flour,
eggs, egg yolk, sugar, lard and a pinch of salt.
Mix to obtain a compact and smooth dough.
Cover with a kitchen towel and let rest for
at least 1 hour.

Form the dough into ropes about 1/2-inch
(1 cm) thick and 6 inches (15 cm) long. Fold
them in half and twist the two halves together
to form shapes like skeins of wool.

Heat the sunflower oil and fry the twists over
medium heat, without letting them color
too much. Drain and dry on paper towels.

In a separate saucepan heat the honey until
it liquefies. Add the twists and stir with a
wooden spoon they have absorbed all the honey.

Arrange on a serving plate and serve, sprinkled
with sugar if desired.

Gattò
Almond Brittle

Serves 6

2 ½ cups (1 lb 2 oz or 500 g) sugar
juice of 1 lemon
5 cups (1 lb or 500 g) sliced almonds, toasted
3 Tbsps extra-virgin olive oil
1 whole lemon
colored sprinkles

Preparation time **15 minutes**
Cooking time **20 minutes**
Level **easy**
Wine **Moscato di Cagliari**

Melt the sugar over very low heat with
the lemon juice. When the sugar starts
to caramelize, add the almonds and stir
with a wooden spoon until well-mixed.

   Pour onto an oiled work surface, preferably
marble or resin, and using the whole lemon
like a rolling pin spread out to a thickness
of about 1/2-inch (1 cm).

   Let cool, then cut into shapes and top
with colored sprinkles before serving.

Matassine dolci

Gattò

Regional index

Regional index

Regional index

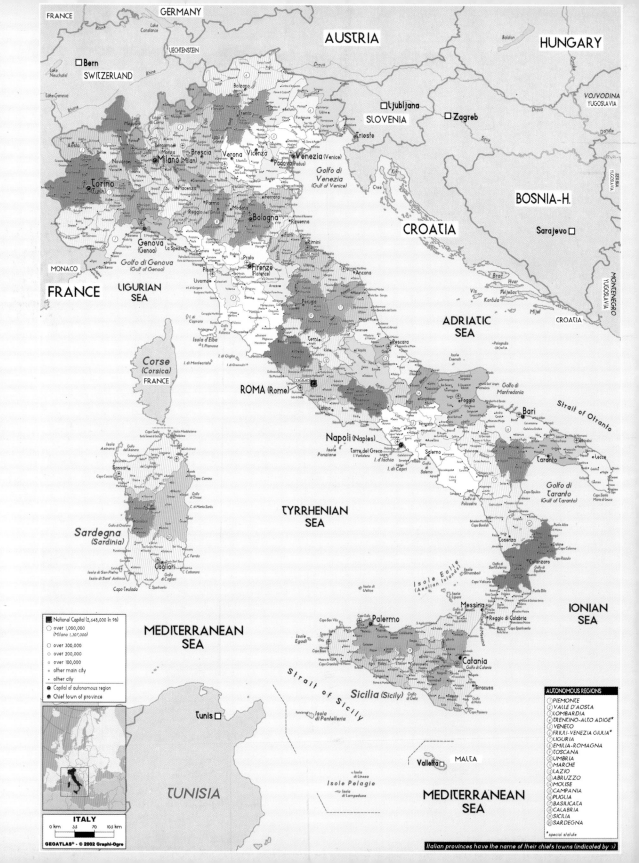

FRANCE GERMANY
AUSTRIA HUNGARY

SWITZERLAND
□ Bern

LIECHTENSTEIN

□ Ljubljana
SLOVENIA
□ Zagreb
Trieste

VOJVODINA
YUGOSLAVIA

BOSNIA-H.

MONACO

FRANCE

Aosta

Torino
(Turin)

Milano (Milan)
Bergamo
Monza
Brescia
Novara
Verona
Vicenza
Padova (Padua)

Venezia (Venice)

Golfo di
Venezia
(Gulf of Venice)

Sarajevo □

CROATIA

Genova
(Genoa)

Piacenza
Parma
Reggio nell'Emilia
Modena

Bologna

Ferrara

Ravenna

Forlì

Rimini

Ancona

CROATIA

LIGURIAN
SEA

La Spezia

Prato

Firenze
(Florence)

Livorno

Pisa

Perugia

ADRIATIC
SEA

Corse
(Corsica)

FRANCE

Isola d'Elba

Terni

Pescara

MONTENEGRO
YUGOSLAVIA

ROMA (Rome)

VATICAN

Napoli (Naples)

Salerno

Foggia

Bari

Lecce

Taranto

Golfo di
Manfredonia

Strait of Otranto

Torre del Greco
I. di Ischia

I. di Capri

Sassari

Golfo di
Taranto
(Gulf of Taranto)

Sardegna
(Sardinia)

TYRRHENIAN
SEA

Cosenza

Cagliari

Catanzaro

IONIAN
SEA

National Capital (2,648,000 in 98)
○ over 1,000,000
(Milano 1,307,000)
○ over 300,000
○ over 200,000
○ over 100,000
○ other main city
+ other city
● Capital of autonomous region
● Chief town of province

MEDITERRANEAN
SEA

Messina

Palermo

Reggio di Calabria

Isole Eolie
(Aeolian Islands)

Catania

Sicilia (Sicily)

Siracusa

Strait of Sicily

Tunis □

Isola
di Pantelleria

AUTONOMOUS REGIONS
① PIEMONTE
② VALLE D'AOSTA
③ LOMBARDIA
④ TRENTINO-ALTO ADIGE*
⑤ VENETO
⑥ FRIULI-VENEZIA GIULIA*
⑦ LIGURIA
⑧ EMILIA-ROMAGNA
⑨ TOSCANA
⑩ UMBRIA
⑪ MARCHE
⑫ LAZIO
⑬ ABRUZZO
⑭ MOLISE
⑮ CAMPANIA
⑯ PUGLIA
⑰ BASILICATA
⑱ CALABRIA
⑲ SICILIA
⑳ SARDEGNA
* special statute

Valletta □ MALTA

MEDITERRANEAN
SEA

Isole Pelagie

TUNISIA

ITALY
0 km   35   70   105 km

GEOATLAS® - © 2002 Graphi-Ogre

Italian provinces have the name of their chiefs towns (indicated by ♦)